D1563947

Complex Economic Dynamics

Complex Economic Dynamics

Volume I

An Introduction to Dynamical Systems and Market Mechanisms

Richard H. Day

The MIT Press
Cambridge, Massachusetts
London, England

This book was set in Times Roman by Windfall Software using ZzTEX, and was printed and bound in the United States of America.

Library of Congress Cataloging-in-Publication Data
Day, Richard Hollis, 1933–
  Complex economic dynamics / Richard H. Day
     p.   cm.
  Includes bibliographical references and index.
  Contents: v. 1. An introduction to dynamical systems and market mechanisms
  ISBN 0-262-04141-3 (v. 1)
  1. Economics, Mathematical. 2. Statics and dynamics (Social sciences). I. Title.
  HB135.D389   1994
  330′.01′51—dc20   93-30291
                                                         CIP

To Barbara
the necessary and sufficient condition

Contents

List of Figures

Foreword

Isaac Newton achieved unique fame for successfully analyzing the dynamics of planets and projectiles. Building on the innovations of Copernicus, Kepler, and Galileo, Newton made obsolete the theories of Aristotle and Ptolemy; he launched the marvelous researches of Euler, Lagrange, Hamilton, and Poincaré. But the job was never finished. In our own day Edward Lorenz discovered (and rediscovered) the beauties of *chaos* and Benoit Mandelbrot created understanding of *fractals*—both exciting developments with potential applications to engineering, biology, and economics, and neither revolution possible without the availability of the modern high-speed computer.

Richard Day has filled an urgent need for economists. The public has been blessed with fine popularizations of the new breakthroughs. But where are researchers or students in economics to find help in mastering what we need to know in optimally applying these new tools—or in judiciously rejecting them—for the basic questions of *our* trade? Can the "strange attractors" of chaos theory be a partial answer to our conundrums about the irregularity of macro *business cycles*? After the Great Stock Crash of October 1987, talk exploded about how the new chaos theory might help us understand that pathology, might aid in its control, and might be useful in augmenting and protecting our precious nest eggs. Writers from departments of mathematics, physics, and meteorology can take the informed economist only so far along the research trail to grapple with questions like these.

Dick Day is an economist, one who has devoted his career to investigating economic change. And he is no Johnny-come-lately in the study of these new dynamic paradigms. He has taken the time to translate for economists and social scientists the content and possible relevances of the new theories for our real-life economic problems. The present work, by design, is less than a treatise but more than a textbook. When my own *Foundations of Economic Analysis* was published in 1947, its author's bookshelf had no useful reference like the present Day work. We are luckier today. But today more is expected of us. Book buyers take notice.

Paul A. Samuelson
Massachusetts Institute of Technology
March 1994

Preface

From the very beginning of my involvement in economics I have been concerned with the study of economic change. In its pursuit, I developed a number of dynamic models each of which when reduced to its simplest possible terms involved a single, nonlinear difference equation. I used these heuristic models to illustrate the kinds of behavior that could take place in the more elaborate theories they exemplified. But even in their simplest forms they possessed many puzzling attributes, and a complete understanding of their possibilities could not be derived with the standard tools of mathematical analysis.

In the meantime, Lorenz in meteorology, Smale in mathematics, May in biology, and Feigenbaum in numerical analysis among others were making breakthroughs in the analysis and interpretation of nonlinear dynamic phenomena.[1] Lorenz's work in particular was brought to my attention by Kenneth Cooke of Claremont College at a conference at Santa Fe in September 1978 at which I was discussing my work on dynamic economic models. Exactly the kind of equations that had been my concern many years before were yielding a host of startling secrets. Of special importance, obviously, was the existence of erratic, turbulent, or chaotic fluctuations. At the University of Southern California Jess Benhabib (now at New York University) had run across the seminal paper of Li and Yorke.[2] We recognized a common interest immediately and set out to see if the mathematical existence of chaos could be established in some standard models of economic theory.

Our first two candidates were the endogenous preference model of Georgescu-Roegen[3] and Samuelson's overlapping generations model in the form given it by David Gale.[4] At the same time I began exploring the same question in the context of classical and neoclassical growth models, in Keynesian models of the business cycle, and in various models of market feedback. This book is based on this series of studies. Its basic purpose is to show how various types of stable and unstable behavior, including structural change, erratic fluctuations, and evolution, arise naturally in dynamic economic theory. The general message is that complex dynamics must be considered as a possibility in *any model that retains essential nonlinearities*. Each type of behavior derives, usually robustly, from the underlying parameters of demand, supply, technology, and so forth. It is a fact, demonstrated in a wide variety of contexts, that complex dynamics is not a peculiar artifact but a generic phenomenon in economic processes.

My initial concern with nonlinear dynamics was motivated by an interest in the general processes that explain economic adaptation and evolution. From the point of view of these much more general considerations chaos, per se, is a sideshow, but what a fascinating sideshow it is! It is little wonder that interest quickly escalated.

Indeed, the economic literature on chaos is by now quite extensive. Much of it goes well beyond what is done here and the interested reader will want to look into the work of Barnett, Benhabib, Boldrin, Brock, Chen, Dana, Gabisch, Gaertner, Goodwin, Grandmont, Hans-Walter Lorenz, Majumdar, Malgrange, Medio, Montrucchio, Nishimura, Pajohla, Saari, Stutzer, Woodford, Yano, and many others in economics, not to mention the works of Guckenheimer, Lasota, Pianigiani, Smale, Yorke, and the other mathematicians who have given us the tools.

This study is presented in two volumes. This volume contains in part I a nontechnical introduction to the theoretical ideas for describing economic change. This is followed in part II by a survey of the mathematical tools used throughout the subsequent chapters. Part III then introduces competitive dynamics in individual markets.

In volume II, which is concerned with macroeconomic dynamics, the economy as a whole is considered. Simplification is achieved by ignoring details of price adjustment, as in part IV on business cycles, or by assuming temporary or intertemporal equilibrium in supply and demand, as in part V on economic growth and part VI on economic development. Volume II is concluded by part VII on dynamical economic science. It provides a brief history of the subject, a guide to current developments, and a summary and reflection on the significance and limitations of the basic concepts of dynamic economics.

The seven parts are closely related and complementary. Though they form a natural sequence, I have written them so they can be read more or less independently. The implications of contemporary dynamical systems for economic theory are profound. These implications are fully illustrated in a variety of specific economic settings. I would hope that no one who reads this book would any longer confine himself or herself to the traditional tools of static analysis. It is high time that dynamics be given an equal standing with statics and that students be given equal training in its concerns. It is, indeed, high time for economics, along with other sciences, to adapt its way of thinking to a world that is changing at an ever increasing pace, one in which the only certainty is that of change itself.

When Jess Benhabib and I began our research on the existence of chaos in an economic context, we knew we were on to something that was "hot," but in the early years so much skepticism, so much hostility even was expressed in the profession that it was hard to anticipate the interest that eventually erupted.

Events goaded the profession into attention. The stock market "crash" of October 1987 served a catalytic role. Abruptly, nonlinear dynamics and chaotic economics entered the flow of "pop" science. General scientific journals, business publications, newspaper and television specials began to appear; all of which gave the subject a somewhat trendy or faddish veneer. Even serious professionals, whose central research interests lie far afield, joined the flock of new entrants, some going so far as to raise the banner of a "new scientific paradigm."

I do hope that this study will indeed contribute to the redirection of economic theory and that it will help bring about an expansion in the scope of research and teaching in graduate, perhaps even undergraduate, education. As one gains familiarity with the concepts, tools of analysis, and economic applications, it becomes evident that, far from being a fad, complex dynamics emerge naturally in the very heartland of the subject.

R. H. D.
Orcas Island
At various times

Acknowledgments

The research on which this book is based was begun at the Institute for Advanced Study in Princeton in 1978. Work continued intermittently during subsequent years at the University of Southern California, whose administration has been uncommonly generous in its support through the years. A year at The Netherlands Institute for Advanced Study in 1984–1985 was especially useful in developing the material in part IV (volume II). Brief but effective periods of study were facilitated by Jean-Pierre Aubin's Centre de Recherche de Mathématiques et de la Décision at the Université de Paris, IX–Dauphine (Spring 1979, Spring 1982), at Gunnar Eliasson's Industrial Institute for Economic and Social Research in Stockholm (Summer 1984, Summer 1985, and various months in 1986 and 1987), and with the sponsorship of Richard Goodwin and Giulio Pianigiani at the Istituto di Matematica and the Faculty of Economics and Banking of the University of Siena in May–July of 1988. A grant from the Electric Power Research Institute in 1989, monitored by JoneLin Huang, was helpful in developing the material for chapters 9 and 13.

As I make clear in the Preface and throughout the book, I have benefited from the collaboration of various individuals, especially Jess Benhabib, Wayne Shafer, and Giulio Pianigiani. Thanks to Luigi Montrucchio, also, who read the manuscript and supplied numerous suggestions. I have also drawn on various published pieces. In particular, a preliminary survey of some of the material is contained in *Complejos Dynamicos*, a series of lectures I presented to—and which were published by—the Mexican Academy of Engineering in March 1985 in Spanish translation by Javier Marquez Diez-Canedo.

In addition to the colleagues mentioned above, I have enjoyed the collaborative assistance of a number of students and former students, including Kenneth Hanson, Federico Segura, Tzong-Yau Lin, Weihong Huang, Raymond Wai-Man Tse, Kyoo-Hong Kim, Jean-Luc Walter, Mu Gu, Larry Powell, Gang Zou, Zhigang Wang, Edward J. McCaffery, Min Zhang, Tong Li, and Stephen J. Conroy. They carried out the numerical experiments that are copiously scattered throughout the book to illustrate the analytical concepts. In more than a few cases, these experiments suggested analytical results that were subsequently verified mathematically. All of these students studied one model or another, checking many of the detailed calculations, ferreting out errors, and in some cases, deriving specific mathematical results. I have cited this collaborative work in the usual way in the text.

I owe a broader intellectual debt to my teachers: Howard Hines and the late Geoffrey Shepherd who, while I was still an undergraduate at Iowa State University, encouraged me to think about dynamic economic theory; then, Wassily Leontief at Harvard University whose essays and occasional lectures on dynamic economics were among the stimulating inputs of my graduate education. Many great economic scientists have provided a long-lived stimulus for the development of economic dynamics, but especially Paul Samuelson, Richard Goodwin, Nicholas Georgescu-Roegen, and Jay W. Forrester. They understood earlier and more deeply than most the explanatory power of nonlinear dynamics.

Finally, I wish to thank Barbara Gordon Day who found a way to accomplish a horde of administrative, editorial, and computational tasks without which I could never have completed this book.

An anecdote: I am not sure the seven substantive parts of this book constitute the seven pillars of dynamical wisdom—to paraphrase T. E. Lawrence's title. But not unlike the experience of that famous author, four chapters in penciled draft were lost along with a valise that was stolen at a train station in Milan in May 1988. Bathed in the hospitality of Richard Goodwin and Giulio Pianigiani, however, my immobilizing depression soon evaporated into the crisp Tuscan air. I set to work again in the cloistered charm of the Certosa Pontignano. Looking back, I marvel at the chaos that is "the life" and how much order is engendered by friendship and goodwill.

Notations

Within a given chapter, equations and diagrams are numbered sequentially. References to equations or diagrams are preceded by the appropriate chapter number. For example, equation (10.6) is equation (6) in chapter 10. Likewise, figure 3.8b is diagram b in figure 8 in chapter 3.

References to sections within chapters is made by the notation, §X.Y, which means chapter X, section Y.

$=$	equals
$\equiv$	is identically equal to
$:=$	is defined to be
$\in$	"is an element of" or "belongs to"
$\subset$	is contained in
$\supset$	contains
$\backslash$	set subtraction: $A \setminus B$ the set of points in A that are not in B
$\backslash$	complement: $\setminus A$ is the set of points not in A
$\mathbb{N}$	the set of integers
$\mathbb{N}^+$	the set of nonnegative integers
$\mathbb{N}^{++}$	the set of positive integers
$\mathbb{R}$	the set of real numbers
$\mathbb{R}^+$	the set of nonnegative real numbers
$\mathbb{R}^{++}$	the set of positive real numbers
$]a, b[$	the complement of (a, b)
$)a, b($	the complement of $[a, b]$
$\tilde{x}$	a stationary state of the variable x
$\tilde{x}^p$	a periodic or cyclic point of period p
$\bar{x}$	a fixed value of the variable x
x^e	estimate or forecast of the variable x
$E(\cdot)$	statistical expectation of the terms in parentheses
λ	price adjustment parameter or the natural rate of population growth
$\max\{a, b\}$	the larger of the terms a and b
$\min\{a, b\}$	the smaller of terms a and b
$\chi_S(x)$	the indicator function $= 1$ if $x \in S$ and $= 0$ if $x \notin S$

M	the supremum or maximum of a function
m	the minimum or infimum of a function
$\lambda(\cdot)$	Lebesgue measure
$\mu(\cdot)$	a measure function
$c\ell(S)$	closure of the set S, namely, the set of its limit points
$\text{supp}_X f$	the support of a function on a set X : $\text{supp}_X f :=$ $c\ell\{x \mid f(x) > 0\}$
$\text{supp}_X \mu$	the support of a measure on the set X = the smallest closed subset of X with positive measure
$\text{supp}\,\mu$	the smallest closed set in the domain of the process with full measure $(= \mu(D))$
$\mathcal{P}(S)$	the power set of a set S: the set of all subsets of S. Also denoted 2^S

I PURPOSE AND METHOD

Being and becoming
are life
States and rates
are forms
the mind creates

1 Introduction

So do flux and reflux—the rhythm of change alternate and persist in everything under the sky.
—Thomas Hardy, *Tess of the D'Urbervilles*

A picture of economic instability might go into the utmost detail, covering the smallest units of economic flux, or the observation might refer to annual changes of broad aggregates.
—Erik Lundberg, *Instability and Economic Growth*

This book is about complex economic dynamics.

Dynamics in its broadest terms is the systematic study of change and the forces generating it; it is the attempt to determine how things change, why change occurs, and what kinds of change might come to pass in the future. Because change must always be considered in reference to nonchange, dynamics is concerned also with determining when and why things don't change and under what conditions things may persist without change in the future.

Economic dynamics is the systematic study of economic change, that is, the study of changes in production, consumption, trade, resource allocation, prices, and welfare. The *dynamic theory of markets* is concerned with the behavior of supply and demand when prices and/or quantities adjust to unfolding conditions. The *theory of business cycles* is concerned with fluctuations in macroeconomic data. The *theory of growth* is concerned with long economic expansions. The *theory of development* is concerned with the evolution of economic structures, including changes in technology and in forms of economic organization.

Many qualitatively distinct patterns of change can be identified. These include *stationary states*, which repeat a given situation endlessly; *periodic states or cycles*, in which distinct situations are repeated at fixed intervals of time; *steady states*, in which all aspects of a system change by the same proportion, as in *balanced growth*, where all variables grow at the same geometric rate, or *balanced decline*, where all variables diminish proportionally.

These are examples of *simple dynamics* because these patterns can all be characterized in a finite or simple way. Patterns of change that are not exactly like any of these types may as time passes become indistinguishable from one of them. Such paths are said to converge, or to be stationary, periodic, or steady in the long run. These possibilities, too, will be referred to as simple dynamics.

In addition to these, however, are other types of change that are not periodic and not balanced, and that do not converge to a periodic or balanced pattern.

Such paths are called *complex*. In particular *complex dynamics* include processes that involve

- nonperiodic fluctuations,
- overlapping waves,
- switches in regime or structural change.

These types of change are very different than the stationary states, periodic cycles, and balanced paths of growth. But they are ubiquitous phenomena in the economics of experience.

The purpose of this book is to mobilize the theory of dynamical systems and the tools of economic analysis in order to explain, interpret, and understand how these complex phenomena emerge in economic processes. It would be impossible, of course, to consider everything of empirical interest. But there are several salient facts that compel attention and command an explanation. Let us begin with this empirical background.

1.1   Some Salient Facts of Economic Change

The central fact is that economic variables change: they do not hold still; they change more or less continuously. What are these changes like?

1.1.1   Microeconomic Fluctuations

First of all, most economic variables, whether they are prices or quantities, oscillate. For example, consider the production of a particular food, such as beef, or the construction of new homes. Or consider stock market transactions: both the level of prices and the volume of trades change from hour to hour, indeed, from one minute to the next. The oscillations that time series of these data display are not regular but highly irregular in nature. These and many other examples are frequently shown in the financial pages of major newspapers and are readily available in periodicals published by the United States government, by various agricultural and industrial associations, and by the several Federal Reserve banks.[1]

1.1.2   Macroeconomic Fluctuations

What is true of individual commodity prices and quantities is also true of macroeconomic indexes of production, consumption, investment, employment capacity utilization, and the general level of prices, wages, interest rates, and the money supply. These indexes, which can be obtained from the sources just cited and which are illustrated in most principles of economics texts, give an average picture of the economy as a whole. Sometimes they reflect a widespread increase in economic activity; at other times they reflect a general decline. These alternating periods of expansion and contraction in the general level of the aggregate economy, like that in the microeconomic variables described above, are not cyclic in nature. They don't exhibit any definite pattern at all.

1.1.3 Growth and Growth Cycles

Many economic variables, such as industrial production, capital stock, and population, show a general upward trend over relatively long periods of time, but interspersed with periods of relatively faster or slower growth or occasional downturns. Such fluctuations are usually called growth cycles but, as in other measures of aggregate activity, the movements of virtually any growing economic variable are quite irregular. Thus, even when it is growing, the economy exhibits much greater complexity of behavior than can be described by simple dynamics.

1.1.4 Development

Economic development involves changes not only in the level of various variables but in an economy's structure, that is, changes in the way the economy works. Such changes can involve advances in technology, modification in organization, or the introduction of new rules of behavior. It could involve the adoption of available but previously unutilized activities or resources, or, contrastingly, the abandonment of previously utilized ones. All such changes induce a shift in the way things are done and in the constraints that impinge on the level or intensity of various activities. As a result, the active forces governing the economy shift in some fundamental way. These kinds of change occur almost continuously as the list of commodities consumed changes or the menu of production processes is modified, and as the rules governing economic intercourse evolve.

If one stands back and looks from decade to decade or from generation to generation, then one perceives an evolution of epochs, waves of consumption, technology, and socioeconomic organization that emerge, overwhelm preexisting practices, grow to dominance, and then, growth having abated, decline absolutely, often precipitously, in the face of a new emerging wave.

From a broad perspective of the very long run, these waves appear as great stages in the evolution of human culture, from hunting and food collecting to the establishment of cities and small-scale agriculture to irrigated agriculture, literate civilization, and trading empires to the modern age of machine technology and high energy production. Although developments within these vast epochs have taken a long time relative to the span of a single human life, the pace of progress through succeeding epochs has quickened.

The first of these epochs lasted at least 40,000 years, the second perhaps eight millennia, the third some two or three millennia, while the most recent is only some two or three centuries old and is already undergoing a fundamental shift to a new computer, robotic, information-dominated age.

The period of transition from one epoch to another often occurs relatively rapidly compared to the duration of the epoch itself, and this period of transition is also quickening. For example, it took several thousand years for agriculture to spread throughout the globe, but a mere two centuries for industrialization to do so. The new information age may spread almost everywhere in only a few decades. Evidently, economic development should no longer be thought of as something that takes a very long time, but rather as something of contemporary and immediate interest.

1.1.5 Explosive Change

From a still more abstract perspective, viewed from the time scale in which biologists reckon the origin and evolutionary progress of living forms and by which astronomers calculate the birth and death of planets, economic development and the growth of human numbers must be seen as explosive processes. When population is plotted on one diagram in this time scale, we have a picture in which all the details of human history, the neolithic and agricultural revolutions, the rise and fall of all previous civilizations, the subsequent waves of technology, and all the vicissitudes of economy and state—all are lost within the thickness of a vertically exploding line![2]

1.1.6 The Fundamental Properties of Change

To summarize, the following facts broadly characterize economic change:

• Individual commodity prices and quantities fluctuate with irregular period and amplitude.

• Aggregate indexes representing the economy as a whole likewise exhibit irregular fluctuations.

Economic growth does not follow a smooth trend but rather one with fluctuating rates of change.

Economic activity follows overlapping waves of consumption, technology, and organization.

Aggregate economic development is an explosively unstable phenomenon when measured on a bio-astronomical time scale.

Putting all these together we arrive at a corollary fact of monumental importance for the construction of economic science: *there is little if any evidence that economic data converge to stationary states, to steady growth or to periodic cycles.* Such evidence as there is would appear to be of a temporary kind, that is, stationary or steady states and regular cyclical behavior are only occasionally approximated and such types of change appear always to be interrupted.

1.2 Explanation

1.2.1 The Modeling Strategy

The question to be answered is, why? What explains the facts just described? The basic strategy to be followed in this book is to build mathematical models based on economic forces that can generate these facts. If we succeed in doing so, we shall have shed some light on the issue. Complete answers within the framework of the simple models to which we shall be confined will not be possible. In particular, no attempt is made to explain the numerical data in exact, quantitative terms. Instead, our goal will be more limited—but more useful. We shall strive to explain the central *qualitative* features of the data that we have identified: irregular microeconomic fluctuations, erratic macroeconomic fluctuations (business cycles), irregular growth, structural change, and overlapping waves of economic development.

Once a given set of economic hypotheses, assumptions, or axioms has been specified, mathematical analysis can derive the specific conditions for which a given qualitative kind of behavior will occur within the model framework. Numerical experiments can then be used to illustrate the analytical results.

1.2.2 Intrinsic versus Extrinsic Explanation

An explanation derived in this way is called an *intrinsic explanation* because the phenomenon of interest is shown to be inherent in the model structure. It is derived from specific hypotheses or assumptions about the economic process. Another way of putting this is to say that the complex dynamic behavior can be explained in terms of *endogenous variables.*

The phenomena we are talking about are often explained in a different way. The economist specifies a model whose endogenous variables—in the absence of "external" forces—behave in simple ways (attain stationary equilibria, periodic cycles, or steady balanced growth). The model is then augmented with exogenous "shock" variables whose behavior is assumed to come from forces outside the economic system under consideration but that influence its working. These shocks are often assumed to be random so that the endogenous variables display irregular behavior. Typical external influences that are treated as random shocks are weather variables (such as droughts, floods, blizzards), political events (such as wars, revolutions, assassinations), and other human factors (such as "irrational acts," innovations, or reorganizations). Simple dynamics become transformed into complex dynamics by the imposition of these exogenous shocks. The result is an *extrinsic explanation* of complex economic behavior in which the irregularity or complexity is caused by external factors and not by the internal dynamics of the economic system itself.[3]

In contrast to this view the hypothesis pursued in the present work is that the complexity of observed economic phenomena can be explained at least in part by the intrinsic working of economic forces and that complex dynamics is endogenous to the way economic systems behave. Exogenous variables are treated as *parameters.* They are held constant so as to make possible controlled analytical experiments to see how a model behaves when exogenous forces are not changing. This enables us to separate out the intrinsic from the extrinsic explanation of different kinds of behavior. This method, which is called "comparative dynamics" or "bifurcation theory" will be made precise and illustrated over and over again throughout the book.

1.2.3 Past Modeling Studies

The mathematical modeling approach has become a basic method of most theoretical sciences. In economics it has long been used to expound theoretical ideas, and in particular it has long been used to explain simple dynamics as it is described above. These developments have given us some of the essential tools: difference and differential equations, the analytical concepts of fixpoint theory and of stability analysis, and the theoretical tools of equilibrium and optimality.

Until recently, however, mathematical methods have not been exploited to explain the phenomena of special interest in this book. The physical and biological sciences were somewhat in advance of economics in this regard but that picture has changed. The study of complex economic dynamics using mathematical models and formal analysis is well established and expanding rapidly. Some of this work will be touched on as we go along, and a survey of contemporary work is contained in volume II.

1.2.4   New Wine in Old Skins

In presenting an introduction to this promising new field, I have tried to depart as little as possible from classic economic thinking. One must first learn to think dynamically and to master the basic concepts that enable change to be described precisely and analyzed rigorously. This can be done by reinterpreting market adjustment, business cycle, macroeconomic growth, and economic development theories that have emerged during the past development of economic science. These classic theories, when reduced to precise mathematical forms, employ abstraction and simplification. Yet they retain essential features of such importance that anyone who wants to have a broad understanding of the subject must know something about them. They provide insights of continuing relevance generation after generation.

With relatively minor modification, classic theories can be employed to introduce some new ideas about economic adaptation, disequilibrium, structural change, and evolution. These new ideas are of considerable importance for the further development of the discipline. Their introduction is an important theme of the book. In the process, every effort is made not only to explain qualitative patterns of change that are familiar from experience but also to derive the explanation from assumptions that are plausible. If the equations have some basis in the way people really behave and in how economic mechanisms actually work, model inferences take on more meaning.

It must be understood that this is just a starting point for the analysis of change. A great deal of work must be done to bring economic dynamics up to the level of generality with which static economics has been expounded. As the work continues the basic concepts and methods of analysis discussed here will have to be exploited again and again. They are fundamental and therefore likely to be of enduring interest whatever the fashion of theory and whatever problems hold popular attention for the time being.

2 Dynamics

May the spirit of Newton give us the power to restore unison between . . . reality and the profoundest characteristic of Newton's teaching—strict causality.
—Albert Einstein, quoted by Abraham Pais in *"Subtle Is the Lord—": The Science and the Life of Albert Einstein*

. . . it is the dynamics that count. All else would merely be a sort of word painting.
—Werner Heisenberg, *Tradition in Science*

Before getting into the details of dynamic analysis in part II, this chapter reviews the basic concepts that will be involved using a minimum of technical machinery. This will enable readers who don't want to plough through more mathematics than absolutely necessary to skip part II and move directly to the economic models in part III and in volume II.

2.1 The Systematic Study of Change

2.1.1 The Dynamic Principle

The systematic study of change can be undertaken in a variety of ways. The study of past human history is one of the most important. Historians and archaeologists often concentrate on the description and analysis of some past situation. They ask, what happened at such a time and such a place? What was it like then and there? When they have constructed answers to such questions for many places and times, a dynamic picture of history emerges. This dynamic picture is a sequence of events describing the movements of peoples, cultures, political organizations, and economic changes. An example of dynamic history that graphically portrays change in the human domain is the *Times Atlas of History*. This book displays in a series of striking, colored maps with directed curves and arrows the development and movement of major peoples and cultures through fifty millennia.[1]

Many quantitative aspects of historical movements were captured even in the ancient and medieval era in the form of inventory, transaction, and financial records, and in various head counts and early census taking. In modern times the accumulation of quantitative economic records of all kinds has become a vast enterprise in all developed and developing countries, giving detailed numerical pictures of change within and among industries, regions, countries, and the world as a whole.[2]

Forecasting how things will change in the future has been an important part of the study of change and is reflected in a great variety of systematic approaches that include divination, astrology, and, more recently, statistics. Pure statistical forecasting methods attempt to predict what will happen in the future on the basis of historical data under the hypothesis that the sequences of situations that have been observed or estimated in the past reveal the directions of change in the future. Although forecasting methods are of considerable importance, the results derived in this book suggest that their success in economics will continue to be severely limited.

Analytical dynamics, with which this book is concerned, involves a fundamental perception common to any field of empirical inquiry that life presents itself as a system of phenomena: perceived facts and objects connected by relationships, and as time passes, as a system of things interrelated by a network of cause and effect: things at one point in time are related in some definite way to things at an earlier time. To put it differently but more or less equivalently, *the way things are (and have been) determines the way things change*. Superficially, this *dynamic principle* would seem to be the basis for forecasting. But this need not be the case. It can also be the basis for an explanation of why we do so poorly at the forecasting art most of the time.

The basic strategy in applying this principle is to identify systems of interrelated parts that influence each other so as to generate behavior. The parts are described by *state variables* that express in quantitative terms various properties of the system under consideration. A sequence of such variables dated by a time index describes the system's behavior and constitutes its history. The interrelationships among the parts consist of causal effects that determine how parts are related at a given instant of time or how values at one time influence changes at succeeding times. These relationships constitute the *structure of the system*. A system so identified may be represented mathematically. This provides a precise means for describing the system's structure and for analyzing its properties. The problem of dynamic analysis is to derive how the behavior of the model is related to its structure.[3]

From the scientific point of view, such a mathematical system is a *model* of the empirical perceptions that underlie it and which it is our purpose to understand and predict. Model-generated behavior can be compared with historical information about "real world" phenomena. It is the task of econometricians to devise methods for carrying out such comparisons in a scientific manner. That is not our task here. As we have already emphasized, our objective is the more limited one of mimicking qualitative attributes of economic data and explaining how various types of change observed in reality can be caused by economic forces.

2.1.2 An Example: Walras's Producer's Tatonnement

In order to illustrate these concepts in the simplest possible way, consider Walras's concept of "tatonnement for producers," which postulates a competitive market with a finite number, say n, of identical firms, none of whom has any knowledge of demand.[4] Each produces an amount x at a total cost $C(x)$ during period t. The total supply, nx, is "trucked to and bartered" on a purely competitive market so that each producer's output is sold at the same market clearing price $p = D^{-1}(nx)$ where $D^{-1}(\cdot)$ is the inverse demand curve. Each producer therefore receives a revenue of $R(x; n) = xD^{-1}(nx)$. The firm's pure profit is its revenue minus its costs $C(x)$ and minus the opportunity cost of the funds invested in production, $iC(x)$. Let us denote this pure profit by $\pi(x) = R(x; n) - (1 + i)C(x)$.

Typical total revenue and total cost functions are shown in figure 2.1a. The corresponding profit functions are shown in figure 2.1b.

When the "internal" rate of return on investment exceeds that outside the industry where the latter "external" rate of return is represented by i, further investment is justified because if existing firms did not take advantage of the opportunity, others who are currently earning less would eventually enter. But, firms don't know where the equilibrium is because they don't know their revenue functions. Suppose that in order to take advantage then of the pure profits available, firms change output in proportion to the pure profit they actually receive. Let κ be constant. Then

$$\Delta x = f(x; n) := \kappa \pi(x; n) = \kappa \left(R(x; n) - (1 + i)C(x) \right). \tag{2.1}$$

Positive profits stimulate investment; negative profits depress it. This causes output to change in the direction of the arrows as shown in figure 2.1b.[5]

Here we have an exact analog of the dynamic principle: how things change depends on the way things are. To solve the problems of dynamic analysis completely, however, some further mathematical ideas are necessary.

2.2 Difference Equations

2.2.1 The First-Order Difference Equation

Imagine that a state variable x (the firm's output in the example) is measured at regular intervals. Let this interval be a unit period such as a minute, hour,

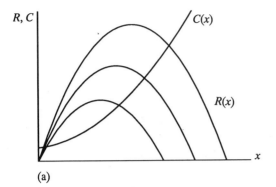

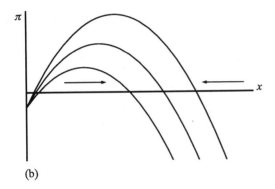

Figure 2.1
Cost and revenue functions for the firm. (a) The revenue function shifts up and out as the demand
parameter a increases. (b) The profit functions shown correspond to the revenue functions in (a).

month, quarter, year, decade, or generation. The base period at which the
measurement is made is denoted 0. The sequence

$$(x_t)_{t=0}^{\infty} := (x_0, x_1, x_2, x_3, \ldots, x_t, x_{t+1}, \ldots) \tag{2.2}$$

is the *trajectory* of the system beginning at time zero. This trajectory or history
describes the behavior at finite intervals of time, so it is referred to as a *discrete
trajectory*.

The change in the behavior of the system between unit intervals is

$$\Delta x_t := x_{t+1} - x_t, \qquad t = 0, 1, 2, \ldots \tag{2.3}$$

If the change Δx_t at time t is determined (or "caused") by the state at time t, then we can write the dynamic principle as

$$\Delta x_t = f(x_t), \tag{2.4}$$

where $f(\cdot; n)$ is called a difference or change operator and n is a parameter. An equivalent form is defined by

$$x_{t+1} = \theta(x_t) := x_t + f(x_t; n). \tag{2.5}$$

This equation states that the state of the system at one point in time determines the state one unit of time later. Equation (2.5) is called a *first-order difference equation*. The function $\theta(\cdot)$ is called the *structure* of the process under consideration. For Walras's producers' tatonnement (2.1), the difference equation is

$$x_{t+1} = \theta(x_t) := x_t + \kappa \pi(x_t) = x_t + \kappa[R(x_t; n) - (1+i)C(x_t)]. \tag{2.6}$$

Note that if $\theta(\cdot)$ is specified, the equivalent dynamic principle (2.4) can always be stated by defining

$$f(x_t; n) = \theta(x_t) - x_t. \tag{2.7}$$

2.2.2 Functional Forms

In much theoretical analysis it is quite sufficient to express models in a general qualitative form. In the example just illustrated, the qualitative form of the total revenue function is that it is single-peaked or bell-shaped, while that of total cost is monotonically increasing and convex. It is extremely helpful, however, in gaining an intuitive feel for what is going on to illustrate the ideas not only graphically but also numerically, and to do this specific functional forms are needed.

As a case in point, the total revenue and cost function shown in figure 2.1 is given by

$$R(x; n) = ax - bnx^2, \tag{2.8}$$

where $R(x; n) = xD^{-1}(nx)$ and $D^{-1}(nx) = a - bnx$, and where

$$C(x) = h + cx + dx^2. \tag{2.9}$$

The profit function is

$$\pi(x) = -(1+i)h + [a - (1+i)c]x - [bn + (1+i)d]x^2, \qquad (2.10)$$

so the difference equation that describes output over time is

$$x_{t+1} = -\kappa(1+i)h + [1 + \kappa a - \kappa(1+i)c]x_t - \kappa[bn + (1+i)d]x_t^2. \quad (2.11)$$

Three graphs of this equation are shown in the upper part of figure 2.2. Each example is obtained using a different total revenue curve and hence a different profit curve.[6]

2.2.3   Behavior: The Derivation of History from Structure

The behavior of a system can be derived recursively, step by step, because the function θ defined by (2.11) maps the space of possible "present" output states into the space of possible "future" output states. To see how this can be done, begin at some initial output x_0 as shown in the upper part of figure 2.2. The next state is $x_1 = \theta(x_0)$. This value is projected via the 45° line onto the horizontal axis that becomes the next "present" state. The "future" state is now $x_2 = \theta(x_1)$. By using the map to obtain the future state from the present, then projecting the future onto the present as a graphical analog for the passage of time, you arrive at a sequence of steps x_0, $x_1 = \theta(x_0)$, $x_2 = \theta(x_1), \ldots, x_{t+1} = \theta(x_t), \ldots$. This sequence represents the unfolding history implied by the system's structure when it begins at the initial state x_0. The unfolding history of states can be converted directly into a graphical function of time by defining the explicit, real-valued function of the integers $(0, x_0)$, $(1, x_1)$, $(2, x_2), \ldots, (t, x_t)$, which may be represented as a map $t \rightarrow x_t$ as shown in the lower part of figure 2.2. By convention the points have been connected. This can be interpreted as meaning that the rate of change of x is constant in the unit interval of time, changing only from discrete period to discrete period.

This graphical process or "paper and pencil simulation" is the visual analog of solving the difference equation (2.5). In general the trajectory of a difference equation is obtained recursively given an initial condition x_0 according to the scheme

$$
\begin{aligned}
x_1 &= \theta(x_0) \\
x_2 &= \theta(x_1) &&= \theta(\theta(x_0)) \\
x_3 &= \theta(x_2) &&= \theta(\theta(x_1)) &&= \theta(\theta(\theta(x_0))) \qquad (2.12)\\
&\ \ \vdots && \ \ \vdots && \ \ \vdots && \ \ \vdots \\
x_{t+1} &= \theta(x_t) &&= \theta(\theta(x_{t-1})) &&= \theta(\ldots(\theta(x_0))\ldots).
\end{aligned}
$$

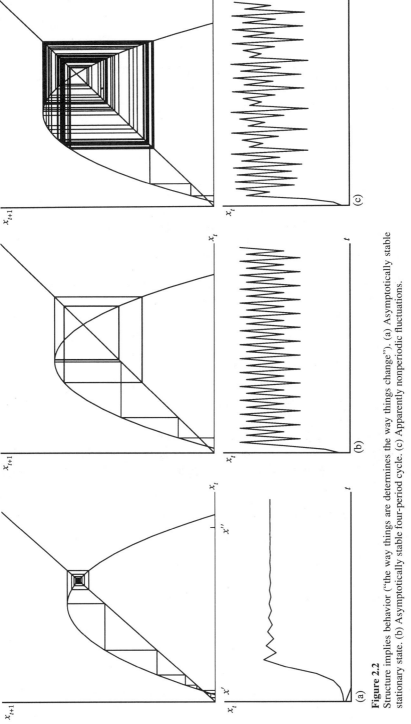

Figure 2.2
Structure implies behavior ("the way things are determines the way things change"). (a) Asymptotically stable stationary state. (b) Asymptotically stable four-period cycle. (c) Apparently nonperiodic fluctuations.

You can see that the terms on the right side are functions of x_0 and must become extremely complicated with the passage of time unless they can be simplified in some way. When $\theta(\cdot)$ is *affine*, which means that its graph is a straight line, this can be easily done (as shown in part II). In general they cannot be simplified in any convenient way.

Fortunately, even when these recursive maps are hopelessly complicated, there are analytical ways to figure out how the system behaves. They shall be developed in part II and applied in the remainder of the book. The computer makes the calculation of (2.12) easy, however, so we can augment the theoretical analysis with numerical experiments without much effort.

2.2.4 The Domain of Definition and Viability

The character of the history generated by the structure depends in general on the initial condition. For example, in figure 2.2a any initial condition smaller than x' or larger than x'' would have led to a sequence of declining values until x became negative. In our example this would indicate bankruptcy and the demise of the industry. The point x' is the *break-even point*. Those points above (but close enough to) x' allow for growth.

For Walras's producer's tatonnement, only positive outputs are meaningful. The half line $D = \{x \geq 0\}$ is thus the *domain of definition* for the process. If $\theta(x) > 0$ for all $x \in D$, the successive output generated from any initial output is positive, so the system is *viable* on its domain D. If, however, $\theta(x) < 0$ for some $x \in D$, the successive output would be negative, which is impossible, so the system is *inviable* for that initial condition. The implication of all this is that

• a viable dynamic system works indefinitely

• an inviable dynamic system stops working or self-destructs by escaping its domain of definition.

The latter possibility arises naturally in economics.

2.3 Dynamic Analysis

2.3.1 Qualitatively Different Histories

The preceding possibility shows that the history generated by a given structure depends on where that history "begins," that is, on the initial condition x_0.

It also depends on the *profile* of the structure. This fact was illustrated in figure 2.2, which showed histories of three quite different types associated with the output adjustment equation (2.11) for three different sets of parameters. In figure 2.2a two trajectories are shown. One converges to a positive stationary state; one declines and "goes negative," that is, escapes the domain of definition D. In figure 2.2b the trajectory converges to a four-period cycle. In figure 2.2c the trajectory has not converged even after many periods. In this case there would seem to be a very high-order cycle, or perhaps no cycle at all. Perhaps the output level continues to wander, sometimes growing, sometimes declining, but continually fluctuating. Because output increases when profits are positive and decreases otherwise, fluctuating output is associated with fluctuating profits.

2.3.2 Simple and Complex Dynamics

The two convergent examples shown in figure 2.2a,b exhibit ultimately periodic behavior. (A stationary state is just a cycle of period 1.) Periodic behavior is *simple* because it can be characterized by the finite number of periodic values that are repeated. This is not quite the case if a system escapes its domain of definition, as in the declining trajectory of figure 2.2a, or if it wanders in an erratic pattern, as in figure 2.2c, never converging to a cycle of some order. Both the latter cases are of obvious empirical and, therefore, theoretical relevance. If firms *do* go bankrupt, if industries *do* disappear, and if economic variables *do* fluctuate in a nonperiodic way, then we want to find models that explain such behavior. These are examples of *complex dynamics* that illustrate how behavior or model histories are derived from model structure.

2.3.3 Comparative Dynamics

The different qualitative histories shown in figure 2.2 were obtained by shifting or bending the total revenue curve and, hence, the profit function and the structural equation (2.11). In the discussion of viability we also saw that the history implied by a given system depended on the initial condition. For a given equation a different history follows for each initial condition. For example, in each of the graphs if we had begun with an initial value x_0 that lay at an intersection of its graph of $\theta(\cdot)$ and the 45° line, the trajectory would have been stationary and its graph would have been a straight line with a constant level.

The study of how history changes when initial conditions or the causal structure are changed is called *comparative dynamics*. It is a subject important for a number of reasons.

• It shows how a given theory can be adjusted to fit a great variety of distinctly different empirical situations.

• It enables us to see how a system's behavior could be modified if its structure were adjusted, and this suggests how the system could be influenced or controlled by policy.

• Comparative dynamics enables us to tell if a qualitative type of behavior is robust, that is, if its general character (periodic cycles, stationarity, erratic fluctuation) persists when the initial condition or structure is perturbed, when errors enter the calculations, or when policy controls are exercised.

• It provides hints of the kinds of change that can occur if some of the parameters—which may have been assumed to be constant as an analytical convenience—are treated as variables. In this way, the comparative dynamic analysis of a single state variable system can provide insight about the behavior of a higher-order system with several state variables and/or lags of different length in which it could be imbedded.

All of these uses of comparative dynamics will be involved in the study of economic models below. To give a more specific idea of what can be involved, let us consider the above example.

2.3.4   The Bifurcation Diagram

In figure 2.3 the results of a detailed, numerical, comparative dynamics experiment is shown. Each point along the horizontal axis is a value for the parameter a in equation (2.11). This parameter is the "demand shifter" and has the effect of moving the revenue curve $R(x)$ upward and outward as it increases. We could say that it represents the "extent of the market," to use Adam Smith's phrase. For each value of a equation (2.11) is simulated for 350 iterations. The first 200 are discarded and the remaining data plotted vertically just above the point a. This gives an estimate of where trajectories go in the long run. By throwing away the early values, we can leave transient changes out of the picture.

For relatively small values of a (below roughly 8.2), trajectories converge to a stationary state; for values up to roughly 9, two-period cycles appear and then four-period cycles. Around 9.2 or so, many points remain that in the long-

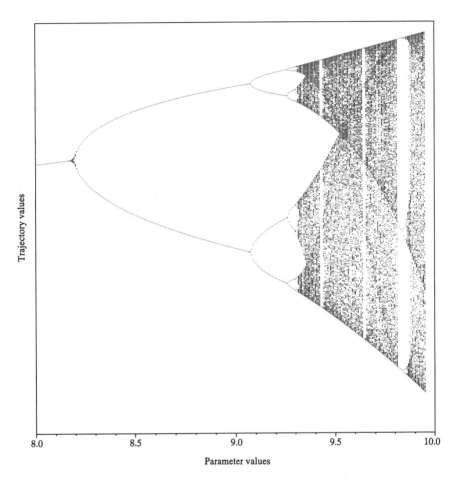

Figure 2.3
A bifurcation diagram for equation (2.11)

run behavior must surely converge to a very high-order cycle or perhaps not even to a cycle of any order. At about 9.5 a stable three-period cycle exists, but for many values between 9.2 and about 9.8, long-run behavior is high-order cyclic or nonperiodic.

The points at which the periodicity of the cycle changes, or at which the qualitative behavior switches from cycles to nonperiodic behavior, are called *bifurcation points* and the diagram is called a *bifurcation diagram*. Roughly speaking, as the extent of the market grows in Walras's tatonnement for pro-

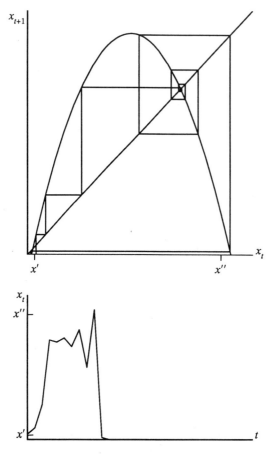

Figure 2.4
A self-destructing trajectory

ducers, market behavior becomes increasingly complex and the qualitative pattern increasingly unstable.

2.4   Complex Dynamics

2.4.1   Multiple-Phase Dynamics

We have observed that a given system can self-destruct. Another such possibility is shown in figure 2.4. Although the trajectory comes close to the equilibrium, it then experiences expanding oscillations, declines precipitously, and falls to zero. Any trajectory that expands above x'' must experience a demise in this fashion.

When this happens in reality, a firm often has recourse to another technology, one that is cheaper and that can keep it going if a switch in production can be made. Or, the economy has rules of bankruptcy that permit a transfer of resources from a bankrupt firm to a different, financially viable enterprise. In general, at critical junctures, the economy switches from one structure to another. Certain conditions, of course, have to induce such a change.

A closely related phenomenon is the switch from one qualitative mode of behavior to another. For example, a variable may exhibit prolonged growth, then switch to a fluctuating behavior. Or, a variable that has been fluctuating may begin a new course of steady growth—or, perhaps, steady decay. After some time it may eventually reach a position of near stationarity.

These are examples of *multiple-phase dynamics* or *regime switching*. In order to formalize these ideas within the framework we have been using, let the economic system under consideration continue to be described by a single state variable x that takes on values in the real numbers. Imagine that this space can be partitioned into subsets called *phase zones*. Suppose further that a distinct difference equation governs change in each of these zones, where each difference equation is determined by a causal structure θ_p, one for each phase zone. We can then investigate the conditions under which behavior may

• escape one zone after another in a progression of evolutionary phases,

• eventually repeat a fixed sequence of phase zones, or

• become trapped in a given zone so that, after this occurs, the system behaves like a single phase system.

In our discussion of the stock market in chapter 10, we look at switching "bear" and "bull" regimes and alternate phases in which caution or financial constraints rule behavior. When we look at the business cycle in volume II, we will see that multiple-phase dynamics formally captures situations in an economy in which monetary factors may have very little influence during one phase of the cycle but play a crucial role in a second phase. Then, when we look at economic development, also in volume II, the concept will provide a natural formalization of the concept of structural economic change in economic development. Indeed, we shall find phase switching fundamental in the analysis of complex dynamics generally. It is one of the key ideas around which this book is built.

2.4.2   Nonperiodic Behavior: Statistical Description

When a history is periodic or converges to a periodic cycle, then it can, at least in the long run, be characterized by a finite number of states equal to the period of the cycle. When a history is nonperiodic this is not the case. How then can the behavior be characterized conveniently?

One possibility is to study the history statistically; for example, by describing the proportion of state values that fall in certain intervals, by the frequency with which states fall below a certain value, or by the mean value and variance of the trajectory. If the densities are stable, that is, if they don't shift around as time progresses but instead converge to fixed numbers, then they provide a way to say something definite about a trajectory as a whole. Systems with this property are called *ergodic*.

Suppose, for example, we compute values for many periods of equation (2.11) using the three examples shown in figure 2.2. We can count the number of values that fall in each of a number of small intervals that partition the state space. Then we can plot the fraction of data points that fall in each of these intervals.

For the first case, the one that converges to the stationary state $\tilde{x}$, consider an interval $I := [\tilde{x} - \epsilon, \ \tilde{x} + \epsilon]$ where ϵ is a small positive constant and count the number of values that belong to I. Let that number be m. Then, because the stationary state is asymptotically stable, for any $\epsilon > 0$ the fraction of points that belong to I, which is $\frac{m}{n}$, converges to 1 as n becomes large. All the density piles up over the stationary state.[7]

For the second case, let $I_1, \ldots, I_4$ be four distinct intervals, each containing one of the cyclic points, each of width ϵ. Now the histogram of values must converge to four spikes of height $\frac{1}{4}$, *i.e.*, if we let m_i be the number of trajectory values that lie in interval I_i, then $\frac{m_i}{n} \to \frac{1}{4}$. In general, for a globally asymptotically stable cycle of length p, the fraction $\frac{m_i}{n}$ of trajectory values in a small interval containing a cyclic point—no matter how small that interval is—must converge to $\frac{1}{p}$.[8]

In case 3 shown in figure 2.3c the trajectory seems to wander all over the place or perhaps to a cycle whose periodicity is extremely large. Indeed, in this example, several hundred values in the trajectory have been computed recursively and their frequencies accumulated for each of 100 small intervals. Roughly, half of these have positive frequencies. Now, if the trajectory were periodic of period less than 50 and if the intervals were small enough, the frequency over each interval would be the same and the density function would look like a set of spikes of equal height. Because it is uneven, we know that (a) the system must be converging very, very slowly to a period lower than 50; or (b) it is converging to a cycle of period greater than 50; or (c) it is wandering without converging to any periodic cycle. Nonetheless, in the latter event the fractions falling in any interval $I := [a, b]$ could converge. If this were so, the histogram of trajectory values would give an approximate statistical character-ization of the trajectory in the long run.

Figure 2.5 shows the computed numerical density function and cumulative distribution for the examples shown in figure 2.2. As surmised, the density for the convergent stationary state is a single spike; its associated cumulative distribution function (c.d.f.) is a rectangle with unit height. The density for the convergent four-period cycle is four spikes and its c.d.f. is a step function with four steps of height $\frac{1}{4}, \frac{1}{2}, \frac{3}{4}, 1$. The nonperiodic case gives an irregular shape of the computed density that is typical when the conditions for chaos are satisfied. We shall see in chapter 8 that this kind of statistical characterization can be used to describe the long-run behavior of many types of models, and 'in the later sections of the book that these types arise generically in economic applications.

2.4.3   Laws of Large Numbers for Deterministic Systems

Granting this possibility, anyone familiar with the statistical theory of stochas-tic models, that is models that *assume a nondeterministic, random component*, would ask if certain kinds of "laws of large numbers" hold. For example, sup-pose we consider a "sample mean"

$$\bar{x}(m) := \frac{1}{m} \sum_{t=0}^{m-1} \theta^t(x_0)$$

of a trajectory beginning from the initial condition x_0. Will it converge to the mean of a long-run density function?

Or, could a central limit theorem hold? This idea involves the distribution of the sample means of a process in which each sample is drawn randomly from a population characterized by a fixed density or distribution function. Here we let the first sample be the first N, say, values in a trajectory $N \cdot p$ periods long. The second sample is the next N trajectory values, and so on.

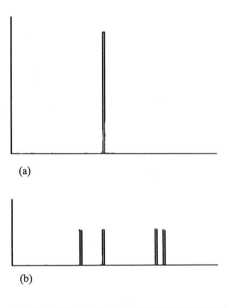

(a)

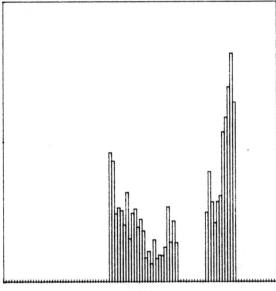

(b)

(c)

Figure 2.5
The density for a trajectory. (a) Stationary state. (b) Four-period cycle. (c) Nonperiodic fluctuations.

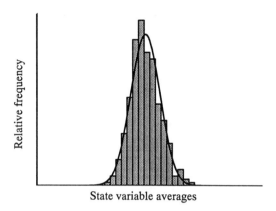

Figure 2.6
A distribution of time averages. The smooth curve is the normal density function.

The sample means are

$$\bar{x}_1 := \frac{1}{N} \sum_{t=0}^{N-1} \theta^t(x_0)$$

$$\bar{x}_2 := \frac{1}{N} \sum_{t=0}^{N-1} \theta^{N+t}(x_0)$$

$$\vdots$$

$$\bar{x}_p := \frac{1}{N} \sum_{t=0}^{N-1} \theta^{N(p-1)+t}(x_0).$$

What is the distribution of the values $\{\bar{x}_i\}_{t=1}^p$? We shall see that when the underlying trajectory can be characterized by a stable distribution (that satisfies certain properties), the answer is that the distribution of sample means converges to a normal distribution, just as in the case of a stochastic process generated from independent random drawings from a stable distribution. And this is true even though the dynamic system has no random component and each item in every sample depends deterministically on its predecessor. This possibility is illustrated in figure 2.6, which gives the distribution of sample means taken from the trajectory whose density is shown in figure 2.5c.

It is shown in this book that this type of "deterministic randomness" occurs in a wide variety of models with "classic" features, that is, whose assumptions are consistent with those used in theories of long-established importance. We want to emphasize that although this property of "deterministic randomness" emerges in a model only with the indefinite passage of time, its existence—when established in theory—provides a deterministic explanation of short-run irregularity in economic data.

It should be noted that, strictly speaking, ergodic behavior of the kind we have been speaking of, which gives nonperiodic, hence complex behavior, need not display highly irregular trajectories, but in certain well-known examples may show a kind of regular "drift."[9] To give irregular fluctuations, the trajectories must have a further property called *mixing*. All of the cases in this book that give ergodic behavior also have this property, and it is this fact that justifies the terms "random-like" or "stochastic-like" behavior.[10]

2.4.4 Nonperiodic Behavior: Chaos

It is often difficult to determine the distributional character of trajectories except numerically, and numerical simulations, while suggestive, are not definitive. A second concept for characterizing nonperiodic behavior is "chaos."

Chaotic trajectories are those whose values belong to an uncountable scrambled set S such that

• no trajectory that begins in S is periodic;

• any trajectory in S wanders away from any cyclic trajectory no matter how close it comes to one; and

• any two trajectories that begin in S and that wander close to one another (no matter how close) wander away from each other.

Thus, chaotic behavior is nonperiodic, does not converge to a cycle of any order, and is unstable with respect to small perturbations or shocks, i.e., it is sensitive to initial conditions.

These properties are closely related to the ergodic behavior discussed in §2.4.2. They derive their importance from the fact that several very simple criteria have been derived for establishing their existence. These are called chaos *overshoot conditions*, which will be discussed in chapter 7. When these conditions are present for a given model, then we know that there is an uncountable number of initial conditions for the model that will "produce" nonperiodic, highly irregular, or erratic trajectories.

Unfortunately, there is a problem with this approach.

When a system is not only ergodic but strongly ergodic in a precise sense that is explained in part II, we know that nonperiodic trajectories must occur with positive probability for initial conditions drawn at random from the model's domain of definition. In this case it is sometimes said that chaos is *strong* or *thick*.[11] Or, in more conventional mathematical terms, it can be said that chaos occurs *almost surely*. When the chaos overshoot conditions are satisfied and a scrambled set is known to exist, we do not know on that basis alone that chaos occurs with positive probability even though the scrambled set has more points than there are rational numbers. In fact, sometimes convergent cycles emerge almost surely even when chaos exists. In this case the mere "existence" of chaos does not mean that it is "important," so in this case the chaos is called *weak* or *thin*.

It can be said, however, that when the chaos overshoot conditions occur, complex dynamics seems to arise very often. That is, numerical simulations often show evidence of very erratic behavior that can only occur with very high-order cycles or nonperiodic motion, and small changes in parameters often cause large changes in behavior measured, say, by the mean of the histogram of values. But now we are getting into details that are better deferred to part II where the necessary background will be developed.

What should be emphasized here is that the fundamental notion of importance for complex dynamics in general and for economic applications in particular is that of nonperiodic, irregular, or erratic change. To characterize it using ergodic theory or chaos theory requires limiting concepts, which requires an analytical experiment based on imagining that a system can be run forever. The duration of an individual human life is pitifully short by comparison. Even human existence as a whole is still but a moment on such a scale.

The importance of these ideas for economics rests, therefore, not on their statistical prediction of what a system will or will not do in the long run but rather on their intrinsic explanation of why behavior over whatever time frame is relevant, is irregular and more or less unpredictable.

2.4.5 Escape from Chaos

A type of mathematical behavior that is of considerable potential importance in understanding economic change—as will be shown in the chapters that follow—is a kind of multiple-phase dynamics in which (at least) one regime produces trajectories that are erratic for a number of periods, but that eventually escape to another regime where growth, decay, or demise can occur. Behavior within the erratically fluctuating regime will be very much like the statistical kind of behavior just described in the preceding section. It differs, however, in having a positive probability of switching to another regime. Under some conditions this probability can be one, even though erratic fluctuations could occur for a long time. Behavior in the succeeding regime could be more stable, or it could also be erratic but in a discernibly different way. Applications of these possibilities will be found below in the analysis of stock market prices, business cycles, and economic development.

This, indeed, is another central theme of the book, the possible movement into and out of irregular fluctuations from and to other qualitative modes of behavior, namely, growth and decay in a sequence of switching regimes.

2.4.6 Deceptive Order

A common character of chaos and of ergodic behavior is the simultaneous existence of unstable cycles and nonperiodic trajectories. If we start precisely at an unstable cyclic point, a finite set of points is repeated indefinitely; but if we perturb this trajectory a tiny bit, a chaotic solution may emerge. But these chaotic trajectories will wander among at least some of the periodic trajectories, coming close but always veering away only to return later *but in a nonperiodic manner*. This means that apparently periodic values will occur and pass through several cycles only to be "disrupted" and replaced by another apparently periodic sequence later. Such a "cyclic" episode will invite an inference of order and suggest the possibility of extrapolating from past data to predict the future. But this order will be deceptive, for it will be short-lived. To summarize, nonlinear systems that satisfy conditions of ergodic, chaotic behavior will exhibit deceptive order in the sense of apparent cycles, but these apparent cycles will change periodicity in a more or less random way and are interspersed with erratic fluctuations.

This property emerges in a model of the stock market to be studied in chapter 11. In that context deceptive order has especially interesting implications.

2.4.7 Path Dependence

Another name for instability or sensitivity to initial conditions and perturbations is *path dependence*. To put it in common parlance, where you go and where you end up depends on what happens along the way. Many examples of this phenomenon will be shown to arise in specific economic models.

Historians have a particular interest in path dependence. Its interpretation would seem to be that the history of human affairs can be explained in part by more or less mechanical, more or less impersonal economic and social forces, but that actions by individuals (which might be considered to be small perturbations) can have a powerful influence much like catalysts in chemical processes. Thus, it has been said that when Alexander turned from pursuit of Darius toward the south and Egypt, he demonstrated how an individual decision could change the course of history forever.[12] The catalytic role of individuals in economic development has also been recognized by economists, especially Schumpeter whose theory describes how the inventiveness of entrepreneurs launches waves of adoption and resource reallocation.

2.5 A Philosophical Note

That unstable, complex phenomena can now be characterized mathematically leads to a vast extension in the domain of potential application of rigorous analysis. But at this point, early in the foray into that domain, a note of caution should be sounded.

The mathematics of complex dynamics is of relatively recent origin and much remains to be done to advance our knowledge in this field. More effort still is required to study its scientific relevance and to determine which aspects of empirical experience can be effectively mimicked in these mathematical terms.

We can be virtually certain that current models and methods will be found wanting, that new models and new methods will be discovered and applied in ways we cannot now imagine. Nonetheless, what we are doing here is not a fad or a fashion, but rather a pushing forward of the potential understanding of why experience appears as it does, in this way both testing the utility of a new way of thinking and reinforcing our respect for classic theories by showing how they contain an explanatory potential that goes far beyond what their originators conceived.

One should be careful, however, in the interpretation of this intellectual advance. Scientists, some of the greatest, have viewed their "laws of nature" not just as theories that give a measure of human understanding to what is an infinitely complex, unfathomably mysterious existence. They have regarded their laws almost as if they were the same thing in essence as the "real" world itself.[13] This, however, is an illusion of conscious perception. Mathematical models and theories are the *products* of human cognition. They are not laws of the external world or laws of nature but symbols and relationships of our internal world, that is, the world of our human imagination. How can it be that these artifacts of language and thought are sometimes able to represent so realistically our perceptions of the external world? This question is itself one of the great challenges for science, but we can't go into it here. What we do know is that mathematical models can provide insight into how the world works, and they help us communicate that understanding with each other in precise and logical forms. In particular we can use models both to explain how economies work in some essential regards, and to explain why our ability to predict must necessarily be limited.

3 Methodological Issues

When the effect produced is no longer in direct relation with nor in exact proportion to the cause, disorganization sets in.
—Honoré de Balzac, *The Rise and Fall of César Birotteau*

We now have before us some of the most important analytical concepts involved in the study of complex economic dynamics. Before giving a more complete and rigorous development of them, there are several methodological issues that need to be mentioned. The first has to do with causation and nonlinearity. The second concerns how single-variable theories can be used to provide insight into more complicated multivariable systems. The third has to do with the role of stochastic shocks in economic processes; the fourth, with problems of empirical inference; the fifth, with the distinction between discrete and continuous time; and the sixth, with the central role of instability for understanding real-world processes.

3.1 Causation

3.1.1 Functions

As we have seen, the fundamental basis for dynamic analysis in science is the identification of systems of cause and effect. Mathematically, cause and effect is represented by functions that define the relationships among the parts of a system. Let us consider them in some detail. If A is a cause and B the effect, one writes A causes B or $A \rightarrow B$. For purposes of mathematical analysis one associates with A and B state variables, say x and y, that characterize the relevant quantitative attributes of a system under consideration. Causal effect is now represented by the binary relationship or function f that maps values of x in a possible set of values (the domain of f) into values of y in a set of possible values (the image of f). In this case one writes $x \rightarrow y$ or $x \rightarrow f(x)$. This notion of causality, represented by functions or mappings, requires that a given argument (cause), x, has one and only one image (effect)

$$y = f(x), \tag{3.1}$$

though this does not preclude a given image having more than one argument.[1]

3.1.2 Aggregation of Fine Structure

When a function is used to characterize an empirical relationship, it generally aggregates or summarizes a finer dynamic structure of relationships in which

A influences *B*, but in a way that takes time and that actually works itself out through an array of intermediate variables. For a static functional representation of causality to be valid this underlying dynamic process must rapidly converge so that its duration can be ignored without serious distortion to the purpose at hand. Given this very important technical prerequisite, an extremely wide range of causal phenomena can be represented by functions, including numerous examples of a physical, biological, social, and psychological nature as well as examples in economics. Indeed, the ability to do so is an essential reason why mathematics has such a wide application in science.

3.1.3   Examples of Causal Effect

In order to emphasize the importance of this point let us consider several specific instances. First, consider the molecular force among atoms that lies at the basis of much of our immediate experience in the physical world. This force depends on the properties of the atoms and upon their distances from one another. The resulting attraction or repulsion depends on a complex dynamic system of relationships among the atoms and among their nuclei and electrons. This system is so complicated that it cannot be represented in any simple way. Nonetheless, throughout a wide range of experience it leads to an empirically valid, causal effect or functional relationship between distance and force. This relationship, taken from Feynman (1963), is shown in figure 3.1.[2]

Figure 3.2 illustrates a second example drawn from social psychology in which a measure of student performance ("pupil growth") is related to a characteristic of teacher behavior ("teacher indirectness"). Identification by Soar

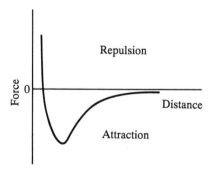

Figure 3.1
Atomic force. Source: Feynman (1963, 12–16.)

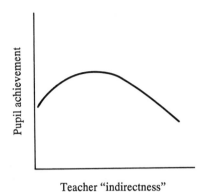

Teacher "indirectness"

Figure 3.2
Educational effectiveness. Source: Soar (1972, 510).

of this "inverted U" phenomenon helped resolve a number of apparently contradictory findings of educational experimenters. The relationship clearly and simply summarizes the outcome of a dynamic interaction among students and teachers that involves communication, reading, study, discussion, examinations, and so forth, all recurring over a prolonged period that allows for accumulated effects. The "inverted U" is thus a static, aggregated representation of an integrated process of change.

Figure 3.3 presents a biological nutrient response curve that reflects the fact that virtually all nutrients have a toxic effect that overwhelms their nutrient value when taken in sufficiently large doses. Thus, grain yields, for example, often decline precipitously when excess amounts of nitrogen are applied in the growing season, a phenomenon called "burning." Similar functional relationships have long been established for various growth processes in plants and animals. Here again we have the integrated, aggregated effect of a complex process of tilling, fertilization, nutrient uptake, and cellular development that commences some time prior to planting and continues through the harvest. Nonetheless, for many purposes the nutrient response function gives an adequate representation.

In figure 2.1 an economic example was given, that of the "total revenue function" for a given commodity obtained from an underlying demand curve. When the price is zero the producers of the commodity can earn nothing. At the other extreme, at some high enough price nobody can afford or, if affordable, nobody would want the commodity, so again nothing can be earned

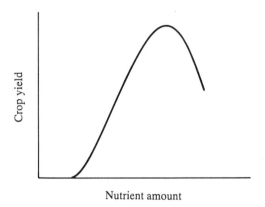

Figure 3.3
Nutrient response. Source: Russell (1950, chap. 3).

by offering it for sale. In between these extremes demand is positive, with revenues rising in the elastic portion of the demand curve, then falling in the inelastic portion. Underlying a total revenue function there must be a dynamic substratum of earning, shopping, purchase, payment, and so on. But none of these details is important for most purposes of economic analysis and can be ignored—at least for constructing relatively simple explanations as a first approximation.

All of these examples represent empirical relationships that summarize interacting systems of great structural complexity and that are only understood in part. Each represents a rigorous hypothesis that can serve as a basis for analytical theory. Science in any field progresses by identifying such functional relationships of cause and effect. They serve as postulates from which various logical implications may be drawn. Also, they express hypotheses that can be subjected to empirical testing. Finally, they stand as phenomena to be derived from an identification of finer, more fundamental states and causal relationships in subsequent research.

3.1.4   Causal Effect Reversal

The four examples just described share a common property, namely that the direction of influence by the independent variable on the magnitude of the dependent variable reverses. In the case of molecular force the causal relationship with distance is such that extremely close atoms are repelled while those very far apart are barely attracted; in between the force of attraction grows until some point of maximum attraction is reached. As the atoms move closer the force of attraction weakens. At some point the net force of attraction is nil. Still closer the force is strongly repelling and the atoms are driven apart. In each of the other examples similar ranges of data can be identified, where the direction of effect is different from one to the other range. In the economic example it is the effect of price increases on total revenues that reverses. This phenomenon is so important in dynamic theory that we shall give it a name, that of *causal effect reversal*.

As we have already shown, causal effect reversal in mathematical models induces complex patterns of change qualitatively like those observed in many areas of experience. Causal effect reversal is the result of *essential nonlinearity*, which means that the effect of one variable on another does not bear a constant proportional relationship nor can it be reduced by transformation to one that is proportional.[3]

The situation is very much different when the relationship between two variables is *affine* and can be represented by a straight line graph as shown in figure 3.4. In this case the direction of effect does not change and the change in y "caused by" a change x is a constant proportion. In dynamic models linear relationships can only exhibit simple patterns of change.

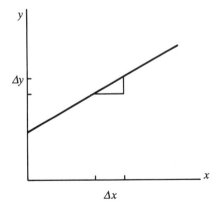

Figure 3.4
Linear causation. The ratio $\Delta y / \Delta x$ is constant.

3.2   System Reduction

Certainly, in economics any single-variable system is bound to be a drastic simplification if not oversimplification of the empirical process of interest. One way to incorporate somewhat more realism is to begin with a multivariable system and reduce it to a single-variable one. This can be done in at least the following ways.

3.2.1   Dependence on a Slow Variable

First, assume some of the variables are constant. This is a mathematical analog of the controlled experiment. Suppose

$$x_{t+1} = f(x_t, y_t), \tag{3.2}$$

where y_t is determined by some unspecified process. Then by assuming $y_t = y$, a constant, we obtain a first-order difference equation in which y plays the role of a parameter. An example that uses this approach is the macroeconomic model, to be discussed in volume II, in which prices and capital stock are assumed fixed in the short run so that changes in aggregate demand caused by an adjustment lag can be studied in isolation.

In order to see how changes in y influence the progress of x a comparative dynamic analysis can be carried out. This will not yield a complete understanding of the system's behavior, but it will provide clues about how the behavior of x may change as interactions with y occur. Generally, this approach is most appropriate when y changes relatively slowly compared to x. Even then, however, it must be remembered that the analysis of the reduced system is an approximation and that the accumulated influence of the excluded variables can, after a sufficient period of time, alter, perhaps drastically, the qualitative performance of the single-variable equation if their changes were taken into account. This is one reason why comparative dynamic analysis is a crucial part of dynamic analysis.

3.2.2   Dependence on a Rapidly Converging Variable

A second approach for reducing a multivariable system is to assume that all variables but one are always in a "temporary equilibrium." For example, suppose we have a two difference equation system with state variables x_t and y_t as before, but in which in addition to (3.2) it is assumed that y is governed by a very rapidly convergent process within the unit interval involved in the change of x. Then, given x_t, y (approximately) achieves an equilibrium

$$y_t = g(x_t, y_t), \tag{3.3}$$

which can be solved in terms of x_t to get

$$y_t = h(x_t). \tag{3.4}$$

Then, substituting into (3.2) we get a first-order difference equation in x alone

$$x_{t+1} = f[x_t, h(x_t)]. \tag{3.5}$$

This method, in contrast to that of assuming y is constant, assumes that y changes very rapidly compared to x in a stable adjustment process that can, as a first approximation, be ignored.

Suppose, for example, there are two interacting markets one of which clears each period and one of which does not. Suppose demands $D^1(p^1, p^2)$ and $D^2(p^1, p^2)$ and supplies $S^1(p^1, p^2)$ and $S^2(p^1, p^2)$ depend on prices in both markets and that the first market clears each period at a price p_t^1 given the price p_t^2 so that

$$D^1(p_t^1, p_t^2) = S^1(p_t^1, p_t^2).$$

Given appropriate conditions, this implicit function can be solved in terms of p_t^2 so that

$$p_t^1 = g(p_t^2).$$

Then in the second market we get demands and supplies $D^2[g(p_t^2), p_t^2]$, $S^2[g(p_t^2), p_t^2]$ whose adjustments over time can now be analyzed in isolation. The price of the second good will then change out of equilibrium in response to temporary gluts or shortages, while the first market clears period after period. Each price p_t^1 clears the market at a given time, but only temporarily. It is a *temporary partial equilibrium*. The term "partial" is used because it specifies that only one of the two markets is cleared.

The concept of temporary equilibrium will arise in the context of business cycles and economic growth in volume II of this study. In studying the real/monetary business cycle, money markets are assumed to clear in each period but commodity markets are allowed to adjust with a lag. In studying economic growth we think of a sequence of markets for capital goods. Agents save and invest on the basis of a current known rate of return and a guess of future rates of return. In contrast to the business cycle model we suppress the complicating action of short-run disequilibrium fluctuations, and assume that the current markets for capital goods and for labor clear at the current wage and rate of return on capital. We suppose also that the guesses for future wages and interest rates are imperfect. When the time comes, market wages and interest rates for future periods may differ from those estimated. The growth path of the economy is thus represented by a sequence of temporary (general) equilibria. Although markets are assumed to clear, estimates about future conditions are not realized and have to be revised period after period as time passes. Because each current outcome is based in part on these unrealized estimates, the sequence is not an intertemporal or dynamic equilibrium. Instead, each element in it is merely a temporary equilibrium. The agents, if they had it to do over again, would want to revise their expectations to avoid these disparities if they could.[4]

3.2.3   Aggregating Variables

A third, standard method often used in economic theory to simplify analytical problems is to assume that a multiple-equation system can be reduced by aggregation; that is, by adding variables and equations together to get a smaller number of variables and equations. Aggregation lies implicitly at the foundation of all of macroeconomics. One application of this approach was used already in §2.1.2 where we discussed Walras's producer's tatonnement. There the market supply was assumed to be provided by n identical firms whose output could be added together (or, what is the same thing, the representative firm's output could be multiplied by n). By assuming each agent is like every other one in economic essentials, the behavior of any one can be used as a basis for aggregate dynamic analysis that is very much simplified over what it would be if individual differences were introduced. This method has a long history of use and is called the *representative agent* (firm or household) method. Like the others it has its limitations, but like them it is useful.

3.2.4   Model Simplification and Analytical Experimentation

In each of the procedures for model simplification outlined above, one is introducing into economic theory an analytical analog of the controlled experiment. Experimental economics is a growing field of considerable scientific and practical importance. Using laboratory methods that exclude all kinds of complicating interactions in the "real world," relatively simple, empirical economic organizations and markets can be constructed and their behavior over time observed. The methods just outlined fulfill the same purpose for analytical theory, namely, that of simplifying the real-world system that we really want to comprehend so that some of the essential features of that world can be understood.

Each way of reducing a complex system to a simple mathematical model gives a different model and each such model may behave differently from one of its relatives. None is likely to tell the whole story about the complex system ultimately of interest, but each may yield useful insights that could not be obtained in any other way. In this book we study relatively simple mathematical systems or models. *We do not study complex systems.* Nonetheless, simple systems will be seen to produce the fundamental types of behavior, including complex dynamics, that are observed in the economic world.

3.3 Random Shocks and Intrinsic Stochasticity

It is common in many sciences, and especially in much of economics, to assume that empirical experience can best be explained by dividing its systematic representation into two parts. One part is the deterministic part that can be treated as an equation like those being discussed above. The second part is the "stochastic part," which is assumed to be some kind of random variable generator. Until now in economics the latter mechanism has seldom if ever been specified as a dynamic structure. Instead, random variables are simply treated as exogenous (unexplained) events that satisfy certain laws of probability.

For example, consider the crop-nutrient response example discussed in §3.1.3 and illustrated in figure 3.3. Let the causation between nutrient x and crop yield y be represented by

$$y_t = f(x_t, z_t), \tag{3.6}$$

where x_t is a deterministic nutrient variable and where z_t is a random "weather" variable. Equation (3.6) might have the form

$$y_t = g(x_t) + z_t, \tag{3.7}$$

where z_t behaved as if it were drawn from a probability density function with certain known properties. In some cases, for example, it might be assumed that $z_t \sim LN(\mu, \sigma^2)$, that is, that z_t was distributed like a log-normal distribution with mean μ and variance σ^2.

Alternatively, suppose, following Lorenz, that the weather variable was generated by a dynamic process that could be described by a nonlinear, deterministic first-order difference equation

$$z_{t+1} = h(z_t). \tag{3.8}$$

Beginning with some initial state z_0 a sequence of weather states $z_0, \ldots, z_t$ could be generated *endogenously*. If the equation (3.8) is ergodic and chaotic in the sense described in §2.4.2, then the variable y will appear to be generated by a stochastic process that could look just as if z were generated randomly from an assumed distribution function.

Assuming stochasticity of z and hence y in (3.7) is quite different from *deriving* stochasticity of y by an explicit specification of a dynamic process (3.8). The former is an *extrinsic* explanation, the latter an *intrinsic* one because the property of interest, in this case randomness, is derived from a deterministic causal structure; that is, one that does not contain any exogenous random inputs. For many purposes of theoretical and empirical research, an extrinsic assumption of randomness is useful. But that approach is well developed, well understood, and continues to receive adequate attention from scholars. The possibility for understanding complex dynamic processes in terms of intrinsic explanations is, however, still rather new and much less widely understood. For that reason an emphasis on that possibility seems well justified.

This book is entirely devoted to the intrinsic theory of dynamic behavior, that is, to the derivation of behavior from an explicit specification of deterministic dynamic structure.

3.4 Inference and Deduction

The immediately preceding discussion raises an issue of profound scientific importance that should be touched on, though we cannot go into the matter deeply in an introductory book. Suppose we have a finite time series of estimated values for a state variable x, say $x_1, \ldots, x_n$. Can we tell if these data have been generated by a first-order difference equation of the kind we are talking about in this book and, if so, how?

One answer that comes immediately to mind is, "Yes, by plotting the pairs (x_j, x_{j+1}), $j = 1, \ldots, n - 1$, on a diagram." If the correct model is equation (2.5), the points will fall on a continuous line. If the correct model is (3.7), the points will be scattered and will form a "fuzzy" shape. This approach is being investigated by several scholars and a number of interesting results have been obtained. Some of this work will be summarized in volume II.

If these methods are appropriate, then they would enable very simple economic models of the kind we are going to be studying to be tested and verified—or disconfirmed—using methods of statistical inference from empirical observations.

In taking this approach, however, it must be remembered that we do not study low-dimensional or single-variable models primarily because we think that empirical data are in fact generated by such simple systems. Quite the contrary! Economic theory generally holds that economies involve many interacting individuals, organizations, technological mechanisms, and natural processes. Consequently, we should expect that real-world data for a given variable would, because of the interaction of many state variables, usually exhibit considerable scatter, even if they are generated by a completely deterministic process. Even an approximate description of this complicated interaction requires a multidimensional system. But this is very difficult.

In an effort to make progress we deal with low-dimension, relatively simple analytical models that retain some of the salient features of the complicated world and that exhibit some of the salient characteristics of that complicated world's behavior.

To this point we may add that a finite series of points may and in general will only reflect some part of the structure that generates it. A quite erratic finite sequence could later switch to a pattern of monotonic growth or decay. In nonlinear systems the presence of multiple-phase dynamics places extreme limits on inference. This may be put as a general methodological proposition:

History does not completely reveal structure. For a given finite number of periods a given nonlinear system can in general exhibit only some of its potential patterns of change.

This is why empirical science augments observation of natural experience wherever possible by controlled experiments that can suggest underlying structure. It is why science is concerned with the direct analysis of how things work—not just how they behave. It is concerned with the deduction of behavior from a specification of structure, just as Galileo and Newton were concerned with a study of the *mechanics* of motion—not just the observation of stars.

3.5 Continuous Time and Discrete Dynamics

In Newtonian mechanics and in many other sciences, time is usually thought of as a continuous variable that can be represented by the real number system. The latter forms a "continuum." It contains no gaps so it poses no difficulty in explaining what happens between moments because there is always "time" between any two moments. In discrete time, which is widely used in economic theory, the situation is quite different. There, as we have seen, time is represented by moments separated by finite intervals, or equivalently by the integers.

As pointed out by various authors, discrete time is to continuous time what a moving picture is to our intuitive idea of activity in real time.[5] The moving picture is a series of discrete events that, when viewed sequentially, portrays motion. If the time interval between discrete events is rather long the picture is jerky; behavior seems to jump from one position to another. When the time unit is short the portrayal of motion is smoother and the flow of behavior from one position to another seems continuous in the same way as our visual perception of real life.

The choice between discrete and continuous time is partly a matter of mathematical convenience, one or the other being logically easier to deal with for particular questions. On the other hand, some real-world processes seem more naturally modeled using one or the other. The distinction between them involves some deep philosophical issues. Some authors claim that continuous time is the only correct assumption and that discrete time is artificial. Others note that in some biological processes and especially in social processes the use of discrete intervals is the better analog of experience. Even in physics it has been argued that there is a smallest duration within which change cannot be observed so that time is something like a pulse or a quantum.[6] The fact is that virtually all of the basic concepts of dynamics can be developed in discrete time more simply than in continuous time, so that even if one regards it as an approximation, it is pedagogically useful in the development of dynamic theory.

So that one is aware of the relationship between these two points of view and to understand the advantage and disadvantage of each, let's consider the difference explicitly. The differential equation accumulates continuous change to obtain changes in state over finite intervals of time. The difference equation treats the rate of change during the finite unit interval as a constant. If the unit interval is "short" relative to the change accumulated over much longer periods of time, then the approximation will be good. Otherwise, it will be poor. (See §3.9.)

Of course, if the rate of change *is* constant over unit intervals, then the approximation is perfect and there is no difference in the two formulations.

Because industrial processes usually operate at more or less constant speeds, which are only modified after more or less regular intervals like quarters (as in the automobile industry), the assumption of discretely changing rates of output is sometimes a reasonably accurate representation of the facts. In cases where there are seasonal periods, as in crop production, where the inputs are applied at specific times and outputs harvested at later times within the crop year, the discrete time is also quite natural.

A more fundamental difference between discrete and continuous time formulation is in the complexity of behavior allowed. In the former case a history is a sequence of discrete points. There is room, even in a finite interval, for an infinite number of completely different points. As we have seen, cycles of any order and even completely nonperiodic behavior are possible in which points jump back and forth within an interval without touching. The orbits of continuous time dynamic models, however, are continuous curves in state space. These curves cannot intersect each other. In a single dimension they can only avoid crossing by moving in a single direction, or converging to a point.

Thus, monotonic growth and decay, either convergent or explosive, are the only possible patterns of change that can be represented in a continuous-time single state variable model.[7]

In three-space all of the types of behavior possible in the discrete one-space case are possible in continuous time. There is enough room then for a curve to wander endlessly without ever touching itself. Three-space, however, is more difficult to represent graphically and to analyze mathematically. Somewhat more advanced techniques are required. For that reason it is pedagogically more convenient to introduce the subject of complex dynamics by using the first-order difference equation, and that is what we do in this book.

3.6   Instability and Relevant Dynamics

By *relevant dynamics* I shall mean dynamical systems that work something like salient aspects of experience. For a considerable period of time and until very recently many if not most mathematicians believed that "only *stable* mathematical models or features of models can be relevant for describing nature."[8] It was a convenient intellectual opinion because it seemed to justify exclusion of complex behavior and unstable phenomena in the mathematical and scientific study of experience.

This is not the place to go into an analysis of that period of intellectual history, but it does deserve a comment because that period is so recent and because that opinion is still so widely held.

It is now generally thought by astronomers that the physical universe evolved and is evolving in physical structure; by nuclear physicists that a profusion of subatomic particles exist for minute periods of time and then cease to exist; by biologists that living systems evolve in their genetic and morphological character, and that most species that have existed are extinct and the current rate of species extinction is very high; by archaeologists that human organizations have evolved into ever more complex systems; and, finally, in growing force by economists that market behavior tends to be complex and that economic institutions change their forms over time.[9] Take a deep breath, pause, and then recognize that many processes in nature—including human nature in general and human economic nature in particular—are unstable! They are unstable in the precise mathematical sense of not converging to stationary, steady, or periodic states.

We can take it as fact then that experience of the phenomenal world includes the complex—this is why a concern with complex dynamics must be central to the mission of science.

3.7 Newtonian Dynamics

The dynamic principle for which the difference equation is a discrete-time mathematical analog was framed by Newton in continuous time. For our purposes, however, the distinctions between continuous and discrete time, between differential and difference equations, are not critical. Although it has been emphasized that these two points of view *are not equivalent*, the kinds of behavior derived from one of them can also be derived for the other given the right dimensions and nonlinearities.

Given this interpretation, the dynamics of this book can be called Newtonian: in the real number system, given exact initial conditions for a given point in time, the entire history generated by the structural equation can be determined exactly in principle. That is, its entire history can be shown to exist in a mathematical sense. It is this property that has been the basis of philosophical determinism.

A good deal is being written about this philosophy. Since I have associated Newton with what we are doing here, I want to make clear my own position, so I shall permit myself a few brief remarks.

First, it must be emphasized that it is a *mathematical history* that is exactly determined. Such a history unfolds in the real number system, most members of which have no finite representation and in fact cannot even be computed. Consequently, we can rarely "see" such a history. We can only represent to ourselves a numerical approximation using rational numbers. That is to say, almost all of the mathematical histories implied by the dynamic principle are not representable because they cannot be computed. *All* of the "numerical experiments" reproduced in this book are approximations in this sense.

Second, chaotic histories as defined in chapter 2 are sensitive to initial conditions: the tiniest error that is introduced in any parameter, initial condition, or in the recursive computation of successive states will change the future histories—and drastically—so much so that prediction very far into the model's future—even approximate prediction—is impossible. Since our computations are supposed to be performed in the real numbers but are in fact only performed in the rationals, prediction of chaotic trajectories is impossible. Indeed, a numerical trajectory is not a solution of a given structural model at all but a sequence of points, each one of which has been perturbed by approximation and so lies on a different "true" trajectory than its predecessor.

The implications of the nonrepresentable nature of Newtonian determinism is therefore that accurate prediction of the distant future using the dynamic principle is not possible whenever chaotic trajectories are implied.

Third, "thick" chaotic trajectories whose "long-run" behavior can be characterized by density functions behave something like stochastic or random processes and mimic or explain erratic change. It is in this sense that the so-called Newtonian paradigm has been revived in the modern work on nonlinear dynamics and found to possess an explanatory power that goes far beyond that possessed by linear examples of the dynamic principle.

But we are not speaking here of Newtonian *mechanics*. That is the subject matter of physics and nowhere will we make use of Newton's equations of motion for physical bodies. Moreover, in the statistical dynamics of ergodic processes that will be derived from nonlinear economic models, we are not employing the methods of theoretical physics in general or of thermodynamics or quantum mechanics in particular. We are instead exploiting the dynamic principle in Newton's mathematical sense—using discrete time for convenience—to study equations of change that arise in *economic* theory.

Fourth, and finally, it is not unusual for physicists to consider Newtonian time as "reversible" and so incapable of explaining "time's arrow." This view is equivalent to saying that the world is essentially the same as our mathematical thoughts about it, a view that I reject (§2.5). One physicist likens the "reversibility" of Newtonian time to a prediction of water molecules spilled on the floor reassembling themselves and refilling the glass on the table as they were before the glass was knocked over.[10] The time of our economic experience, however, does not run backward, but inexorably forward. When we use the dynamic principle to look into the past, we need not interpret it as saying that time moves backward. Instead, the model can estimate what the state of the system was at an earlier time, or in the case of nonlinear discrete time models, what the possible states of the system could have been from which the present emerged. In the case of the water molecules one could run the physical equation backward to estimate the position of the molecules in the glass before the spill; the molecules themselves do not return to the glass but continue to seep into the floor. From this point of view, time's forward arrow is a postulate of and is not derived from the dynamic principle.

To summarize, in drawing on the dynamic principle this book is manifestly not an application of concepts from physics to economics. Rather, it is a reconsideration of the heartland of economic analysis using the dynamic principle. Nonetheless, it is a testament to the interdisciplinary power of nonlinear dynamics because the mathematical tools used here are applicable in any science that uses the dynamic principle and in which nonlinearities play an intrinsic role.

3.8   Genericity

In several contexts by now, a concept central to any theoretical program has been touched upon that deserves more explicit elaboration. When a given result is obtained from a model, for example the occurrence of chaotic behavior, it is essential to know if that result was obtained for a special configuration that was peculiar, or implausible, or that would disappear if the model components were slightly perturbed. This would mean that the result would be obtained only if that very special configuration was constructed, and it would mean that if a model component were altered slightly to improve the realism of its general form or the accuracy of its numerical coefficients, the result would no longer occur. In these cases the result is called an *artifact*. An artifact may still be of some theoretical interest, but it is of much less scientific importance than would otherwise be the case.

A result is of far greater significance if it occurs for a range of numerical coefficients. Specifically, if a result occurs for an interval of parameter values, it is called *robust* with respect to those perturbations. If a result occurs robustly for a general class of structural components, we shall say that the result is *generic*.

The emphasis throughout the present book is on the existence of robust, generic properties. For example, in Walras's producer's tatonnement it can be shown that chaos occurs for an interval of parameter values for virtually any combination of demand and cost functions that lead to causal effect reversal in the profit function. Similar genericity is obtained for the full repertoire of classic economic models when intrinsic nonlinearities are retained and not assumed away for analytical or statistical convenience.

3.9   Appendix: The Relationship between Continuous and Discrete Time

Imagine a continuous time index $s \in \mathbb{R}$ and let Δs be an interval of fixed duration. If x changes continuously and smoothly with s we can write

$$\dot{x} := \lim_{\Delta s \to 0} \frac{\Delta x}{\Delta s} = \frac{dx}{ds},$$

where $\Delta x = x_{s+\Delta s} - x_s$. The variable $\dot{x}$ is the rate of change of x with respect to time. The continuous time Newtonian analog of equation (2.4) is

$$\dot{x} = \frac{dx}{ds} = f\left(x(s)\right).$$

The state at time $t + \Delta t$ is then

$$x(t + \Delta t) = x(t) + \int_{t}^{t+\Delta t} f\left(x(s)\right) ds.$$

This equation asserts that the change in state between any two points of time $t, t + \Delta t$ is the accumulated effect or integration of the instantaneous changes over that interval. Suppose $\Delta t = 1$ so that t is measured in a "natural" unit (say a year). Then

$$x_{t+1} = \theta(x_t) := x_t + \int_{t}^{t+1} f\left(x(s)\right) ds,$$

where $x_t = x(t)$. Thus, the first-order difference equation might be thought of as measuring the progress of a continuous system at discrete intervals of time.

There is a problem with this interpretation, however. Return to equation (2.5) but consider the difference equation at interval Δt, namely,

$$\frac{x_{t+\Delta t} - x_t}{\Delta t} = f(x_t).$$

Then

$$x_{t+\Delta t} = \theta\,(x(t)) = x_t + \Delta t\, f(x_t).$$

Thus, $\theta(\cdot)$ depends not just on x_t but on Δt because $\Delta t\, f(x_t)$ is an approximation of $\int_t^{t+\Delta t} f(x_s)ds$. The bigger (smaller) Δt, the more course (fine) is the approximation.

II DYNAMICAL SYSTEMS

Initial state
structure of things and force
the pulse of time
unfolding

4 Dynamical and Semidynamical Systems

[Born] therefore gave me the task of studying difference equations. I did this with considerable aesthetic satisfaction. . . .
—Werner Heisenberg, *Tradition in Science*

In order to get to the bottom of why and how complex change arises in economic theory, an appeal must be made to a number of purely analytical concepts that have been developed by mathematicians. This part of the book presents a survey of these ideas. Those readers who want to hasten to the economic part of the story may want to jump straight to part III. You can always turn back to this part if you want the underpinnings.

For the introduction to dynamic theory and to the machinery of complex dynamic analysis presented here, a minimum of mathematical preparation is needed: the basic set operations, some calculus and algebra. A few advanced concepts will have to be used and a few proofs of some of the simpler results have been given, but this is not a comprehensive mathematical treatise. Appropriate references are provided for the reader who wants to plumb the depths of dynamical systems theory. Given a willingness to follow a considerable amount of mathematical notation, however, this introduction should be useful as a survey and reference to readers with varied backgrounds and interests.

Discrete time dynamics has only recently been given systematic treatment as a subject in its own right. Difference equations were usually treated as numerical tools for solving equations and for computing continuous time differential equations. Recent developments in chaos and ergodic theory can now be integrated into the fundamentals of the discrete time approach, and, using the concept of a dynamical system, difference equations can be given an elegant development. Moreover, many of the concepts carry over to continuous time models, so what one learns for one approach is of considerable help in learning the other.[1]

To analyze the stability of dynamic models, the linear difference equation is necessary. But in this book linearity is only a means to the more general objective of understanding nonlinear dynamics. Nonlinearity is fundamental in economics, and rather than follow the traditional approach of extending linear models in one dimension to higher dimensions with a corresponding emphasis on matrix algebra, we remain within the single state variable framework and introduce the powerful concepts of semidynamical systems, bifurcation analysis, chaos, ergodic behavior, and multiple-phase dynamics. The reader should note, however, that most of the concepts and many of the results described here can be extended to higher-dimensional systems. Indeed, the ability to do so has been a criterion in the choice of methods covered.

4.1 Systems

4.1.1 Difference Equations and Domains

Begin with a map or function $\theta : D \to \mathbb{R}$ where D is called the *domain of admissible* or *feasible* states and is defined to be a subset of the real numbers $\mathbb{R}$. Then

$$x_{t+1} = \theta(x_t), \quad x_t \in D, \ t \in \mathbb{N}^+ \tag{4.1}$$

is the first-order difference equation where $\mathbb{N}^+$ is the set of nonnegative integers. The pair (θ, D) is a *system*. The *null domain* is the set $D^0 := \mathbb{R} \setminus D$. It represents the part of the real numbers where states are not defined or allowed.

4.1.2 Examples

Here are several examples of functions that can be used to define θ directly or that are involved in the derivation of the map θ in various cases. They will all play various roles later. To get a difference equation directly from one of these functions, just write $x_t = x$ and $x_{t+1} = \theta(x)$. The domain is determined by economic considerations in particular applications. In the examples that follow, the domains given are just illustrative.

The linear system. For a parameter $a \in \mathbb{R}$,

$$\theta(x) = ax, \quad D := \mathbb{R}^+. \tag{4.2a}$$

The graph of (4.2a) is a straight line through zero with slope a.

The affine system. For parameters $a, b \in \mathbb{R}$,

$$\theta(x) = ax + b, \quad D := \mathbb{R}^+. \tag{4.2b}$$

Its graph is like figure 3.4 where the intercept is b and the slope is a. The affine system is essentially like the linear one, as can be seen by setting $z = x + b/(a-1)$. Then we get $\theta(z) = az$. From a qualitative point of view, therefore, (4.2b) behaves like (4.2a). For that reason it is often called linear and we shall do so here.

The hyperbolic system. For $a > 0, b/c \neq 0$,

$$\theta(x) := \frac{ax}{b + cx}, \quad D := \mathbb{R} \setminus \{-b/c\}, \ D^0 := \{-b/c\}. \tag{4.2c}$$

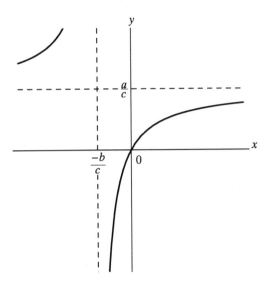

Figure 4.1
The hyperbolic function

The graph of (4.2c) is shown in figure 4.1. Note that $\theta(x)$ is defined every-where in $\mathbb{R}$ except at $x = -b/c$. This point is a *singularity* at which $\theta(-b/c)$ is unbounded.[2] Note also that $\bar{x} = a/c$ is a horizontal asymptote.

The quadratic system. For $\alpha \leq 0$, $\beta > 0$, $\gamma < 0$,

$$\theta(x) := \alpha + \beta x + \gamma x^2, \quad D = [x', x''], \quad D^0 = \mathbb{R} \setminus D, \tag{4.2d}$$

where x', x'' are the two roots of $\alpha + \beta x + \gamma x^2 = 0$.

Walras's producer's tatonnement used in chapter 2 can serve as an example. Let $\alpha = -\kappa(1 + i)h$, $\beta = [1 + \kappa a - \kappa(1 + i)c]$, $\gamma = \kappa[bn + (1 + i)d]$. Re-member that i is the interest rate, n is the number of firms, h is overhead cost, a is the intercept, b is the slope of the demand function, and k is an adjust-ment coefficient. Substitute these expressions for α, β, and γ in (4.2d) to get (2.11). The point is that the parameters in (4.2d) when applied to this example are derived from the parameters of demand, cost, and the adjustment of output to profits. The process is restricted to $[x', x'']$ because outside this range the implied output would be negative, which doesn't make sense.

The quadratic function can be given the simple form

$$\bar{\theta}(y) := my(1 - y), \quad D = [0, 1], \quad D^0 = \mathbb{R} \setminus D, \tag{4.2d'}$$

where m is a complicated expression of the parameters α, β, and γ in (4.2d).
For many illustrative purposes this is convenient.[3] To see how this can be
done, let $y = A + Bx$. Substitute this expression into the right side of (4.2d').
Expand and collect parameters. Multiply both sides of (4.2d) by B and add A
to both sides. You now have two expressions for $A + Bx$ and can associate the
parameters on the right side of each to get

$$A + B\alpha = mA(1 - A)$$
$$\beta = m(1 - 2A)$$
$$\gamma = -mB.$$

Solving for m in terms of α, β, and γ, you get

$$m = 1 + \left[1 - 4\alpha\gamma + \beta(2 - \beta)\right]^{\frac{1}{2}}.$$

The power system. For $c > 0$, $0 < a < 1$, $D = [0, \infty)$,

$$\theta(x) = cx^a. \tag{4.2e}$$

It has the appearance shown in figure 4.2.

The generalized power system. For $c > 0$, $a_1, a_2 > -1$ and $0 < b_1 < b_2$,

$$\theta(x) := c(x - b_1)^{a_1}(b_2 - x)^{a_2},$$
$$D := [b_1, b_2], \tag{4.2f}$$
$$D^0 := (-\infty, b_1) \cup (b_2, \infty).$$

The map $\theta(x)$ in this case is the well-known Pearson Type I function used in

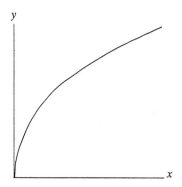

Figure 4.2
The power function

statistical distribution theory. It also arises naturally in a variety of economic settings and led one of my students to call it my "secret weapon" because it can assume many different forms with correspondingly many kinds of dynamic behavior. This is seen in figure 4.3, which shows the system for various values of the parameters a_1, a_2.

Just as for the quadratic system, an appropriate transformation leads to a simpler form. Let $y = \alpha + \beta x$ and set $\alpha = \frac{-b_1}{b_2-b_1}$, $\beta = \frac{1}{b_2-b_1}$. Solving for x, substituting into (4.2f), and rearranging and collecting terms, we get

$$\bar{\theta}(y) := A y^{a_1}(1-y)^{a_2}, \quad D = [0, 1], \quad D^0 = \mathbb{R} \setminus D, \tag{4.2f'}$$

where A depends on b_1, b_2, and c of the version given in (4.2f). This form is known as the β-function.

The piecewise linear system. Let $a_0, \ldots, a_n, b_0, \ldots, b_n$, be sequences of real numbers with $a_{i-1} < a_i, i = 1, \ldots, n$. Then $D := [a_0, a_n]$ and

$$\theta(x) := b_i + \beta_i(x - a_i), \quad a_i \leq x \leq a_{i+1}, \tag{4.2g}$$

where $\beta_i = (b_i - b_{i-1}/(a_i - a_{i-1}) = 1, \ldots, n$. The function $\theta(x)$ is here made up of n linear (affine) segments that are pieced together to form a continuous map on the interval $[a_0, a_n]$. Figure 4.4a shows an example with five segments that will arise in the discussion of stock market dynamics in chapter 11. Figure 4.4b gives another example, this time with four segments. It occurs in the study of business fluctuations in volume II.

The special piecewise linear systems. Special cases of the piecewise linear system that are pedagogically illuminating and that also arise in economic applications of part III are the *shack* and *check* maps with two linear segments shown in figures 4.5a and 4.5b.

Closely related are the *tent* and *V* maps shown in figures 4.5c and 4.5d. Note that the shack and check maps are isomorphic up to a linear transformation. The tent and V maps are also isomorphic. This means that results established for one obtain for the other.

4.1.3 Nonlinear, Essentially Nonlinear, and Essentially Linear Systems

A system (θ, D) is *nonlinear if it is not affine.* Some systems are nonlinear but can be transformed to linear ones. If there exists a transformation $f : x \to f(x)$ and an affine map $\lambda : f(D) \to f(D)$ such that

$$(f \circ \theta)(x) = (\lambda \circ f)(x) \quad \text{for all} \quad x \in D, \tag{4.3}$$

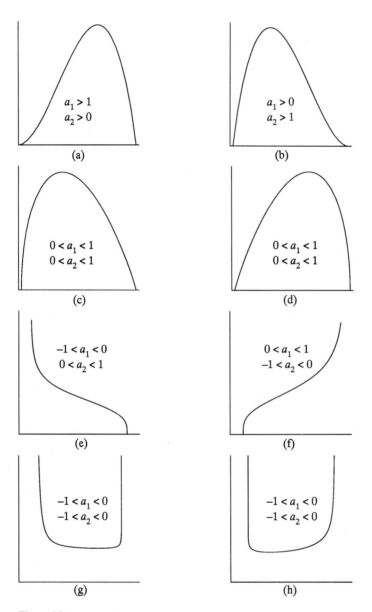

Figure 4.3
The generalized power function

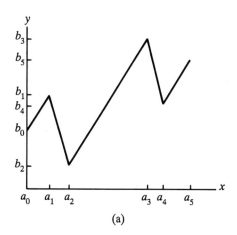

(a)

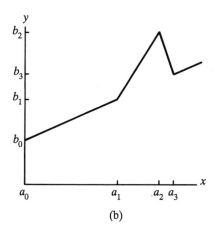

(b)

Figure 4.4
Piecewise linear maps

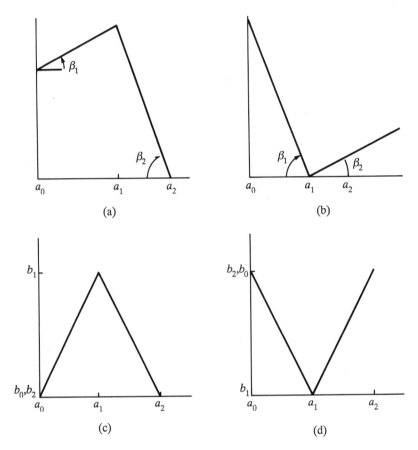

Figure 4.5
Special piecewise linear maps. (a) Shack. (b) Check. (c) Tent. (d) V.

then θ is said to be *essentially linear*. Given this, it is natural to define an *essentially nonlinear system to be one that is not essentially linear*.

As an example, consider the *power system* (4.2e). Taking logs, we get

$$\log(\theta(x)) = \log c + a \log x.$$

Let $y = f(x) := \log x$ and let $\lambda(y) = \log c + ay$. Then

$$(f \circ \theta)(x) = f(\theta(x)) = \log \theta(x)$$
$$= \log c + a \log x = \lambda(f(x)) = (\lambda \circ f)(x).$$

Consequently, the power system is essentially linear. The log transformation, however, will not work for the generalized power system. It is essentially nonlinear.

As another example, consider the hyperbolic system (4.2c). Let $y_t = f(x_t) = \frac{1}{x_t}$ and $\lambda(y_t) = \frac{b}{a}y_t + \frac{c}{a}$. Then—perhaps surprisingly given the profile of the original map—you can easily show that (4.2c) is essentially linear.

4.1.4 Qualitative Systems

Obviously, there are as many systems as there are functions. Studying the dynamics generated by each one is out of the question. To get around this, mathematicians define classes of maps that share well-defined but general properties. The same is true in economics. Often in economic theory a system may not be specified by an explicit formula as in the examples of §4.1.2, but only by certain qualitative properties. For example, suppose we can say that θ is continuous on an interval $[a, b]$ with $\theta(a) = \theta(b) = 0$ and $\theta(x) > 0$ all $x \in (a, b)$. Such maps are called *stretchable* and are discussed in §5.5.2. A stretchable map could look like the quadratic map or like some members of the Pearson family shown in figure 4.3, or like some more complicated shape. In some examples, it might also be known that θ is differentiable and concave, and so forth.

Wherever possible we shall provide an analysis of qualitative systems. Specific functional forms are used primarily for illustration. Fortunately, it is often possible to derive the types of behavior of which a given system is capable from its qualitative properties alone. The exact formula need not be written down. For purposes of pure theory, qualitative results are good enough. For purposes of empirical description and forecasting, qualitative estimates may be the best we can do.

The following give some other important classes of qualitatively defined systems that figure prominently in the economic applications.

Monotonic and strictly monotonic systems. A map θ defined on D is *monotonic* if for all $x, y \in D$ either

$$\theta(x) \leq \theta(y) \quad \text{for all} \quad x < y \qquad \text{or} \qquad \theta(x) \geq \theta(y) \quad \text{for all} \quad x < y.$$

In the first case it is *monotonic increasing*; in the second, *monotonic decreasing*. The map is *strictly monotonic* (respectively *increasing* or *decreasing*) if either

$$\theta(x) < \theta(y) \quad \text{for all} \quad x < y$$

or

$$\theta(x) > \theta(y) \quad \text{for all} \quad x < y.$$

For example, the affine system is monotonic and it is strictly monotonic for $a \neq 0$. In figure 4.2 the power function is strictly monotonic increasing. Such systems play an especially important role in the theory of economic growth.

Piecewise monotonic and piecewise strictly monotonic systems. Let $\mathcal{I} :=$ $\{I_i, \ c\ell I_i = [a_{i-1}, a_i] \text{ for } a_{i-1} < a_i, \ i = 1, \ldots, n\}$ be a set of n intervals that form a partition of an interval $I = [a_0, a_n]$. (Here each I_i can be closed, open, or semiclosed.) Let $\theta_i, i = 1, \ldots, n$ be a set of maps with each θ_i defined on $= [a_{i-1}, a_i]$. Define

$$\theta(x) := \theta_i(x), \quad x \in I_i.$$

Then (θ, I) is *piecewise monotonic (piecewise strictly monotonic)* if each θ_i is monotonic (strictly monotonic) on I_i. The piecewise linear map (4.4a) is an example of a piecewise strictly monotonic map that arises in a model of the stock market price adjustment mechanism developed in chapter 11, while the one shown in figure 4.4b arises in the business cycle theory to be developed in volume II.

Single-peaked and single-troughed systems. Let I be an interval with θ defined on $c\ell I = [a, b]$. The system (θ, I) will be called *single-peaked* if there exists $c \in (a, b)$ such that θ is strictly increasing on $[a, c]$ and strictly decreasing on $[c, b]$. It will be called *single-troughed* if θ is strictly decreasing on $[a, c]$ and strictly increasing on $[c, b]$. If (θ, I) is single-peaked or single-troughed, it will be called *bitonic*.

Note that if (θ, I) is single-peaked and continuous, then $M = \max_{x \in I} \theta(x)$ $= \theta(c)$. If it is single-troughed and continuous, then $m = \min_{x \in I} \theta(x) = \theta(c)$.

The generalized power functions shown in figure 4.3 are all bitonic, except cases (g) and (h) which are monotonic. The shack and tent maps are single-peaked. The check and V maps are single-troughed. Both are bitonic.

4.1.5   Extension to $\mathbb{R}$

Define $\theta(x) \equiv 0$ for all $x \in D^0$. Now (θ, D) is extended to $(\theta, \mathbb{R})$. All of the examples in §4.1.2 can be extended in this way. Note that in some cases the extension of θ to $\mathbb{R}$ is continuous on $\mathbb{R}$ and in some cases not. For example, the tent map is continuous on $\mathbb{R}$, but not the shack map. This extension of θ to $\mathbb{R}$ will be called the *usual extension*.

4.2   Semidynamical and Dynamical Systems

4.2.1   Iterated Maps and Semiflow

In §2.2.3 we saw how a system generates behavior, beginning with an initial condition $x_0 = x$. From the recursive application of equation (4.1) we get the sequence

$$x_0 = x$$
$$x_1 = \theta(x)$$
$$x_2 = \theta(\theta(x))$$
$$x_3 = \theta(\theta(\theta(x))) \qquad\qquad (4.4)$$
$$\vdots$$
$$x_t = \theta(\dots(\theta(x))\dots).$$

in this way, the state of the system for any period can be derived starting from an arbitrary initial condition x.

It is clear from this procedure that the state of the system at any time t is a well defined function of the initial condition x and the period t. It is convenient to have a name for this functional relationship. Define the *identity map* θ^0 by $\theta^0(x) := x$ for any x. Define $\theta^1(x) := \theta(x)$ for any x. Then define $\theta^2(x) := \theta(\theta^1(x)), \theta^3(x) := \theta(\theta^2(x))$ and in general $\theta^{t+1}(x) := \theta(\theta^t(x))$ for $t = 1, 2, 3, \dots$ for any x. The new function θ^t is called the tth *iterated map*. The function

$$h\colon (t, x) \to h(t, x) := \theta^t(x), \quad t \in \mathbb{N}^+$$

is called the *semiflow*. For any initial condition x and any nonnegative integer t it gives the subsequent state t periods later.

The left-side diagrams of figure 2.2 illustrated the recursive generation of successive states. The right-side diagrams presented the graphs of the associated semiflows.

4.2.2 Trajectories and Orbits

A finite sequence $\tau_n(x) = (x_i)_{i=0}^{n}$ of recursively generated states can be written

$$\tau_n(x) := \left(x, \theta(x), \ldots, \theta^n(x)\right)$$

and is called an n-period (finite) *history* from x. A recursively generated sequence $\tau(x) := (x_n)_{n=0}^{\infty}$ can be written

$$\tau(x) := \left(x, \theta(x), \theta^2(x), \ldots, \theta^t(x), \ldots\right)$$

and is called a *trajectory*. Because θ is a single-valued function, any finite history from x and the trajectory from x are unique.

The *orbit* of a trajectory $\gamma(x)$ is the set of points through which the trajectory passes; that is, $\gamma(x) = \{x, \theta(x).\theta^2(x), \ldots\}$. If a trajectory repeats any point after a finite number of time intervals, then $\gamma(x)$ is a finite set.

4.2.3 Malthus's Example

For the linear difference equation (4.2a) the iterated maps are easily computed. The semiflow is $h(t, x) = a^t x$ and you get the trajectory

$$\tau(x) = (x, ax, a^2x, \ldots, a^t x, \ldots) \tag{4.5}$$

for each $x \in \mathbb{R}^+$.

Malthus, in his *Essay on Population*, argued that populations of biological species in general and humans in particular would, in the absence of resource limitations, natural checks, or social restraint, grow according to a geometric law defined by the linear difference equation (4.2a). He estimated that population in the early nineteenth century was about 1 billion and that, unrestrained, it would double roughly every "generation" of 25 years. Using a quarter-century as the time unit, this implies that $a = 2$ and that the trajectory would be $\tau(x) = \{1, 2, 4, 8, 16, 32, 64, 128, 256, \ldots\}$. This explosive behavior could clearly not be realized. Sooner or later checks of some kind would have to come into play.

The actual doubling time during the last two centuries has been closer to 50 years, which, using the generational time unit, implies that a has been roughly equal to $\sqrt{2}$. If world population was approximately 4 billion in 1975, then beginning with $x = 4$ and letting 0 indicate 1975, we get $\tau(x) = \{4, 4\sqrt{2}, 8, 8\sqrt{2}, 16, \ldots\}$. Thus, at its current growth rate world population would be 8 billion in 2025 and more than 11 billion by 2050. Issues like this are part of the theory of economic growth to be taken up in volume II.

4.2.4 Existence of Semiflows and Viability

Semiflows need not exist. Figure 4.1 illustrates this case for the hyperbolic system. A singularity occurs at $x = -b/c$ where $\theta(-b/c)$ is undefined, so trajectories do not exist for this initial condition. Any x in the interval $(\infty, -b/c)$ maps into $(\bar{x}, \infty)$. Likewise, "most" points in $(-b/c, 0)$ map into $(-\infty, -b/c)$ and thence into $(\bar{x}, \infty)$. All points in $(0, \infty)$ map into $(0, \bar{x})$. Thus, almost all points in $\mathbb{R}$ map into $(0, \infty)$ and hence into $0, \bar{x}$. There are, however, a countable number of points in $(-b/c, 0)$ that map onto $-b/c$ after a countable number of periods. But $\theta(x)$ is undefined at this point, so a semiflow does not exist for these initial conditions. On the other hand, trajectories do exist everywhere except the points that eventually hit $-b/c$, that is, they exist "almost everywhere."

If for all $x \in D$, $\theta(x) \in D$, then θ is called *into*, i.e., $\theta(\cdot)$ maps D *into* D. In this case as $\theta(x) \in D$ for all x in D, then, recursively, $\theta^n(x) \in D$ for all $n \in \mathbb{N}^+$. Moreover, if $\theta^t(x) \in D$ for all x and for all t, then in particular $\theta^1(x) = \theta(x) \in D$ for all x in D so θ is *into*. To summarize, a unique semiflow

$$h(t, x) = \theta^t(x), x \in D, t \in \mathbb{N}^+$$

exists for all x in D if and only if θ maps D into D. In this case (θ, D) will be called viable, or we shall say that θ is viable on D. In the hyperbolic example illustrated in figure 4.1, $(\theta, \mathbb{R}^+)$ is viable but $(\theta, \mathbb{R})$ is not.

4.2.5 Semidynamical Systems

Consider two iterated maps θ^s and θ^t beginning from two points x and y with $z = \theta^s(y)$ and $y = \theta^t(x)$. By substitution, $z = \theta^s(\theta^t(x))$. Because y is the state that occurs t periods after x and z occurs s periods after y, evidently z occurs $s + t$ periods after x, that is,

$$z = \theta^s \circ \theta^t(x) := \theta^s(\theta^t(x)) = \theta^{s+t}(x), \tag{4.6}$$

where θ^{s+t} is just the $(s + t)$th iterated map. In this way iterated maps are composed to obtain another iterated map. The set of maps $\{\theta^0, \theta^1, \theta^2, \ldots,$

$\theta^n, \ldots\}$ is a *semigroup*, with the group operation "$\circ$" defined by (4.6) and the identity element θ^0. As we saw in §4.2.2, this set of maps determines the unique trajectory from any initial condition. A viable system and its associated semigroup of iterated maps is called a *semidynamical system*. Because it is generated by the dynamic structure θ will denote both the underlying system and the semidynamical system that it generates.

4.2.6 Dynamical Systems

Inverse elements of each map θ^n, $n \geq 0$ can be defined by $\theta^{-n}(x)$, $n \geq 0$ using the group composition operation. Thus, $\theta^{-n}(\theta^n(x)) = \theta^{n-n}(x) = \theta^0(x) = x$. The set of maps $G := \{\theta^n, n = 0, \pm 1, \pm 2, \ldots\}$ is now a *group* because, using the composition operator (4.6), for any $\theta^p, \theta^q \in G$, $\theta^{p+q} \in G$, and for any $\theta \in G$ its inverse $\theta^{-p} \in G$. If a map θ^p has a negative exponent, then it is called a *backward iterate*; otherwise it is called a *forward iterate*. A backward iterate θ^{-p} gives the states p periods earlier from which the state at the initial period can be reached. The viable system and its associated group of forward and backward iterates is called a *dynamical system*.

The backward iterates of a nonlinear map are, in general, not single-valued. In figure 4.6a, for example, the state x_0 could have been arrived at either from x' or from x''. Each of these could in turn have been arrived at from either of two preimages.

The set-valued map or correspondence θ^{-n} is defined recursively by

$$\theta^{-1}(x) := \{y | \theta(y) = x\}$$
$$\theta^{-2}(x) := \{y | \theta(y) \in \theta^{-1}(x)\}$$
$$\vdots$$
$$\theta^{-n}(x) := \{y | \theta(y) \in \theta^{1-n}(x)\}.$$

(4.7)

A single-valued map $h : (x, t) \to h(x, t)$ such that $h(x, t) \in \theta^t(x), t \in \mathbb{N}$, where we define $\theta^t(x) := \{\theta^t(x)\}$ for $t \in \mathbb{N}^+$, is called a *flow* of the dynamical system (θ, D). A sequence $\varphi(x) := (h(x, t))_{t=-\infty}^{\infty}$, where $h(x, t)$ is a flow of the dynamical system (θ, D), is called a trajectory *through* x. Let $z \in \theta^{-n}(x)$. Then $\theta^s(z) \in \theta^{s-n}(x)$, $s = 0, 1, \ldots, n-1$, and $\theta^n(z) = x$. This sequence gives a finite history from z to x. Any finite history from any other point in $\theta^{-n}(x)$ will also lead to x but by a different route.

For the affine map with $0 < a < 1$, $b > 0$, and with $D := \mathbb{R}^+$, there is an interval of nonnegative points containing zero for which the inverse map is

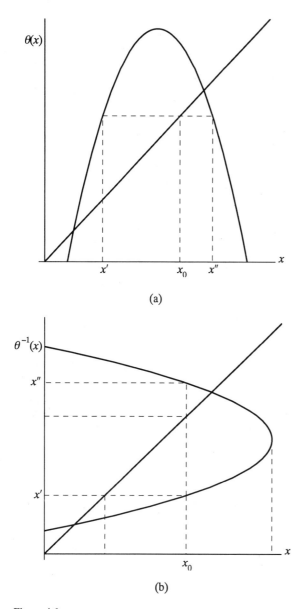

(a)

(b)

Figure 4.6
Preimages and the inverse map. (a) Multiple preimages. (b) The inverse map.

empty. Although trajectories can emanate from such points, they cannot be reached from any initial condition in the domain. This means that flows need not always exist in the domain of the system even though semiflows do.[4]

The moral is that for a discrete time nonlinear dynamical system, even though the trajectory *from* a given point is unique, that point could have been reached from many different paths, or it might not be reachable from any other point in the domain.

In chapter 1 it was observed that history does not reveal structure. Now we have a converse proposition.

Structure cannot reveal history; it can only reveal possible histories.

All this does not mean that history in the real world is nonunique. It just means that understanding how a discrete time system gets from one state to another after a unit interval of time *does not in general enable one to derive how the system got to any given starting point.* A knowledge of system structure can at best only enable one to derive the possible ways it might have done so.

4.2.7   Example: The Tent Map

The tent map shown in figure 4.5c is a convenient one for illustrating iterated maps because successive ones are easy to construct. The critical points (endpoints and turning points) are $\{0, \frac{1}{2}, 1\}$. Two points map into 0, which is a fixpoint (i.e., $\theta(0) = 0$). They are 0 and 1. There is one point, $\frac{1}{2}$, that maps onto 1. Therefore, θ^2 must have the three critical points that touch the horizontal axis. The point $\frac{1}{2}$ has two, and only two, preimages, $\frac{1}{4}$ and $\frac{3}{4}$, so θ^2 maps onto 1 from these two points. The second iterated map, therefore, has linear segments on $[0, \frac{1}{4}]$, $[\frac{1}{4}, \frac{1}{2}]$, $[\frac{1}{2}, \frac{3}{4}]$, $[\frac{3}{4}, 1]$. This process of construction is shown in figure 4.7a. Figure 4.7b shows the third iterated map.

The tent map is onto, but as each preimage of any point in [0, 1] has two preimages, $\theta^{-1}(x)$ is double-valued, and $\theta^{-n}(x)$ has 2^n points so it is not one-to-one. The system $(\theta, [0, 1])$, therefore, is only a semidynamical system. But $(\theta, \mathcal{P}[0, 1])$, where $\mathcal{P}[0, 1]$ is the power sets of [0, 1], is a dynamical system. What this means is that every point in [0, 1] is reachable. Semiflows are unique. Flows are not.

4.2.8   Existence of Unique Flows

Obviously, for flows to be unique the backward iterates of θ must be nonempty and single-valued. When this is the case θ is said to be *one-to-one onto*. That

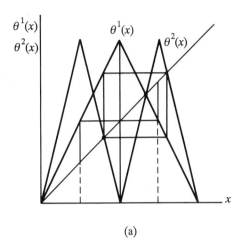

(a)

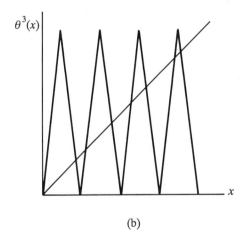

(b)

Figure 4.7
Forward iterates of the tent map. (a) First and second iterated maps. (b) Third iterated maps.

is, each x in D has one and only one preimage, so that $\theta^{-1}(x)$ exists in D and is single-valued. Such maps are highly restricted. In fact the necessary and sufficient condition for a continuous map to be one-to-one on a set $I \subset D$ is that it be *strictly monotonic*.

Suppose θ is strictly monotonic. By definition there exist no distinct points x, y such that $\theta(x) = \theta(y)$ (because either $\theta(x) < \theta(y)$ or $\theta(y) < \theta(x)$). This means that $\theta^{-1}(x)$ (or $\theta^{-1}(y)$ is single-valued. Consequently, θ must be one-to-one. Suppose θ is one-to-one but *not* strictly monotonic increasing. Then there must exist distinct x, y, z such that $x < y < z$ with $\theta(x) < \theta(y)$ but with $\theta(y) \geq \theta(z)$. Suppose $\theta(z) < \theta(x)$. By continuity θ must assume all values between $\theta(y)$ and $\theta(z)$. In particular there must exist a $v \in (y, z)$ such that $\theta(v) = \theta(x)$. By assumption $x < y$ so $x < v$. Therefore, $\{x, v\} \subset \theta^{-1}(\theta(x))$ so θ is not one-to-one, which is a contradiction.

The implication of this fact can be seen by defining the *backward difference equation*

$$x_{t-1} = \theta^{-1}(x_t), \quad t = 0, -1, \ldots$$

If $\theta(\cdot)$ is a map that is *one-to-one onto* D, then for every $x \in D$ there is a unique $y \in D$ with $\theta^{-1}(y) = x$. Let $s = |t|$. Then $x_{s+1} = \theta^{-1}(x_s), s = 0, 1, \ldots$ is a difference equation that has a unique semiflow. And if so, $\theta(\cdot)$ is strictly monotonic. To summarize, we have:

THEOREM 4.1   *A viable system* (θ, D) *has a unique flow if and only if the map* θ *is one-to-one onto or, equivalently, is strictly monotonic and onto.*

Therefore, any state $x \in I$ has a unique, discrete trajectory passing through it; there is only one path leading to—as well as from—any given state. The flow $h(t, x) \to \theta^t(x)$ is therefore defined on $\mathbb{N}$ (not just $\mathbb{N}^+$) and is unique.

The linear systems based on (4.2a) and the power system (4.2e) are monotonic for $D = \mathbb{R}^+$ (and one-to-one). Moreover, both are onto, so unique flows exist through any point x for each system. The affine system based on (4.2b) is monotonic (and one-to-one) but is not onto. It is only into. Therefore, only semiflows exist in $D = \mathbb{R}^+$. Of course, for $D = \mathbb{R}$ the affine map is onto, so flows do exist through any given point. The hyperbolic system (4.2c) is monotonic for $D = \mathbb{R}^+$ but not for $D = \mathbb{R}$. The quadratic or piecewise linear systems based on (4.2d) and (4.2g) are not monotonic. Some examples of the generalized power or Pearson system (4.2f) are monotonic on their domains but others are not.

4.3 Explicit Solutions

4.3.1 Definition

When a flow or semiflow exists and can be reduced to a formula, that formula is called an *explicit solution*. Or putting it the other way around, suppose $\sigma : (s; x) \rightarrow \sigma(s; x)$ is an explicit formula defined for all $s \in \mathbb{R}$, $x \in D$ such that

$$\sigma(0, x) = x$$

and

$$\sigma(t + 1, x) = \theta[\sigma(t, x)], \qquad t \in \mathbb{N}.$$

Then $\sigma(s, x)$ is called an *explicit solution* of the system (θ, D) if $\sigma(t, s) \in D$ for all $x \in D$.

4.3.2 Examples

The linear system. For the linear system (4.2a), it was found, using (4.4), that

$$\sigma(t, x) = a^t x, \tag{4.8}$$

which is a differentiable function for $t \in \mathbb{R}$. On differentiating with respect to t one gets

$$\frac{d \log \sigma}{dt} = \log a,$$

so a trajectory from a point x exhibits a constant proportional rate of growth or decay. If $\sigma(t, x)$ is growing (decaying), the absolute rate of growth (decay) increases (decreases) because

$$\frac{d\sigma}{dt} = (\log a)a^t x.$$

(Here we have imbedded t in the real numbers, something we can't do in general.)

The affine system. Now consider the affine system (4.2b) and let $z = x - b/(1 - a)$. Then $z_{t+1} = az_t$, so $\sigma_t(t, z) = a^t z$ or $x_t - b/(1 - a) = a^t(x - b/(1 - a))$. Hence

$$\sigma(t, x) = a^t[x - b/(1 - a)] + b/(1 - a) \tag{4.9}$$

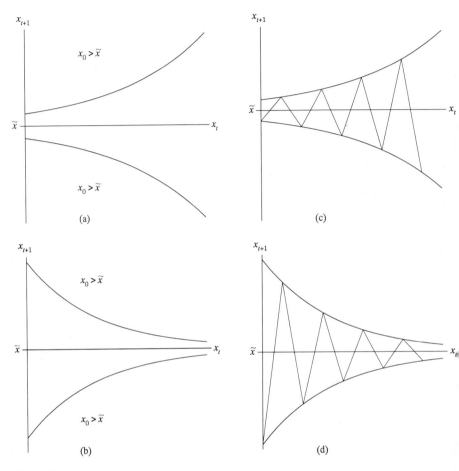

Figure 4.8
Explicit solutions of the affine map. Note: $\tilde{x} = b/(1-a)$. (a) $a > 1$. (b) $0 < a < 1$. (c) $a < -1$.
(d) $-1 < a < 0$.

is the explicit solution of (4.2b), which is easily checked by substitution. It is displayed in figures 4.8a and 4.8b for positive values of a.

Actually, the recursive substitution strategy that led to the explicit solution (4.8) for the linear system can be applied here as well. Thus, beginning at x we get the sequence

$$x_0 = x$$
$$x_1 = ax + b$$
$$x_2 = a^2 x + b(1 + a)$$
$$x_3 = a^3 x + b(1 + a + a^2)$$

$$\vdots$$

which suggests the formula

$$\sigma(t, x) := a^t x + b(1 + a + \cdots + a^{t-1}), \quad t = 0, 1, \ldots \tag{4.10}$$

It is readily verified to satisfy (4.2b). This can be given a more compact form by observing that

$$b(1 + \cdots + a^{t-1}) = \frac{b}{1-a}(1 - a^t).$$

Substituting in (4.10) and collecting terms, we get (4.9).

From the discussion in §4.1.2 it is already evident that the behavior of the affine model is essentially the same as that of the linear one. This is verified by computing its derivative with respect to t, where again we exploit differentiability by imbedding t in $\mathbb{R}$. (This can be done when $a > 0$.) When a is negative, note that a^t is positive for even t and negative for odd t, but $\theta^2(x) = a^2 x + b(2 + a)$ and a^2 is positive. This is an affine difference equation whose explicit solution is the same as (4.9) except that a^2 is substituted for a and $b(2 + a)$ is substituted for b. It gives the value of x *every other period*. From this fact we can graph the flow $h(t, x)$ of the original affine solution as shown in figure 4.8c.

The power system. Because the power system (4.4) is essentially linear (recall §4.1.3), the affine system can be used to find its solution. To see this, let $y_t = \log x_t$; to obtain the affine system, compute

$$y_{t+1} = \log c + a y_t.$$

From (4.9) we find its solution

$$y_t = \sigma(t, x) = a^t \left[y - \frac{\log c}{1 - a} \right] + \frac{\log c}{1 - a}.$$

Substituting $y = \log x$ and taking antilogs, we get the explicit solution for (4.4)

$$x_t = \sigma(t, x) = c^{\frac{1}{1-a}} \left(\frac{x}{c^{\frac{1}{1-a}}} \right)^{a^t}.$$

The hyperbolic system. Using the same technique as for the power system, the explicit solution for the hyperbolic system can also be found, an exercise left to the reader.

4.3.3   Explicit Solutions, Recursive Computation, and Special Solutions

An explicit solution provides a simplified expression for describing a trajectory of states. By analyzing its character directly, one can determine the qualitative properties as well as the quantitative properties of the system trajectories. But the importance of explicit solutions is easily exaggerated. For one thing, explicit solutions are only known for a few difference equations and these are of minor interest in economics. We can, however, find out the qualitative properties of trajectories for systems that are of major interest without ever knowing the explicit solution. For another, it is not necessarily easier to compute the value of the explicit solution for a given t by any algorithm other than direct iteration. Indeed, the iterated solution beginning with x obtained recursively, as shown in expression (4.4) of §4.2.1, is often a satisfactory and sometimes the necessary means for computation even when explicit solutions exist.

Even though explicit solutions may not be known (except in rare instances), *special solutions* may exist that describe trajectories by simple formulas *for special values* of the state variable in D but are undefined elsewhere. The most important examples, those of stationary states and cycles, are given in the next chapter.

5 Simple Dynamics

It is above all clear that the stationary state is not statical . . . *[but a] solution of a dynamical process.*
—Paul A. Samuelson, "Dynamics, Statics and the Stationary States"

The basic observation that commercial crises recur at somewhat regular intervals was made at least as early as 1833.
—Wesley C. Mitchell, *What Happens During Business Cycles? A Progress Report*

We consider in turn stationary states, cycles, and behavior that converges to periodic trajectories.

5.1 Stationary Behavior

5.1.1 Fixpoints and Stationary States

Suppose a trajectory $\tau(\tilde{x})$ emanating from a state $\tilde{x}$ of a system (θ, D) is constant, that is, suppose $\theta^t(\tilde{x}) = \tilde{x}$ for all t. Such a trajectory is called *stationary* and $\tilde{x}$ is called a *stationary state*. In particular $\tilde{x} = \theta(\tilde{x})$ so a stationary state of a system (θ, D) is a fixpoint of the map θ that lies in D. Obviously, if $\tilde{x}$ is a fixpoint of θ in D then by recursive application of θ, $\tau(\tilde{x})$ is a stationary trajectory and $\tilde{x}$ a stationary state. Consequently, there is an exact correspondence between fixpoints of a map and stationary states of the corresponding dynamical system.

Given this fact, it is clear that the stationary states of a (single state variable) dynamical system can be represented by the intersection of the graph of the map $\theta(\cdot)$ with the 45° line as, for example, in figure 2.2 which illustrates the Walrasian dynamical process of producer's tatonnement. This fact can be given a general definition. Let $G(\theta^n, D) := \{(x, \theta^n(x)), x \in D\}$ be the graph of the nth iterated map on the domain D. Note that $G(\theta^0, D) = \{(x, x), x \in D\}$ so it is just a 45° line in $\mathbb{R}^2$. Then the set $P^1 := G(\theta^1, D) \cap G(\theta^0, D)$ is the set of fixpoints and, hence, the set of stationary states of θ on D. See figures 4.1–4.9.

It should be noticed that in applications a stationary state is not a state where nothing happens. It is just a persistent situation.[1] In volume II we shall consider an economic example in which the state variable is interpreted as a rate of accumulation of capital per capita and where a stationary state is associated with a steady rate of economic growth. In that example, saying that the "same thing" happens is to say that a given rate of growth persists indefinitely.

5.1.2 Examples

For the linear difference equation based on (4.2a) the only fixpoint is zero. For the affine difference equation based on (4.2b) the fixpoint is the solution of $x = ax + b$ or

$$\tilde{x} = b/(1 - a), \tag{5.1}$$

which exists as long as $a \neq 1$. For the difference equation based on the hyperbolic map (4.2c) there are two stationary states,

$$\tilde{x} = 0 \quad \text{and} \quad \tilde{x} = (a - b)/c, \ c \neq 0. \tag{5.2}$$

For the quadratic case based on (4.2d$'$) there are also two stationary states,

$$\tilde{x} = 0 \quad \text{and} \quad \tilde{x} = (m - 1)/m. \tag{5.3}$$

The generalized power equation (4.2f) does not yield a convenient formula for its fixpoints as in the preceding cases. Nonetheless, it is possible to provide conditions for which they exist, and we shall do so in §5.1.4.

For the piecewise linear difference equation based on (4.2g) the existence of fixpoints must be examined piece by piece. Thus, if a fixpoint exists in the interval (a_i, a_{i+1}) we must have

$$a_{i-1} < \tilde{x}_i = \frac{b_i - a_i\beta_i}{1 - \beta_i} < a_i, \tag{5.4}$$

where $\beta_i := (b_i - b_{i-1})/(a_i - a_{i-1})$.

5.1.3 Existence of Stationary States

We have seen that the existence of stationary states of a system (θ, D) is equivalent to the existence of fixpoints in D for the map $\theta(\cdot)$. The latter can be based on the fact, discussed in standard texts on analysis, that continuous maps that change sign on an interval have zeros. This fact is called the Intermediate Value Theorem.

INTERMEDIATE VALUE THEOREM[2] *Let $f : D \to \mathbb{R}$ be a continuous function. If there exist $x, z \in [a, b] \subset D$ such that $f(x) \leq 0$, $f(z) \geq 0$ then there exists at least one point $y \in [\min\{x, z\}, \max\{x, z\}]$ such that $f(y) = 0$.*

See figure 5.1.

Let $f(x) := \theta(x) - x$. Then $f(\tilde{x}) = 0$ implies $\tilde{x} = \theta(\tilde{x})$ is a fixpoint of θ, hence a stationary state of (4.1). Consequently, we have the following corollary of the Intermediate Value Theorem.

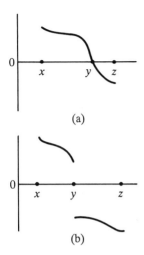

Figure 5.1
Existence of a zero image. (a) Continuous. (b) Discontinuous at y.

THEOREM 5.1 *Let θ be continuous on D. If there exist $y, z \in D$ such that $\theta(y) \leq y$ and $\theta(z) \geq z$ then there exists a stationary state $\tilde{x}$ of the difference equation (4.1).*

Of course, $\min\{y, z\} \leq \tilde{x} \leq \max\{y, z\}$.

5.1.4 Example

As an example, consider the generalized power difference equation (4.2e) with $-1 < a_1 < 0$ and $a_2 > 0$ and rewrite $\theta(x)$ as

$$\theta(x) = \frac{c(b_2 - x)^{a_2}}{(x - b_1)^{-a_1}}, 0 < b_1 < b_2.$$

Then $\lim_{x \to b_1+} \theta(x) = \infty^3$ and $\theta(b_2) = 0$. Thus, for y close enough to b_1, $\theta(y) > y$. Moreover, $\theta(b_2) = 0 < b_2$. By Theorem 5.1 there is a fixpoint and hence a positive stationary state. See figure 4.3e.

5.1.5 Stationary States on Noncontracting and Nonexpanding Sets

Using Theorem 5.1 sufficient conditions for the existence of fixpoints and stationary states can readily be obtained for several important classes of systems.
  Consider an interval $I = [a, b]$. If $\theta(I) \subset I$, then $\theta(b) \leq b$ and $\theta(a) \geq$

a. This implies that $\theta(b) - b \leq 0$ and $\theta(a) - a \geq 0$ so the function $f(x) = \theta(x) - x$ changes sign on I. From Theorem 5.1 a fixpoint exists in I.

A similar argument works if $\theta(I) \supset I$. Let m and M be the minimum and maximum of the function $\theta(\cdot)$ on I. (These exist by continuity.) The minimizer and maximizer of θ are given by

$$\theta(x^m) = m = \min_{x \in I} \theta(x) \qquad \text{and} \qquad \theta(x^M) = M = \max_{x \in I} \theta(x),$$

where $x^m, x^M \in [a, b]$. Since θ is continuous, it assumes all values in $\theta[m, M]$, so $\theta(I) = [m, M]$. By hypothesis $\theta(I) \supset [a, b]$ so

$$m \leq a < b \leq M.$$

Hence

$$\theta(x^m) = m \leq a \leq x^m,$$

also

$$\theta(x^M) = M \geq b \geq x^M.$$

Let $y = x^m$ and $z = x^M$. Then by Theorem 5.1 there exists a stationary state $\tilde{x}$ of (4.1) and $\tilde{x} \in \left[\min\{x^m, x^M\}, \max\{x^m, x^M\}\right]$.

To summarize, we have:

THEOREM 5.2   *Let $\theta : D \to \mathbb{R}$ be continuous on D and let $I = [a, b] \subset D$. If*

(i) $\theta(I) \subset I$ (I is nonexpanding under θ) or

(ii) $\theta(I) \supset I$ (I is noncontracting under θ)

then there exists a fixpoint $\tilde{x} \in I$ and $\tilde{x}$ is a stationary state of the system (θ, D).

Theorem 5.2 is illustrated in figure 5.2a,b.

If $\theta(I) = I$, then I is called an *invariant set*. As a direct corollary of Theorem 5.2, it is clear that if θ is continuous on an invariant set $I \subset D$, then there exists a fixpoint $\tilde{x} \in I$ of θ and hence a stationary state. In figure 5.3a, $\theta(I) \not\subset I$, $\theta(I) \not\supset I$ so Theorem 5.2 does not apply. In figure 5.3b, $\theta(I) = I$.

5.2   Cycles

5.2.1   Cycles and Fixpoints

Suppose there exists a $y \in D$ and an integer $p > 1$ such that

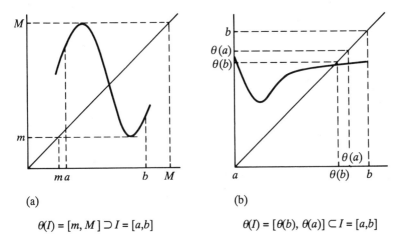

$$\theta(I) = [m, M] \supset I = [a,b] \qquad\qquad \theta(I) = [\theta(b), \theta(a)] \subset I = [a,b]$$

(a)   (b)

Figure 5.2
Fixpoints in noncontracting and nonexpanding sets. (a) Noncontracting sets. (b) Nonexpanding
sets.

$$y = \theta^P(y) \qquad \text{and} \qquad y \neq \theta^n(y), \ n = 1, \ldots, p-1. \tag{5.5}$$

Then y is called p-cyclic because if such a y is chosen as an initial condition it
will be repeated every p periods. Note that a p-cyclic state is a fixpoint of the
pth iterated map. As a consequence and using the notation defined in §5.1.1,
the p-cyclic states belong to $G(\theta^P, D) \cap G(\theta^0, D)$.

If y is p-cyclic, then applying θ to both sides of (5.5), we get

$$\theta(y) = \theta\left(\theta^P(y)\right) = \theta^{1+P}(y) = \theta^{P+1}(y) = \theta^P\left(\theta(y)\right),$$

so $\theta(y)$ is p-cyclic. The set of points or *orbit*

$$\gamma(y) := \left\{ y, \theta(y), \ldots, \theta^{p-1}(y) \right\}$$

is called a *cycle* of period p. Because each cyclic state is repeated every p
periods, we obtain the *special cyclic solution*

$$\sigma_p(t, x) := \theta^{t \bmod p}(x), \ \text{all } x \in \gamma(y),$$

where $t \bmod p$ is the remainder of $t \div p$.

As in the case of stationary states, the p-cyclic points of a map θ are the
fixpoints of the map θ^P. In every case the fixpoints of θ^1 are also fixpoints
of θ^P but these cannot be p-cyclic because $p > 1$. Let n be an integer that
divides p, i.e., $p \bmod n = 0$. Then the fixpoints of θ^n are also fixpoints of θ^P

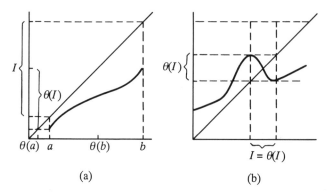

Figure 5.3
Noninvariant and invariant sets. (a) No fixpoint on I. (b) I is invariant.

because $\theta^p = \theta^{mn}$ for some integer m. We shall refer to P^n as the set of pairs $(x, \theta^p(x))$ such that $x = \theta^p(x)$ but $\theta^n(x) \neq x$ for all $1 \leq n < p$.

The nth iterate of the tent map has 2^n fixpoints. For $n = 1$ there are two stationary states. For $n = 2$ there are 2^2 fixpoints of which two are the two stationary states, so there is one two-period cycle. For $n = 3$ there are 2^3 fixpoints. Two are the stationary states. The six remaining are the orbits of two three-period cycles.

As noted above, a stationary state y is a unit cycle, so *periodic behavior includes stationary states*. To avoid confusion we will reserve the term *cycle* for *periodic behavior that is not stationary*.

5.2.2 Examples

The linear system. Consider the dynamical system based on the linear function (4.2a) with domain $\mathbb{R}$. Suppose y is p-cyclic. Then $y = a^p y$. The solution $y = 0$ is a stationary state. If $y \neq 0$ and $p > 1$ then $y = a^p y \Rightarrow a^p = 1 \Rightarrow a = 1$ or -1. Suppose $a = 1$. Then $h(t, x) = x$ for all x. That is, every state is stationary. On the other hand, suppose $a = -1$. Then $h(t, x) = (-1)^t x$ so $h(1, x) = -x, h(2, x) = x, h(3, x) = -x, \ldots$. Consequently, every initial condition is 2-cyclic with orbit or cycle $\omega(x) = \{x, -x\}$ for all $x \in \mathbb{R}$.

The affine system. A similar result can be obtained for the affine map (4.2b). Thus, setting $y = x - b/(1 - a)$ and using the explicit solution (4.9) we get $y = a^t y$ for all t. From this it follows that

$$h(t, x) = (-1)^t (x - \frac{b}{1 - a}) + \frac{b}{1 - a},$$

so every initial condition except $x = b/(1 - a)$ is 2-cyclic and the orbit is

$$\gamma(x) = \{x, 2b/(1 - a) - x\}.$$

The quadratic system (4.2f). The second iterate of the quadratic difference equation based on (4.2f) gives a fourth-degree difference equation

$$x_{t+2} = \theta^2(x_t) = m^2 x_t(1 - x_t)\left[1 - m x_t(1 - x_t)\right]. \tag{5.6}$$

Consequently, the two-period cycles must be zeros or roots of the fourth-degree polynomial

$$P^4(x) := x - \theta^2(x) = x - m^2 x(1 - x)\left[1 - m x(1 - x)\right] = 0.$$

Two roots $x = 0$ and $x = (m - 1)/m$ must satisfy the quadratic expression

$$P_1^2(x) := x - \theta(x) = 0$$

and these must also satisfy (5.6) (because if $x = \theta(x)$ then $x = \theta^2(x)$). Therefore, the roots of

$$P_2^2(x) = \frac{P^4(x)}{P_1^2(x)} = \frac{\theta^2(x) - x}{\theta(x) - x} = 0$$

are the extra roots we are looking for. Upon long division we find that

$$P_2^2(x) = m^2 x^2 - (m^2 + m)x + m + 1.$$

So the roots are

$$y_1, y_2 = \left[m + 1 \pm \sqrt{(m + 1)(m - 3)}\right]/(2m)$$

and the orbit is $\omega(y_1) = \omega(y_2) = \{y_1, y_2\}$. For these to be real it is necessary and sufficient for $(m + 1)(m - 3) > 0$. For both y_1 and y_2 to be positive it is necessary for $m > 3$.

The tent map. You can see that the brute force computation of fixpoints for the higher iterates of the quadratic map involves the roots of successively higher-order polynomial equations, a further study of which is of considerable interest but would send us along a path tangent to our intended trajectory at this point. We want to move on to methods that free us from particular functional forms. Before doing so, however, it is worth considering an example for which it is *easy* to construct cycles of any specified order.

Consider here the following special case of (4.2g):

$$x_{t+1} = \begin{cases} \pi x, & 0 \leq x \leq a, \pi = b/a \\ \rho(c - x), & a \leq x \leq c, \rho = b/(c - a). \end{cases} \tag{5.7}$$

Figure 5.4 displays this map and illustrates the choice of c (or ρ) that yields cycles of orders two, three, and four.[4]

In general, note that the inverse image for any point x in $(0, a)$ is $(a/b)x$ and that there is a unique monotonic prehistory for any such point. Suppose then we want an n-period cycle. Begin with b. Its preimage is a. Now choose an $(n - 2)$-period prehistory of a. This gives the increasing sequence $(a/b)^{n-2}a, \ldots, a, b$. Choose c so that

$$\rho(c - b) = \frac{b}{c - a}(c - b) = \frac{a^{n-2}}{b^{n-2}}a. \tag{5.8}$$

Solving for c we get

$$c = \frac{b^n - a^n}{b^{n-1} - a^{n-1}}. \tag{5.9}$$

Therefore, the sequence $\{(a/b)^{n-2}a, \ldots, a, b\}$ is an n-cyclic orbit. For example, let $c = (b^3 - a^3)/(b^2 - a^2)$. Then $\{a^2/b, a, b\}$ is a 3-cycle orbit.

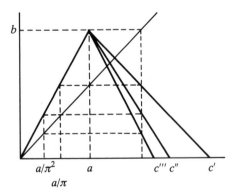

Figure 5.4
Construction of cycles for the tent map. Points c', c'', and c''' show values of c given 2-, 3-, and 4-period cycles.

5.2.3 Existence of Cycles of All Orders

To obtain an n-cycle, it is not enough to know that a point is a fixpoint of an n-iterated map θ^n. We must also know that y is *not* a fixpoint of any lower-order iterated map. It is possible, however, to generalize the approach in the tent map of §5.2.2 so that the stationary state existence theorems of §5.1.3 can be exploited to solve this problem.

Let us stick with viable continuous systems (θ, D) and consider two intervals A and B in D where $B = \theta(A)$, such that

$$A \cap B = \emptyset \tag{5.10}$$

and

$$\theta(B) \supset A \cup B. \tag{5.11}$$

Call these the *expansivity conditions*. First, note that $B \subset \theta(B)$ so B is non-contracting under θ. By Theorem 5.2 there is a fixpoint, hence a stationary state. But note also that $\theta^2(A) \supset A$ so A is noncontracting under θ^2. Again by Theorem 5.2 there is a fixpoint, say $y = \theta^2(y) \in A$. But $\theta(y) \neq y$ because $A \cap \theta(A) = \emptyset$. Consequently, $\{y, \theta(y)\}$ is a 2-cyclic orbit in D.

This argument can be extended to obtain the existence of a cycle of *any order*. To establish this result several intermediate results are required. The first is:

LEMMA 5.1 *If G is a continuous map from an interval $I \subset D$ into $\mathbb{R}$ and if J is any compact (closed, bounded) interval in $G(I)$, then there exists a compact interval $Q \subset I$ such that $G(Q) = J$.*

Proof Choose an interval $J \subset G(I)$ and choose $p, q \in I$ such that $J = [G(p), G(q)]$. Suppose $p < q$. Since G is continuous, it takes on all values between $G(p)$ and $G(q)$ (perhaps some several times). Let $r = \max_{x \in [p,q]}\{G(x) = G(p)\}$ and $s = \min_{x \in [r,q]}\{G(x) = G(q)\}$. Let $Q = [r, s]$. Then $G(Q) = J$. ∎

The lemma is illustrated in figure 5.5.

The next step is:

LEMMA 5.2 *Let (θ, D) be a closed continuous system, and let $I_n, n = 0, 1, 2, \ldots$ be a sequence of compact intervals in D such that $\theta(I_n) \supset I_{n+1}$ for all n. Then there exists a sequence of compact intervals $Q_n, n = 0, 1, 2, \ldots$ such that $Q_{n+1} \subset Q_n \subset I_0$ and $\theta^n(Q_n) = I_n$ for all n.*

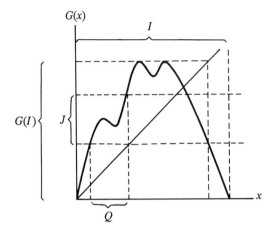

Figure 5.5
Illustration of Lemma 5.1: choosing an interval in I that maps into an interval in $G(I)$

Proof   The proof is by induction. Let $Q_0 = I_0$. Then $\theta^0(Q_0) = I_0$. Suppose there exists Q_{n-1} such that $\theta^{n-1}(Q_{n-1}) = I_{n-1}$. Applying θ to both sides of this equation, we get $\theta^n(Q_{n-1}) = \theta(I_{n-1})$. By hypothesis, $\theta(I_{n-1}) \supset I_n$. Let $G := \theta^n$, $I = Q_{n-1}$, and $J = I_n$. Use Lemma 5.1 to show that there exists a compact interval $Q_n \subset Q_{n-1}$ such that $\theta^n(Q_n) = I_n$.   ∎

Assume the conditions (5.10)–(5.11). Construct a sequence of compact sets $I_n, n = 0, 1, 2, \ldots$ as in the following array with $I_0 = A$, $I_i = B$, $i = 1, \ldots, k-1$, $I_k = A$, and $I_{i+k} = I_i$, $i = 1, 2, 3, \ldots$.

I_0	I_1	$\cdots$	I_{k-1}	I_k	I_{k+1}	$\cdots$	I_{2k-1}	I_{2k}
A	B	$\cdots$	B	A	B	$\cdots$	B	A
Q_0	Q_1	$\cdots$	Q_{k-1}	Q_k	Q_{k+1}	$\cdots$	Q_{2k-1}	Q_{2k}

That is, A's occur every k periods. This sequence is called a *periodic itinerary*.
By (5.11) $\theta(B) \supset B$ and $\theta(B) \supset A$; moreover, $\theta(A) = B$ so $\theta(I_k) \supset I_{k+1}$. By Lemma 5.2 there exists $Q_k, k = 0, 1, \ldots$ such that $Q_{k+1} \subset Q_n \subset Q_0 = I_0$ with $\theta^n(Q_k) = I_k$. Therefore, $Q_k \subset I_0$ and $\theta^k(Q_k) = Q_0 = I_0 \supset Q_k$. This means that Q_k is noncontracting under θ^k and according to Theorem 5.2 has a fixpoint. This fixpoint is a stationary state of period not greater than k. To prove that there can be no cyclic point with period less than k, proceed by contradiction. Suppose there is; then there must exist $p < k$ such that $\theta^{k-p}(x) \in I_{k-p} = B$ but $\theta^{k-p}(x) = x \in A$ by construction. To summarize, we have:

THEOREM 5.3   *Let (θ, D) be a closed continuous system and suppose there exists a set $A \subset D$ satisfying (5.10)–(5.11). Then there exists a cycle of every order $n = 1, 2, 3, \ldots$ in D.*[5]

The conditions of the theorem are illustrated in figure 5.6a.

5.2.4   The Li-Yorke Conditions

An alternative but equivalent result is:

THEOREM 5.4   *Let (θ, D) be a closed continuous system and suppose there exists a point a such that*

$$\theta^3(a) \leq a < \theta(a) < \theta^2(a) \tag{5.12}$$

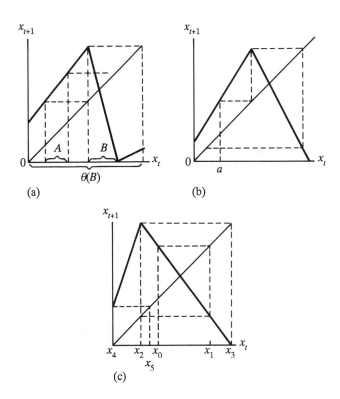

Figure 5.6
Sufficient conditions for an infinite number of periodic trajectories

or conversely, such that

$$\theta^3(a) \geq a > \theta(a) > \theta^2(a). \tag{5.13}$$

Then there exists a cycle of every order $n = 1, 2, 3, \ldots$ in D.

Conditions (5.12)–(5.13) are called the *Li-Yorke overshoot conditions* and a point satisfying (5.12) or (5.13) is called a *Li-Yorke point*. The point a in figure 5.6b is an example.

Theorem 5.4 is useful because it provides a simple computational condition: compute a finite history and search for a point a with succeeding points that satisfy (5.12) or (5.13). To prove it, you show that (5.12)–(5.13) imply (5.10)–(5.11).[6]

5.2.5 Examples

Consider the quadratic system (4.2d′) for $A = 4$ and let $b = \frac{1}{2}$. Then $c = \theta(b) = 1$, $d = \theta(1) = 0$ and $a = \frac{1}{2} - \frac{1}{4}\sqrt{2}$. Consequently, $d < a < b < c$ so Theorem 5.4 is satisfied. The quadratic system with $A = 4$ possesses cycles of all orders.

As a second example, consider the tent map of §5.2.2 that was illustrated in figure 5.4. Consider any positive a, b and let

$$c = \frac{b^3 - a^3}{b^2 - a^2}.$$

We know from §5.2.2 and equation (5.9) that $\{(a/b), a, b\}$ is a 3-period orbit. By Theorem 5.4 cycles of all orders exist.

5.2.6 Existence of Cycles for High-Order Iterates

Suppose the conditions for Theorem 5.3 or 5.4 do not hold for the map θ but do hold for a higher iterated map, $x_{t+p} = \theta^p(x_t)$. Then the results hold for the map θ^p. But a stationary state for θ^p must be p-cyclic. Therefore, we have:

COROLLARY 5.1 *Let (θ, D) be a closed continuous system and suppose that the Diamond or Li-Yorke conditions (5.10)–(5.11) or (5.12)–(5.13) hold for the difference equation*

$$x_{t+p} = \theta^p x_t$$

for some p. Then there exist cycles of order $p, 2p, 3p, \ldots$ for the underlying difference equation (5.1).

In figure 5.7a a shack map is shown. In figure 5.7b its second iterate is given. Although the Li-Yorke condition does not hold for θ, it does for θ^2.

5.2.7   The Švarkovskii Theorem

A famous theorem named after Švarkovskii provides a remarkable result that goes beyond Theorem 5.4. With slight abuse of previous notation, let $P(k)$ be the property that a periodic orbit of order k exists. Then the following is Švarkovskii's Theorem.[7]

THEOREM 5.5 (Švarkovskii)   *Let (θ, D) be a continuous, compact dynamical system. Then*

$$
\begin{array}{llllllll}
P(3) & \Longrightarrow & P(5) & \Longrightarrow & P(7) & \Longrightarrow & \cdots \\
\cdots P(2 \cdot 3) & \Longrightarrow & P(2 \cdot 5) & \Longrightarrow & P(2 \cdot 7) & \Longrightarrow & \cdots \\
\cdots P(2^n \cdot 3) & \Longrightarrow & P(2^n \cdot 5) & \Longrightarrow & P(2^n \cdot 7) & \Longrightarrow & \cdots \\
\cdots P(2^m) & \Longrightarrow & P(2^{m-1}) & \Longrightarrow & \cdots & \Longrightarrow & P(2) & \Longrightarrow & P(1)
\end{array}
$$

For example, if there exists an even cycle of order 2^n, then there exist cycles of every lower power of two. Or, if there exists a cycle of any odd order, then there exist cycles of every higher odd order and cycles of every even order. An important implication of this will be considered in chapter 7 when the existence of nonperiodic trajectories is taken up.

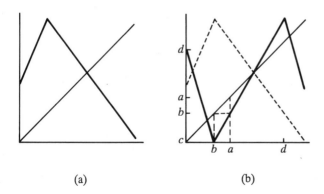

(a)   (b)

Figure 5.7
Li-Yorke condition for the second iterated map

5.3 Stability

Stationary states and cycles represent simple dynamics because they generate patterns that can be described by a finite number of points. Until now we have found that large classes of closed, continuous systems possess stationary states and cycles. If an initial condition is chosen that is stationary or cyclic, then a predictable future is generated. What, however, if an initial condition is nonperiodic? Where do trajectories then go? The examination of this question leads to questions of *stability*.

Roughly speaking, if the trajectories of a system are asymptotically stable then they converge over time to simple dynamics, that is, their behavior is better and better approximated by a periodic solution of some period. This means that asymptotically stable systems become more and more predictable with the passage of time.

5.3.1 Asymptotic Stability

Consider the linear system (4.2a) and suppose $|a| < 1$. Then the difference at any time t between any two trajectories from points $x \neq y$ is just

$$|h(t, x) - h(t, y)| = a^t |x - y|. \tag{5.14}$$

This difference converges to zero as t becomes indefinitely large. If x is the unique stationary state 0, then any trajectory beginning at some other point y must converge to it, so the unique stationary state is "asymptotically stable."

The idea of converging trajectories can be stated for a general system (θ, D). Let $N(x, \delta) := (x - \delta, x + \delta)$ be a δ-neighborhood of x in D. A trajectory $\tau(x)$ is called *asymptotically stable* if and only if there exists a positive δ such that for all $y \in N(x, \delta)$,

$$\lim_{t \to \infty} |\theta^t(y) - \theta^t(x)| = 0. \tag{5.15}$$

In this case the trajectories $\tau(x)$ and $\tau(y)$ are said to *converge* because they eventually get closer and closer together. If $\tau(x)$ is asymptotically stable for all $x \in D$ then (θ, D) is called *asymptotically stable everywhere*. If it is asymptotically stable for some $x \in D$ it is called *locally asymptotically stable*.

5.3.2 Contraction and Convergence

The concept of asymptotic stability is closely related to the idea of contraction for a map that is defined as follows. If there exists an interval $I \subset D$ and a constant $k, 0 < k < 1$ such that for all $x, y \in I$

$$| \theta(y) - \theta(x) | \le k \, | \, y - x \, | \tag{5.16}$$

then (θ, D) is *locally contractive*. If (θ, D) is locally contractive for all $I \in \mathcal{P}(D)$, then (θ, D) is *contractive everywhere* and $\theta(\cdot)$ is called a *contraction map* on D. If you think of x and y as points on two different trajectories or two distinct initial conditions, then the state values in the next period are closer together.

If θ is contractive on an interval $I \subset D$, then because $\theta(x)$ and $\theta(y)$ belong to I

$$| \theta^2(y) - \theta^2(x) | \le k \, | \theta(y) - \theta(x) | \le k^2 \, | \, y - x \, |$$

and, by recursion,

$$| \theta^t(y) - \theta^t(x) | \le k^t \, | \, y - x \, | \, . \tag{5.17}$$

As $0 < k < 1$ so $\lim k^t = 0$. We get (5.15) so $\tau(x)$ and $\tau(y)$ converge.

5.3.3 Asymptotic Stability of Stationary States

Suppose we are concerned with a stationary trajectory $\tau(\tilde{x}) = (\tilde{x}, \tilde{x}, \ldots)$. Then (5.15) becomes

$$\lim_{t \to \infty} | \theta^t(y) - \tilde{x} | = 0. \tag{5.18}$$

What are conditions of the map $\theta(\cdot)$ that will guarantee this convergence? First is a basic condition for continuous but not necessarily differentiable maps.

THEOREM 5.6 *Let (θ, D) be a continuous system. A stationary state $\tilde{x}$ is asymptotically stable if there exists a constant $\delta > 0$ and a constant k with $0 < k < 1$ such that*

$$| \theta(y) - \tilde{x} | \le k \, | \, y - \tilde{x} \, | \tag{5.19}$$

for all $y \in N(\tilde{x}, \delta)$.

This result follows from the fact that (5.19) implies (5.16) and hence (5.17).

As an example, consider the piecewise linear map

$$\theta(x) := \begin{cases} -a_1 x + b_1, & 0 \le x \le b_1/(1 + a_1) \\ -a_2 x + b_2, & b_1/(1 + a_1) \le x, \end{cases}$$

where $1 > a_2 > a_1 > 0$ and $b_2 = \frac{1+a_2}{1+a_1} b_1 > 0$, as shown in figure 5.7a. The
stationary state is $\tilde{x} = b_1/(1 + a_1) = b_2/(1 + a_2)$. It is easy to show that

$$|\theta(y) - \tilde{x}| = \begin{cases} a_1 \, | \, y - \tilde{x} \, |, & y < \tilde{x} \\ a_2 \, | \, y - \tilde{x} \, |, & y > \tilde{x}. \end{cases}$$

Let $k = (2a_2 - 1)/2$. Then you can see that (5.19) is satisfied for all $y \neq \tilde{x}$.
Therefore, $\theta(\cdot)$ as defined is everywhere contracting and $\tilde{x}$ is asymptotically
stable. See figure 5.8.

For differentiable functions a convenient condition can be given. Suppose
that $\theta(\cdot)$ is differentiable on D, and that $\theta'(x)$ evaluated at a stationary state $\tilde{x}$
is strictly less than unity in absolute value. By definition of the derivative, for
all ϵ close enough to zero there exists a $\delta > 0$ such that

$$\left| \frac{\theta(x) - \theta(\tilde{x})}{x - \tilde{x}} - \theta'(\tilde{x}) \right| < \epsilon$$

for all x such that $| \, x - \tilde{x} \, | < \delta$. Choose $\epsilon < 1 - | \, \theta'(\tilde{x}) \, |$ and set $k = | \, \theta'(\tilde{x}) \, |$
$+\epsilon$. Then $| \, \theta(x) - \tilde{x} \, | < k \, | \, x - \tilde{x} \, | < | \, x - \tilde{x} \, |$. So from Theorem 5.6, $\tilde{x}$ is
asymptotically stable. For convenience state this result as:

THEOREM 5.7   *If θ is differentiable at a stationary state $\tilde{x}$ of (θ, D), then $\tilde{x}$ is
asymptotically stable if*

$$| \, \theta'(\tilde{x}) \, | \leq \delta < 1. \tag{5.20}$$

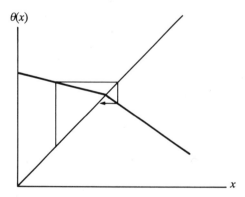

Figure 5.8
Asymptotic stability

5.3.4 Example

Consider the quadratic system. As we know, there are two stationary states 0 and $\tilde{x} = (m-1)/m$. From (5.17) we need to consider $\theta'(x) = m(1-2x)$ at each of these points. $\theta'(0) = m$ so zero is asymptotically stable if $m < 1$. But if this is true the other stationary state is negative for any $0 < m < 1$.

   Suppose $m > 1$; then $\tilde{x} = (m-1)/m > 0$ is asymptotically stable if

$$\left|\theta'(x)\right| = |m - 2(m-1)| = |2 - m| < 1,$$

that is, if

$$1 < m < 3.$$

Actually, for $1 < m \leq 2$ we have monotonic growth converging to $\tilde{x}$ from below. For $2 \leq m < 3$ fluctuations must eventually occur (after a period of growth if x_0 is close to zero), but these will converge to the positive stationary state $(m-1)/m$.

5.3.5 Asymptotically Stable Cycles

Other kinds of trajectories can be asymptotically stable, in particular cyclic ones. Suppose y is p-cyclic. According to Theorem 5.7, each cyclic point x in the orbit $\gamma(y) = \{y, \theta(y), \ldots, \theta^{p-1}y\}$ is an asymptotically stable stationary state of the dynamical system (θ^p, D) based on the pth iterate of $\theta(\cdot)$ if

$$\left|\frac{d}{dx}\theta^p(x)\right| < 1. \tag{5.21}$$

Using the fact that $\theta^p(x) = \theta\left(\theta^{p-1}(x)\right)$ and using the chain rule for partial differentiation, we get:

THEOREM 5.8 *Let θ be differentiable almost everywhere and in particular at the p-periodic points $x \in \gamma(y)$ where y is p-cyclic. A sufficient condition that the cyclic points $x \in \gamma(y)$ are asymptotically stable is*

$$\times_{x\in\gamma(y)} \left|\theta'(x)\right| < 1. \tag{5.22}$$

5.3.6 Example

As an example, return to the quadratic system. When m increases just above 3, two things occur simultaneously: the positive stationary state becomes unstable and a stable, two-period cycle emerges. This can be seen by examining

(5.6). Taking the derivative and using Theorem 5.8 we find that

$$\left|\frac{dx_{t+2}}{dx_t}\right| = 1 - (m+1)(m-3).$$

Consequently, for $0 < (m+1)(m-3) \le 1$ the two-period cycle is approached monotonically, i.e., from "inside" or from the "outside." For $1 < (m+1)(m-3) \le 2$ the two-period cycle is approached cyclically, and for $(m+1)(m-3) = 2$, or $m = 1 + \sqrt{6}$, the two-period cycle becomes unstable and a four-period cycle emerges.[8]

5.3.7 Lyapunov Stability and Instability

A trajectory $\tau(x)$ of a difference equation is *stable* if any other trajectory, $\tau(y)$, $y \ne x$, that passes sufficiently close at some time s remains close after that time. Formally, a trajectory $\tau(x)$ is *stable* if and only if for all $\epsilon > 0$ there exist a time s and a constant δ (which may depend on ϵ) such that if

$$\left|\theta^s(x) - \theta^s(y)\right| < \delta$$

then

$$\left|\theta^t(x) - \theta^t(y)\right| < \epsilon$$

for all $t \ge s$. If every trajectory in the domain D is stable then the system $\{\theta, D\}$ is *everywhere stable*. Such stability is sometimes referred to as Lyapunov stability.[9] Asymptotically stable trajectories are stable but the converse need not be true.

5.3.8 Examples

For the linear difference equation (4.2a), when $|a| < 1$, $a^t y - a^t x = a^t(y-x)$ shrinks so any two trajectories move together at an exponential rate. They are therefore asymptotically stable and so stable. However, it is easy to see that trajectories are everywhere stable for $a = 1$. Of course, the same result holds for the affine difference equation when $a = 1$, even though there are no stationary states. The affine difference equation with $a = -1$ is 2-cyclic as we saw above. But the system $(\theta^2, \mathbb{R})$ is just a linear system with $a = 1$ so every two-cycle is also stable.

5.4 Instability

Systems that are not stable are called *unstable*. We shall see that unstable systems are generic in economic theory. We discuss formal aspects of instability now.

5.4.1 Properties of Unstable Trajectories

Consider the linear system (4.2a) again and suppose that $| a |> 1$. Then the difference between any two trajectories from points $x \neq y$, given by (5.14), grows exponentially and without bound, no matter how close these initial conditions are. Consequently, the zero stationary state is not stable.

In general a trajectory $\tau(x)$ is *unstable* if for any $y \in D,\ \delta > 0, s \geq 0$ such that

$$| \theta^s(x) - \theta^s(y) |< \delta$$

there exists an $\epsilon > 0$ and a $t > s$ such that

$$| \theta^t(x) - \theta^t(y) |> \epsilon.$$

This means that no matter how close one trajectory comes to another, they move apart.

What about *bounded* nonperiodic trajectories that do not converge to a stationary state or to any cycle? Can they be unstable? The answer is yes. Indeed, they play an important role throughout this book as has already been indicated in the brief introduction to chaotic trajectories discussed in chapter 2.

Consider a bounded, nonperiodic trajectory $\tau(x) = \{x_n\}_{n=0}^{\infty}$ that does not converge to a stationary state or cycle. Define

$$x^\sharp = \limsup x_n := \inf_{y} \{y \mid y \geq x_n \quad \text{all} \quad n \geq N \quad \text{for some} \quad N \geq 0\}$$

$$x^\flat = \liminf x_n := \sup_{y} \{y \mid y \leq x_n \quad \text{all} \quad n \geq N \quad \text{for some} \quad N \geq 0\}.$$

Thus, $| x^\sharp |< \infty$ means that for any $\epsilon > 0$ only a finite number of values of $\{x_n\}$ are greater than $x^\sharp + \epsilon$. Likewise, if $| x^\flat |< \infty$, then for any $\epsilon > 0$ only a finite number of elements in the sequence fall below $x^\flat - \epsilon$. Moreover, the trajectory eventually is trapped and fluctuates inside the interval $[x^\flat, x^\sharp]$. The bounds of this *trapping set*, $x^\flat$ and $x^\sharp$, are accumulation points.

Consider two sequences $\{x_n\}$ and $\{y_n\}$. If

$$| y_n - x_n |^\sharp = \limsup | y_n - x_n |> 0$$

then the two series depart from one another by a finite amount infinitely often and

$$| y_n - x_n |^b = \liminf | y_n - x_n | = 0$$

means that the two series approach each other closely infinitely often.

Now consider a bounded unstable trajectory $\tau(x)$. Then for any $\delta > 0$ and for any trajectory $\tau(y)$, $y \neq x$, such that

$$| y - x | < \delta,$$

it is true that

$$\limsup \left| \theta^t(x) - \theta^t(y) \right| > 0.$$

If every trajectory is unstable in D, then (θ, D) is *everywhere unstable*.

5.4.2 Conditions for Instability: Expansivity

A condition for instability of periodic orbits is simply the converse of Theorems 5.8 and 5.9. This is summarized for reference as:

THEOREM 5.9   *Let $\theta(\cdot)$ be differentiable almost everywhere on D and in particular at the p-periodic points $x \in \gamma(y)$ where y is p-periodic. Then a sufficient condition for the periodic trajectories $\tau(x), x \in \gamma(y)$ to be unstable is that*

$$\times_{x \in \gamma(y)} | \theta'(x) | \geq \delta > 1. \tag{5.23}$$

In particular if $\tilde{x}$ is a stationary state, then

$$| \theta'(\tilde{x}) | \geq \delta > 1 \tag{5.24}$$

is sufficient for $\tau(\tilde{x})$ to be unstable.

This theorem suggests the following:

THEOREM 5.10   *Let θ be differentiable almost everywhere on D and assume that there exists an integer $m \geq 1$ such that*

$$\left| \frac{d\theta^m(x)}{dx} \right| \geq \delta > 1 \tag{5.25}$$

for all $x \in D$ where the derivative is defined. Then all trajectories in (θ, D) are unstable. In particular if

$$|\theta'(x)| \geq \delta > 1 \tag{5.26}$$

where the derivative is defined, then (θ, D) is unstable.

A map θ that satisfies (5.26) is called *expansive*. A map $\theta(\cdot)$ such that $\theta^p(\cdot)$ is expansive need not itself be expansive, as we will observe in subsequent work. A map whose pth iterate θ^p is expansive, but whose lower iterates $\theta^0, \ldots, \theta^{p-1}$ are not expansive, will be called *p-expansive*.

5.4.3 Examples

The tent map (5.7) for $\pi, \rho > 1$ is expansive, so it is everywhere unstable. The shack map in figure 5.7a is not expansive but its second iterate is expansive, so every N-period cycle is unstable. Later we will show that it is everywhere unstable.

5.4.4 Global Stability and Global Instability

Suppose the trajectories of a system are bounded. That is, suppose there exists a finite interval $I \subset D$ such that $\gamma(x) \subset I$ for all $x \in D$. Then the system (θ, D) is called *globally stable*. The linear system with $|a| > 1$ is not globally stable. Such systems are called *globally unstable*. Notice, however, that a Lyapunov stable system can be globally unstable (i.e., neither asymptotically stable nor globally stable). For example, the affine system with $|a| = 1, b \neq 0$. Moreover, as is emphasized later, globally stable systems can be unstable in the sense of Lyapunov previously defined. Notice also that asymptotically stable systems can be globally unstable. An example is the Solow one-sector growth model studied in volume II. In that model, population and capital follow an unbounded path that converges to a unique balanced growth path.

5.5 Comparative Dynamics and Bifurcation Analysis

The analysis of the existence and identification of isolated parameter values (or initial conditions) at which qualitative behavior of trajectories switches is called *bifurcation theory*. Samuelson called such analysis *comparative dynamics* in his book *Foundations of Economic Analysis*. We shall use the terms interchangeably.

The importance of comparative dynamic analysis arises from the fact that

the exact values of the parameters or the initial conditions of a system being
studied are seldom, if ever, known. Worse! The exact form of the function $\theta(\cdot)$
is seldom, if ever, known exactly. We may, however, have some confidence
that parameter values should fall in some range. Then it is of interest to find
out what are the possible qualitative modes of behavior in that range.

Or, it may be that a system can be influenced theoretically by a parameter
without reducing it to an explicit formula. Such a parameter may enable one
to study how the qualitative behavior of a general system depends on a shift in
its structure.

5.5.1 Comparative Dynamics for the Affine System

The concept of bifurcation can be illustrated using the simplest linear dynamic
system, because we have already found that the qualitative behavior of a trajectory depends on where the initial condition is and what the slope parameter
value, a, is. Indeed, in the examples involving this system we have found all
the following possibilities:

$a > 1$	unstable	explosive growth or decay	(5.27a)
$a = 1$	stable	all x are stationary	(5.27b)
$0 < a < 1$	asymptotically stable	monotonic growth or decay	(5.27c)
$a = 0$	1-period convergence		(5.27d)
$-1 < a < 0$	asymptotically stable	dampening 2-period fluctuations	(5.27e)
$a = -1$	stable	all x are 2-cyclic	(5.27f)
$a < -1$	unstable	explosive 2-period fluctuations	(5.27g)

Evidently, the values $1, 0, -1$ are special values for the parameter a at
which *the qualitative behavior switches*. These parameter values are called *bifurcation points*.

5.5.2 A Qualitative Example: Stretchable Functions

As a second example, suppose we can define θ as follows:

$$\theta_\beta(x) := \theta(x; \beta) = \beta f(x), \tag{5.28}$$

where $f(x) > 0$ on $D := (a, b)$ and $f(x) = 0$ on $D^0 := \mathbb{R} \setminus (a, b)$. The parameter $\beta \geq 0$ "stretches" the function f. Thus, if $x^* = \arg\max_x f(x)$ and
if $x_f^M = f(x^*)$ then $x_\theta^M = \beta x_f^M$. For obvious reasons the function f (or θ) is
called *stretchable*.

Suppose now that $f(x) < x$ for all $x \in (a, b)$ and consider the difference equation defined by (5.28) with $\beta = 1$. Then we know that $\tau(x)$ must be a declining trajectory that shrinks to the single stationary state $\tilde{x} = 0$.

However, let

$$\beta^* := x^*/f(x^*). \tag{5.29}$$

By construction, x^* is a fixpoint of (θ_β, D) and hence a stationary state. Then for all $\beta > \beta^*, \theta_\beta(x) > x$ for all x close enough to x^*. Consequently, for initial conditions in a neighborhood of x^* growth is possible for some periods. The parameter β^* is therefore a bifurcation point. See figure 5.9.

5.5.3   A Formal Definition

To give these ideas a general expression let $B \subset \mathbb{R}$ be a parameter space and define the one-parameter family of systems $(\theta_\beta; D)_{\beta \in B}$ by

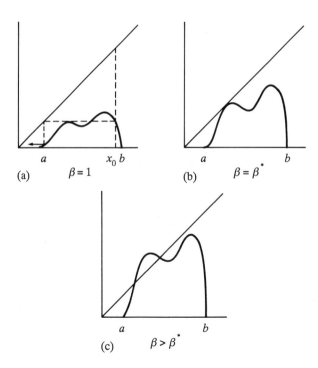

Figure 5.9
Function stretching. (a) $\beta = 1$. (b) $\beta = \beta^*$. (c) $\beta > \beta^*$.

$\theta_\beta(x) := \theta(x; \beta),$

where $\theta(\cdot; \beta)$ is a real-valued function defined on D and dependent on the parameter β. Let

$-\infty \le \beta_0 < \beta_1 < \cdots < \beta_n \le \infty$

such that the qualitative behavior of the system is the same for all

$\beta \in B_i := (\beta_{i-1}, \beta_i)$

but for any $\beta \in B_{i-1} \cup B_{i+1}$ the qualitative behavior is different than for $\beta \in B_i$. The points $\beta_1, \ldots, \beta_n$ are the bifurcation points and the open sets $B_i, i = 1, \ldots, n$ are called *parameter zones*. Systems (θ_β, D), $\beta \in B_i$ will be called *qualitatively similar*. Notice that subfamilies defined by adjacent parameter zones must be different but subfamilies separated by at least one parameter zone can be similar. As we see at various places in this book, qualitative behavior can switch back and forth from one parameter zone to another.

In the linear system we have $\beta = a$, $B = \mathbb{R}$, $\beta_0 = -\infty$, $\beta_1 = -1, \beta_2 = 0$, $\beta_3 = 1$, $\beta_4 = \infty$, so $B_1 = (-\infty, -1)$, $B_2 = (-1, 0)$, $B_3 = (0, 1)$, $B_4 = (1, \infty)$. For all $\beta \in B_1$ we get expanding two-period fluctuations, for all $\beta \in B_2$ we get contracting two-period fluctuations, for all $\beta \in B_3$ we get monotonic convergence to a unique stationary state, and for all $\beta \in B_4$ we get explosive divergence. These form qualitative properties and are therefore robust and in fact generic for the general class of affine systems.

5.5.4 The Quadratic System

To take another example, we have had occasion so far to identify the following bifurcation points for the quadratic system (equation 4.2b) with parameter $\beta = m$. They are $m = 0, 1, 2, 3, 1 + \sqrt{5}, 1 + \sqrt{6}$. It turns out there are many more, as shall be seen in the next chapter.

5.5.5 The Tent Map

For still another example with which we are already familiar, reconsider the tent map of §5.2.2, equation (5.7) and recall figure 5.4. Hold π fixed and vary ρ. For this map $\theta'(\tilde{x}) = -\rho$, so for $0 < \rho < 1$ we get convergence to the stationary state $\tilde{x} = \rho c/(1 + \rho)$. When $\rho = 1$ any initial condition leads eventually to a stable two-period cycle (except, of course, $x_0 = \tilde{x}$ which is the stationary state). When $\rho > 1$ the stationary state is unstable.

Now consider the orbit $\gamma(a) = \{(a/b)^{n-2}a, \ldots, a, b\}$ which is by construction n-periodic. (See §5.2.2.) Note that $\theta'(x) = \pi = b/a$ for each of the $n-1$ points $(a/b)^{n-2}a, \ldots, a$, and that $\theta'(b) = -b/(c-a)$. Now $b/a > 1$ and, as $\rho > 1$ by assumption, $b/(c-a) > 1$. Consequently,

$$\times_{x\in\omega(a)} \left|\theta'(x)\right| = \left(\frac{b}{a}\right)^{n-1} \cdot \frac{b}{(c-a)} > 1.$$

By Theorem 5.8 every cycle is unstable. This means that trajectories whose initial conditions are noncyclic cannot converge to a periodic orbit. To summarize, as ρ increases, higher- and higher-order cycles emerge but they are all unstable. For $\rho > 1$ unstable behavior is generic for the class of tent maps given by (5.7). The value $\rho = 1$ is therefore a bifurcation point separating stable stationary states from unstable behavior of some sort.

What are unstable trajectories like when $\rho > 1$? If they are not periodic and do not converge to a periodic cycle, what do they do? Where do they go? We have dubbed behavior "complex" that is not stationary, not monotonic, not periodic, and not convergent to any of these. What is the character of complex behavior? This question will occupy our attention in the next three chapters.

6 Multiple-Phase Dynamics I

We must face the fact that the form of the equations of a realistic model may have to be regarded as a function of the variables involved.
—Trygve Haavelmo, A *Study in the Theory of Economic Evolution* (paraphrased)

We observe in economics, as in other fields, that quite different forces or relationships govern behavior in differing situations of state. It can also come to pass that behavior in one situation is so different from that in another that we want to distinguish it. Multiple-phase dynamical systems formalize these ideas. Such systems, which arise throughout this book, are discussed in this chapter. Concepts and techniques will be introduced that shall be used subsequently in the study of chaotic behavior and its statistical properties.[1]

6.1 Multiple-Phase Dynamics

6.1.1 Multiple-Phase Dynamical Systems

Consider a family of single-valued mappings $\theta_p: x \to \theta_p(x)$, $p \in \mathcal{P}$, where $\mathcal{P}$ is a set of indexes. Each map $\theta_p(\cdot)$ is called a *phase structure* and is defined on a set $D^p \subset \mathbb{R}$ called the pth *phase domain*. A *regime* is a pair $\mathcal{R}_p := (\theta_p, D^p)$. The dynamics within a given phase domain is given by the *phase equation*

$$x_{t+1} = \theta_p(x_t), \quad x_t \in D^p, \tag{6.1}$$

where it is assumed that $D^p \cap D^q = \emptyset$ for all $p \neq q \in \mathcal{P}$. Defining the map

$$\theta(x) := \theta_p(x), \quad x \in D^p \tag{6.2}$$

with domain $D := \cup_p D^p$, we have the usual dynamical system (θ, D) with dynamics

$$x_{t+1} = \theta(x_t), \quad x_t \in D.$$

Let $\chi_S(x)$ be the indicator function.[2] Then another way to write (6.2) that is the literal analog of Haavelmo's admonition at the head of this chapter is

$$x_{t+1} = \theta(x_t) = \sum_{p \in \mathcal{P}} \chi_{D^p}(x_t) \cdot \theta_p(x_t). \tag{6.3}$$

We shall call the collection $\{\mathcal{R}_p, p \in \mathcal{P}\}$, or the equivalents (6.1) or (6.3), a *multiple-phase* or *multiple-regime dynamical system*.

6.1.2 Example

The piecewise linear map given in equation (4.2h) provides an example that
has already been used for several illustrative purposes. This map was defined
over a set of closed intervals $[a_i, a_{i+1}]$, which gives the phase domains if we
define the latter to be the semiopen intervals

$$D^i := [a_{i-1}, a_i), \quad i = 0, \dots, n, \; D^n := [a_{n-1}, a_n].$$

Let $\mathcal{P} := \{1, \dots, n\}$. The phase structures are

$$\theta_i(x) := b_{i-1} + \beta_i(x - a_{i-1}), \quad x \in D^i,$$

where $\beta_i = (b_i - b_{i-1})/(a_i - a_{i-1})$, $i \in \mathcal{P}$. Thus, the n "pieces" of the
piecewise linear dynamical system correspond to n "phases" of an equivalent
multiple-phase dynamical system.

6.1.3 Regimes and Qualitative Modes

Suppose that the domain of a given dynamical system can be partitioned into
nonintersecting subsets D^p, $p \in \mathcal{P}$ within each of which behavior is distinct,
for example, monotonic growth, monotonic decline, cycles, or erratic behav-
ior. Then the restriction of $\theta(\cdot)$ to D^p can be denoted θ_p and the pair (θ_p, D^p)
can be considered a regime.

For example, consider the generalized power map of equation (4.2f). It
is defined on an interval $[b_1, b_2]$ as shown in figure 6.1 for one particular
case. For any initial condition that falls in $D^1 = [b_1, \tilde{x}^l) \cup (d, b^2]$, monotonic
decline occurs. Any trajectory that enters this set must eventually fall below b_1
and hence into $D^0 := [-\infty, b_1]$. Note that D^1 is not connected. Any trajectory
that falls in D^2 grows. Any trajectory that falls in D^3 is stationary or fluctuates
indefinitely.

6.1.4 The Null Regime

The null domain D^0 means that for all $x \in D^0$ the system is inviable and that
no consistent structure capable of perpetuating behavior has been defined. Define a map θ_0 called the *null phase structure* that has the property that $\theta_0(x) \in$
D^0 for all $x \in D^0$. That is, once a trajectory enters D^0 it cannot escape. For example, $\theta_0(\cdot)$ could simply be the identity map so that $\theta_0(y) = y$ for all $y \in D^0$.

In many applications the null domain includes the set of nonpositive states.
In this case one could define the null phase structure by

$$\theta_0(x) \equiv 0 \quad \text{for all} \quad x \in D^0. \tag{6.4}$$

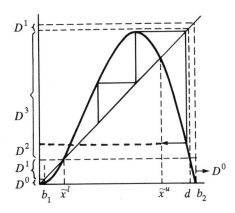

Figure 6.1
Qualitative regimes

For example, in Walras's production tatonnement model used for illustrative purposes in chapter 2, the map θ was a quadratic function that gave output as a function of lagged profits. A negative output level would be impossible, so it would be natural to define $D^0 := \{x|\theta(x) \leq 0\}$ and $D^1 := \{x|\theta(x) > 0\}$. Then any trajectory that entered D^0 would imply bankruptcy of the industry.

Given these definitions, the original dynamical system can now be extended to the real line. Redefining $\mathcal{P} := \{0, 1, \ldots, n\}$, the collection of regimes is $\{(\theta_p, D^p), p \in \mathcal{P}$. When the extension is made by means of (6.4), we shall refer to it as the *usual extension*. From now on we will consider every multiple-phase dynamical system to be extended in the usual way unless otherwise indicated.

6.1.5   Escape and Regime Switching

Suppose that a given trajectory enters a given regime with a value $y \in D^p$ and that there is a least integer n such that $\theta_p^n(y) \notin D^p$; then the trajectory from y is said to *escape* regime p in period n. The map $\theta_p^n(\cdot)$ is the nth iterated map of the map $\theta_p(\cdot)$. If the trajectory escapes regime p, it must enter another part of the domain of the system and hence another regime, or it must enter the null domain. This phenomenon is called *regime switching*. In the latter case when the trajectory escapes the domain of definition and enters the null domain, the system is said to *self-destruct*.

In the example illustrated in figure 6.1, any trajectory in D^2 must escape and enter D^3; any trajectory in D^3 remains there; any trajectory in D^1 self-destructs, i.e., enters D^0. Growth occurs in D^2. Fluctuations are perpetuated in D^3.

6.1.6 Epochal Evolution

Evidently, a trajectory of a system can be characterized by the sequence of regimes through which it passes. Define the regime index of a given state by

$$I(x) := \sum_p p \cdot \chi_{D^p}(x). \tag{6.5}$$

Then the sequence

$$I\left[\theta^t(x)\right], \quad t = 0, 1, 2, 3, \ldots \tag{6.6}$$

gives the dynamics of the system as a sequence of regimes. A given history can now be decomposed into a denumerable sequence of *episodes*, each one of which represents a *sojourn* within a given regime. Let

$$
\begin{aligned}
0 = s_1(x) \le t < s_2(x), \quad & I\left(\theta^t(x)\right) = p_1, \\
s_2(x) \le t < s_3(x), \quad & I\left(\theta^t(x)\right) = p_2, \\
s_3(x) \le t < s_4(x), \quad & I\left(\theta^t(x)\right) = p_3, \\
& \vdots
\end{aligned}
\tag{6.7}
$$

The triple

$$(\theta_{p_i}(\cdot), D^{p_i}, T_i), \quad i = 1, 2, \ldots \tag{6.8}$$

is called the ith *episode*; the period $s_i(x)$ is called the ith *entry time*; the state $\theta^{s_i(x)}(x)$ is called the ith *entry state*; the sequence of integers $T_i := \{s_i(x), s_i(x) + 1, \ldots, s_{i+1}(x) - 1\}$ is the *sojourn*, and the number $s_{i+1}(x) - s_i(x)$ the *duration* of the ith episode. The sequence of episodes (6.8) associated with a given trajectory is an *epochal evolution*.

Suppose in (6.7) the sequence is finite, say n episodes long for $n < \infty$. Then $s_{n+1}(x) = \infty$ and the trajectory is trapped in the phase domain D^{p_n}. The associated epochal evolution converges to phase D^{p_n}. This does not mean that the trajectory converges to a stationary, steady, or periodic state, however, but only that the phase structure governing change does not switch.

Consider the sequence of phase structure indexes

$$p_1, p_2, p_3, \ldots$$

associated with epochal evolution (6.8). If for every p_i (except the last if the sequence is finite) there is a $j > i$ such that $p_j > p_i$, the history of episodes forms a *progression*. If in addition $p_1 < p_2 < p_3 < \cdots$, the progression is monotonic. If for some $k > 0$, $p_{i+k} = p_i$, $i = 1, 2, 3, \ldots$ the evolution is *phase cyclic*. If the sequence (6.7) is not finite and not periodic, then we will call it a *nonperiodic (chaotic) evolution*. A periodic sequence of regimes does not imply that trajectories are periodic. We shall give examples in chapter 9 that are phase cyclic, but in which the trajectories are nonperiodic (chaotic) almost surely.

6.1.7 The Set-Valued Inverse Map

Subsequently, much use is made of the map $\theta^{-1}(\cdot)$ defined by

$$\theta^{-1}(S) := \cup_{y \in S}\{x \in D | \theta(x) = y\}, \quad S \subset D.$$

Analogously,

$$\theta_p^{-1}(S) := \cup_{y \in S}\{x \in D^p | \theta(x) = y\}, \quad S \subset D^p.$$

The inverse maps θ^{-n} are defined recursively. Thus,

$$\theta_p^{-n}(S) := \theta_p^{-1}\left(\theta^{-n+1}(S)\right), \quad n = 1, \ldots, \quad S \subset D^p.$$

Note that $\theta_p^{-n}(S) \subset \theta^{-n}(S)$. In particular it can happen that $\theta_p^{-1}(D^p) = \emptyset$ while $\theta^{-1}(D^p) \neq \emptyset$. Note also that every map in $\{\theta^i, i \in \mathbb{N}\}$ has an inverse so that the set of positive and negative iterates together with the power set $\mathcal{P}(D)$ constitute a dynamical system.

6.2 Stable and Unstable Regimes

The qualitative analysis of a multiple-phase dynamical system is carried out via an analysis of the dynamics of its constituent regimes. For this purpose the ideas of stability and instability need to be defined appropriately.

6.2.1 Stable Regimes

If any trajectory that enters a given regime, say the $\mathcal{R}_p$, remains there, then the regime is called *stable*. Formally, a regime $\mathcal{R}^p$ is stable if and only if for any entry state $y \in D^p$, $\theta^s(y) \in D^p$, $s = 1, 2, 3, \ldots$.
Or, equivalently,

- A regime $\mathcal{R}_p$ is stable if and only if $\theta_p(D^p) \subset D^p$.
- In particular, the null regime is stable.

6.2.2 Locally Stable, Locally Unstable, and Unstable Regimes

It is possible that for some entry states the trajectories escape. We shall call the set of such points the *unstable set* in phase domain D^p and denote it U^p. For any entry state $y \in U^p$ there is a minimum integer $k \geq 1$, such that $\theta^s(y) \in D^p, s = 0, 1, \ldots, k - 1$ and $\theta^k(y) \notin D^p$. The set $S^p := D^p \setminus U^p$ consists of all the entry states whose trajectories remain in D^p. We call it the *stable set*. Of course, $\mathcal{R}_p$ is stable if and only if $S^p = D^p$, that is, if $U^p = \emptyset$. If $U^p \neq \emptyset$, then $\mathcal{R}_p$ is not stable. Suppose $U_p \neq \emptyset$ and $S_p \neq \emptyset$. Then $\mathcal{R}_p$ is called *locally stable* on S_p and *locally unstable* on U_p. Of course, $\theta(S^p) \subset S^p$ and $\theta(U^p) \supset U^p$.

If $U^p \neq \emptyset$, then there must exist a nonempty *escape set* $E^p \subset U^p$. Any trajectory that enters E^p escapes the pth regime in one period, that is,

$$E^p = \{x \in D^p \mid \theta_p(x) \in \setminus D^p\}.$$

If $E^p \neq \emptyset$ there could be a set in D^p, say E_2^p, whose trajectories escape in two periods and so on, recursively, there could be a set that escapes in n periods:

$$E_n^p := \theta_p^{1-n}(E^p), n = 1, 2, 3, \ldots. \tag{6.9}$$

We call E_n^p the nth escape set in U^p, the first one of which is just called the escape set. All these sets could be empty for $n \geq 2$. For example, in figure 6.2a, $E_1^1 = D^1$ so $E_n^1 = \emptyset$ all $n > 1$. In figure 6.2b E_1^1 and E_2^1 are both nonempty and $E_1^1 \cup E_2^1 = D^1$ so $E_n^1 = \emptyset$ all $n > 2$. In figure 6.2c all the sets E_n^1 are nonempty for $n = 1, 2, 3, \ldots$. Figure 6.2d shows three regimes composed of the pieces of the tent map extended to the positive real line. In both $\mathcal{R}_1$ and $\mathcal{R}_2$ all the sets $E_n^1 \subset D^1$ and $E_n^2 \subset D^2$ are nonempty, $n \geq 1$. Note that the destination of escaping trajectories from either regime depends on where in the escape set the trajectory enters. Some enter the null regime and some enter the other non-null regime. Note also that neither E^1 nor E^2 are connected.

Evidently, the set of points that escape a given regime p eventually, that is, the unstable set, is the union of all these escape sets E_n^p, that is,

$$U^p = \cup_{n=0}^{\infty} E_n^p. \tag{6.10}$$

If $U^p = D^p$, then the pth regime is *unstable*.

A given phase domain D^p may contain a set of periodic states, say P^p. Let

$$C^p := \cup_{n=0}^{\infty} \theta_p^{-n}(P^p). \tag{6.11}$$

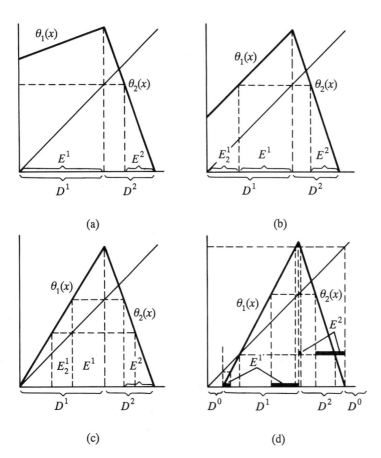

Figure 6.2
Escape sets

This is the set of points in D^p that are *eventually periodic*, so we'll call it the *eventually period set* in D^p. What happens to trajectories whose entry states do not belong to the eventually periodic set? They could converge to a periodic orbit in P^p; or they could wander erratically in D^p, never converging to a cycle of any order. If either event were true for any entry state, the regime would be stable. But even points that come close to a point in C^p might eventually exit and this could be true for almost all points, i.e., for all but a countable number. Note that a periodic orbit may intersect several phase zones. Trajectories with such orbits, or that converge to them, will be phase cyclic.

6.2.3   Sigma Algebras and Measure Spaces

To get a precise notion of what is meant by "almost all," we have to introduce several technical concepts.[3] They will be of use later in various contexts. First is a σ-algebra.

DEFINITION 6.1   *A σ-algebra is a collection of subsets Σ of a set D*

(i) that contains D, i.e.,

$$D \in \Sigma;$$

(ii) that contains the complement of any set in Σ, i.e.,

$$X \in \Sigma \Rightarrow D \setminus X \in \Sigma;$$

(iii) that contains the union of any countable collection of subsets in Σ, i.e., let $\{X_n\}_{n=1}^{\infty}$ be a countable collection of sets with $X_n \in \Sigma$ all n; then

$$\bigcup_{n=0}^{\infty} X_n \in \Sigma.$$

Several facts follow. The empty set $\emptyset$ belongs to Σ; the intersection and difference of sets in Σ belongs to Σ; that is, if $X \in \Sigma$, $Y \in \Sigma$, then $X \cap Y \in \Sigma$ and $X \setminus Y \in \Sigma$.

Sequences of sets in the domain of a dynamical system have been constructed several times in previous discussions using the iterated maps. In doing so, we were in effect operating in a σ-algebra on the domain.

DEFINITION 6.2   *Let $\{X_n\}_{n=0}^{\infty}$ be a countable collection of disjoint sets in a σ-algebra Σ. A measure is a map $\mu : \Sigma \to \mathbb{R}^+$ such that* *(i)* $\mu(\emptyset) = 0$

(ii) $\mu(\bigcup_{n=0}^{\infty} X_n) = \sum_{n=1}^{\infty} \mu(X_n)$.

An example is the Lebesgue measure on the real line, denoted $\lambda(\cdot)$, which associates with an interval its length. Thus, if $I := [a, b]$ is an interval, then $\lambda(I) = \mid b - a \mid$. Obviously, the Lebesgue measure of points is zero. The Lebesgue measure of an open or semiopen interval is, therefore, the same as its closure. In general if a measure μ is zero on points, it is called *continuous* or *nonatomic*.

Lebesgue measure involves the set of subsets of $\mathbb{R}$ that can be obtained as a union of intervals. Here the complement $\backslash[a, b]$ of any interval defined by points $a < b$ is the union of two intervals $(-\infty, a)$ and (b, ∞) so $\lambda(\backslash[a, b]) = \infty$.

DEFINITION 6.3 *A measure space is a triple* (D, Σ, μ) *in which* Σ *is a σ-algebra of subsets of D and $\mu(\cdot)$ is a measure defined on Σ. The sets in Σ are called* measurable. *The measure space is called* finite *if $\mu(X) < \infty$ for all* $X \in \Sigma$. *The measure $\mu(\cdot)$ is called a probability measure if $\mu(D) = 1$, and* (D, Σ, μ) *a* probability space.

Note that Lebesgue measure is not finite on $\mathbb{R}$ but is a probability measure on $[0, 1]$. Obviously, any finite measure can be normalized to lie between 0 and 1. If $\mu(\cdot)$ is a finite measure, then $\mu(X)/\mu(D)$ is a *probability measure* and (D, Σ, λ) a *probability space*. To avoid extra notation, we will not introduce a separate symbol for a probability measure but make clear which is the case in context.

These concepts play a fundamental role in investigating nonperiodic trajectories and will come up in chapters 7 and 8. Here we use them to define stability and instability for regimes.

6.2.4 Stability and Instability

We can now consider the measure of the stable and unstable sets. If $\mu(U^p) = \mu(D^p)$, then $\mathcal{R}_p$ is *μ-unstable*; trajectories that enter any subset of D^p that has positive measure *escape μ-almost surely*. If $0 < \mu(U^p) < \mu(D^p)$, then we say that $\mathcal{R}_p$ is *locally unstable* and that trajectories that enter subsets of D^p that have positive measure D^p *escape with positive measure*. If $0 < \mu(S^p) < \mu(D^p)$, then $\mathcal{R}_p$ is *locally μ-stable* and trajectories are *trapped in*

D^p *with positive measure. If* $\mu(S^p) = \mu(D^p)$, *then* $\mathcal{R}_p$ *is* μ-*stable and trajectories that enter* D^p *are trapped there* μ-*almost surely.*

Note that a regime that is μ-unstable may have a stable subset of Lebesgue measure zero. In particular, this set would contain all the periodic orbits that are strictly contained in D^p. The concept of μ-instability and μ-stability is actually quite limited because a given measure μ may be positive only for some subsets of a given domain and, as already noticed, these could even be finite and therefore of Lebesgue measure zero. We shall deal with this problem in chapter 9 after developing a stronger class of measures of particular relevance for dynamical systems in chapter 8. Here, however, we can give the strongest concept of stability and instability. If a regime $\mathcal{R}_p$ is λ-unstable or λ-stable, we shall say it is unstable or stable, respectively. If a regime $\mathcal{R}_p$ is locally λ-unstable or locally λ-stable, we shall say that it is locally unstable or locally stable, respectively.

6.2.5   Decomposability, Indecomposability, and Switching Regimes

If every regime $\mathcal{R}_p$, $p \in \mathcal{P}$ of a multiple-phase dynamical system is stable, then each regime (θ_p, D^p) is a closed dynamical system and the multiple-phase system is *decomposable*.

Contrastingly, suppose every regime is unstable except the null regime $\mathcal{R}_0$, then every trajectory must involve switching regimes almost surely. The number of episodes in any nondegenerate evolution is countable, either infinite or finite. If the number of episodes is infinite, then every evolution must involve phase cycling or it must exhibit a nonperiodic sequence of regimes. If the number of episodes is finite, then the trajectory must be eventually stationary or cyclic in the "last" phase or it must enter the null domain.

6.3   Possible Evolutions

Later in this book we will consider in detail the kind of evolutions that are possible for multiple-phase dynamical systems that arise in various economic settings, especially when considering economic development. Here we shall investigate the idea abstractly.

6.3.1   Conditional Evolutions

Let $\{\mathcal{R}_p, p \in \mathcal{P}\}$ be a multiple-phase dynamical system and consider an ordering of regimes

$$p_1, p_2, \ldots, p_k, \qquad (6.12)$$

which we shall call a *conditional evolution*. Could there exist a trajectory with initial condition $x \in D$ and sojourns $T_i, i = 1, \ldots, k - 1$, such that

$$I\left(\theta^t(x)\right) = p_i \quad \text{for} \quad t \in T_i, \quad i = 1, \ldots, k? \qquad (6.13)$$

We don't ask about what happens before $s_1(x)$ or after $s_{k+1}(x)$ unless we want to assume that $s_1(x) = 0$ or that $s_{k+1}(x) = \infty$.

6.3.2   Switching and Transition Sets

Obviously, for such a given sequence of episodes to occur, it must be possible to switch from one regime to another *in the specified sequence*. This means that each regime in the sequence up to the last must be locally unstable. Define a *switching set*

$$E^{i,j} := \{x \in E^i | \theta_i(x) \in D^j\}, \quad i \neq j. \qquad (6.14)$$

It is the set of points in the ith regime's escape set E^i that map outside D^i and into the jth phase domain. Obviously, if $E^{i,j} = \emptyset$, such a switch can't occur. Of course, $E^i = \cup_j E^{i,j}$.

Now define a *transition set* $U^{i,j}$

$$U^{i,j} := \bigcup_{n=0}^{\infty} \theta_i^{-n}(E^{i,j}). \qquad (6.15)$$

This is a subset of the unstable set U^i containing all the points in D^i that eventually escape and enter D^j. Of course, $U^i = \cup_j U^{i,j}$.

6.3.3   Existence of Conditional Evolutions

Our question can now be framed in terms of these transition sets. Can there exist an initial condition $x \in D$ and sojourns T_i such that

$$\theta^t(x) \in U^{p_i, p_{i+1}}, t \in T_i, i = 1, \ldots, k - 1? \qquad (6.16)$$

If so, then, of course, $\theta^{s_k(x)}(x) \in D^{p_k}$.

For this to happen it is necessary that each transition set in the sequence be nonempty. This will be true if each escape set in the sequence is nonempty. But this is not sufficient because the trajectory must not only eventually switch from one regime to the next, it must enter each successive transition set. That is, for the entry time $s_i(x)$ it must be that

$$\theta^{s_i(x)}(x) \in U^{p_i, p_{i+1}}, i = 1, \ldots, k - 1. \tag{6.17}$$

For this to happen, $\theta^{s_{i-1}(x)}(x)$ must enter the correct subset of U^{p_{i-1}, p_i}, and this must be true phase by phase so the initial condition x must belong to a special subset of U^{p_1, p_2} that will lead from one transition set to another in the proscribed sequence.

To determine what this special set is, we can proceed backwards from the last regime in the conditional evolution. Thus, we must have

$$\theta_{p_{k-1}}(D^{p_{k-1}}) \cap D^{p_k} \neq \emptyset. \tag{6.18}$$

This implies that the set of points that escape $D^{p_{k-1}}$ and enter D^{p_k} is nonempty, i.e.,

$$E^{p_{k-1}, p_n} := \theta_{p_{k-1}}^{-1} \left(\theta_{p_{k-1}}(D^{p_{k-1}}) \cap D^{p_k} \right) \neq \emptyset \tag{6.19}$$

so

$$U^{p_{k-1}, p_k} := \cup_{n=0}^{\infty} \theta_{p_{k-1}}^{-n} (E^{p_{k-1}, p_k}) \neq \emptyset. \tag{6.20}$$

Any trajectory that enters U^{p_{k-1}, p_k} eventually arrives in D^{p_k}.

To enter U^{p_{k-1}, p_n} from $D^{p_{k-2}}$ we must have

$$\theta(D^{p_{k-2}}) \cap U^{p_{k-1}, p_n} \neq \emptyset. \tag{6.21}$$

This is a subset of $E^{p_{k-2}, p_{k-1}}$ and we now have to get the corresponding subset of its transition set, which we shall denote

$$U^{p_{k-2}, p_{k-1}, p_k} := \cup_{n=1}^{\infty} \theta_{p_{k-2}}^{-n} \left(\theta(D^{p_{k-2}}) \cap U^{p_{k-1}, p_k} \right). \tag{6.22}$$

Any entry state $\theta^{s_{k-2}(x)}(x) \in U^{p_{k-2}, p_{k-1}, p_k}$ will traverse $\mathcal{R}_{p_{k-2}}, \mathcal{R}_{p_{k-1}}, \mathcal{R}_{p_k}$ in succession.

In like manner we can define

$$U^{p_{k-i}, \ldots, p_k} := \cup_{n=1}^{\infty} \theta_{p_{k-i}}^{-n} \left(\theta_{p_{k-i}}(D^{p_{k-i}}) \cap U^{p_{k-i+1}, \ldots, p_k} \right) \tag{6.23}$$

and so on, recursively, $i = 1, \ldots, k - 1$ until we get the condition $\theta_{p_1}(D^{p_1}) \cap U^{p_2, \ldots, p_k} \neq \emptyset$.

We thus arrive at

PROPOSITION 6.1   *The necessary and sufficient condition for a trajectory $\tau(x)$ to follow the conditional evolution defined by $p_1, p_2, \ldots, p_k$ is that*

$$x \in U^{p_1,\ldots,p_k} := \cup_{n=1}^{\infty} \theta_{p_1}^{-n} \left(\theta_{p_1}(D^{p_1}) \cap U^{p_2,\ldots,p_k} \right) \neq \emptyset. \tag{6.24}$$

It should be noted that many (usually most) conditional evolutions among all those sequences that can be written down will not be possible.

6.3.4 Examples

In the two regime examples of figure 6.2 in which both phases were unstable, the only possible sequences are

$$1, 2, 1, 2, \ldots \quad \text{or} \quad 2, 1, 2, 1, \ldots.$$

Consequently,

$$U^{1,2,1,\cdots} = D^1$$

and

$$U^{2,1,2,\cdots} = D^2.$$

Figure 6.3 illustrates two cases of a three-phase system. In figure 6.3a the parameters are given so that just the following sequences of regimes are possible:

$$\mathcal{R}_1, \ \mathcal{R}_2, \ \mathcal{R}_1, \ \mathcal{R}_2, \ \ldots$$
$$\mathcal{R}_3, \ \mathcal{R}_2, \ \mathcal{R}_3, \ \mathcal{R}_2, \ \ldots$$
$$\mathcal{R}_2, \ \mathcal{R}_1, \ \mathcal{R}_2, \ \mathcal{R}_1, \ \ldots$$
$$\mathcal{R}_2, \ \mathcal{R}_3, \ \mathcal{R}_2, \ \mathcal{R}_3, \ \ldots$$

Every evolution is phase periodic with switches between phase p_1 and p_2 or between p_2 and p_3.

The same system but with different parameters is shown in figure 6.3b.

One can see that any trajectory in $\mathcal{R}_2$ must go to $\mathcal{R}_1$ or $\mathcal{R}_3$, while some trajectories in $\mathcal{R}_1$ could escape to $\mathcal{R}_2$ or to $\mathcal{R}_3$, and some trajectories in $\mathcal{R}_3$ could escape to $\mathcal{R}_2$ or $\mathcal{R}_1$. We find, for example, the following are possibilities:

$$\mathcal{R}_1 \ \mathcal{R}_2 \ \mathcal{R}_1 \ \mathcal{R}_2 \ \cdots \ \mathcal{R}_1 \ \mathcal{R}_2 \ \mathcal{R}_3 \ \mathcal{R}_2 \ \mathcal{R}_3 \ \cdots$$

$$\mathcal{R}_1 \ \mathcal{R}_2 \ \mathcal{R}_3 \ \mathcal{R}_2 \ \mathcal{R}_3 \ \mathcal{R}_2 \ \mathcal{R}_3 \ \cdots$$

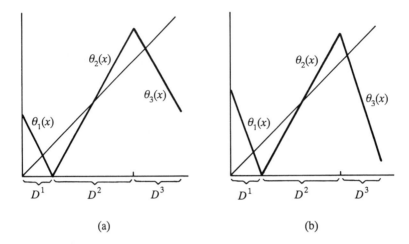

$$(a) \qquad\qquad (b)$$

Figure 6.3
Switching regimes. (a) Cyclic regime switching. (b) Complex possibilities.

and with a little practice you will quickly see that an incredible variety of sequences are possible. Indeed, its number is uncountably infinite. And it includes both phase cycles of any order and nonperiodic phase sequences.

This example has not just been drawn from a trick hat but arises in a particular model of price adjustment that has been used to describe some salient features of the stock market. In that model the different regimes are determined by the kinds of investors who are active in the market and by how their transaction strategies depend on current prices. It will be discussed in detail in chapter 11.

6.3.5 Probable Conditional Evolutions

If initial conditions are not known but can be located with varying degrees of reasonable belief within certain sets, one could then give a precise meaning to the probability of occurrence of a given conditional evolution.

Suppose then that μ is a probability measure on $D^1 = [a_0, a_1]$, the first phase zone. The number $\mu(S)$, $S \subset D^1$ then expresses the degree of reasonable belief that the initial condition $x \in S$. Because trajectories are unique (within the class of dynamical systems discussed in this book), they establish a one-to-one map $x \to \tau(x)$. This in turn enables conditional evolutions to be associated with a degree of reasonable belief. This can be summarized as:

PROPOSITION 6.2   *Let $\mu(\cdot)$ be a probability measure defined on D^1. Consider a conditional evolution (6.12). Then*

$$\text{Prob} \left\{ I \left(\theta^t(x) \right) = p_i, t \in T_i, \ i = 1, \ldots, k \right\}$$
$$= \mu(U^{p_1, \ldots, p_k}).$$

To get a better understanding of these complicated possibilities from a technical viewpoint, we have to take up the theories of chaos and statistical dynamics, which is done in the next two chapters. After that multiple-phase systems will be reconsidered for a more detailed analysis of possible evolutionary patterns.

7 Chaos

It may happen that small differences in the initial conditions produce very great ones in the final phenomena. A small error in the former will produce an enormous error in the latter. Prediction becomes impossible, and we have the fortuitous phenomenon.
—Henri Poincaré, *Science and Method*

Let us now return to the problem of characterizing nonperiodic behavior that does not converge to periodic behavior but wanders erratically. We know from the examples of chapter 2 that numerical trajectories of nonlinear dynamical systems often appear to be nonperiodic. That does not constitute a proof, however, because within any time interval less than the period of a high-order cycle, the trajectory could have an irregular appearance. More fundamental is the fact that the computer does not simulate the exact dynamical system but a rational approximation of it. This introduces numerical round-off error into a given model, which has the effect of acting like an exogenous shock. The behavior we observe is influenced by these numerical errors and can't be exactly like the "true" behavior of the underlying dynamical systems of interest.[1]

In this chapter we present some basic analytical results and use them to establish constructive existence conditions for chaotic trajectories.

7.1 Nonperiodic Trajectories

7.1.1 Recapitulation

Let us recapitulate. The trajectories of a (semi)dynamical system can be generated recursively, a step at a time. Any given state in the sequence, say the tth, can be represented by an iterated map $\theta^t(\cdot)$ so that $x_t = \theta^t(x_0)$, $t = 0, 1, 2, \ldots,$. Each such iterated map, when $\theta(\cdot)$ itself is nonlinear, becomes a successively more complicated function of the initial condition and of time. Except in exceptional cases, it cannot be reduced to a simple formula that expresses the current state at time t as a function of t and x. However, special solutions may exist for particular values of x. In particular, there may exist periodic solutions consisting of a finite orbit of p distinct points $\gamma(x^0) = \{x^0, \ldots, x^{p-1}\}$ such that $x^i = \theta^i(x^0)$, $i = 1, \ldots, p - 1$ and such that for all $x \in \gamma(x^0)$, $x_t = \theta^{t \bmod p}(x)$, $t = 0, 1, \ldots.$ It was seen that not only may such special solutions exist, but for some maps periodic solutions of every period $p = 1, 2, \ldots$ may exist. If trajectories begin away from a periodic point but hit such a value after a finite time, they are called *eventually periodic*. If trajectories do not begin in a periodic orbit and are not eventually periodic but converge to a cycle, then they are asymptotically periodic.

Periodic, eventually periodic, and asymptotically periodic trajectories constitute—in the terminology of this book—simple dynamic behavior. It was then shown that maps exist for which all of the periodic trajectories were unstable. For such maps any nonperiodic initial condition cannot converge to a periodic solution of any order. We left the study of simple dynamics in chapter 5 with the questions: where do such unstable trajectories go, and how do they behave?

In the interim, multiple-phase dynamical systems were considered whose domains are partitioned into phase domains on each of which the dynamic structure takes a distinct form, or the dynamic behavior exhibits a distinct, qualitative pattern of growth, decay, or fluctuation. Qualitative histories were then defined in terms of sequences of regimes, each with a characteristic structure or qualitative behavior. The existence of possible qualitative histories then involved the consideration of the backward iterates of the several phase structures $\theta_{p_i}(\cdot)$ in the specified sequence to obtain the set of initial conditions from which trajectories of the required character would flow.

This technique is now going to be used to study the character of nonperiodic trajectories. To apply it, we use an idea closely related to that of a regime. We construct a sequence of sets called an *itinerary*. To each set in this itinerary is associated the restriction of the map θ to that set. We then consider the existence of trajectories that "pass through" a given itinerary. The passage through a given itinerary is analogous to the passage through a given conditional evolution except that there is one set in the itinerary for each period of time instead of merely for each of several episodes of several periods' duration, and the sets in the itinerary do not form a partition of the domain but satisfy a "nesting property." We construct a "phase structure" for each set in the itinerary and form a nested nonincreasing sequence of sets. The idea is to take a small enough set Q in X_0 so successive iterates of any point in Q will thread their way through the specified itinerary.

7.1.2 Admissible Itineraries

Formally, an itinerary is a sequence of nonempty, compact (closed, bounded) sets $\{X_n\} = \{X_0, X_1, \ldots\}$ each member of which belongs to the domain D. An itinerary is *admissible* if there exists a nonempty compact set, Q say, such that

$$\theta^n(x) \in X_n, \quad n = 0, 1, 2, \ldots \tag{7.1}$$

for all $x \in Q$.[2] Thus, an admissible itinerary "contains" a specific class of trajectories that pass through the designated parts of the domain in the specified order.

Consider an itinerary such that the following "nesting" property holds:

$$X_{n+1} \subset \theta(X_n), \quad n = 0, 1, 2, \ldots \tag{7.2}$$

Let $Q_0 = X_0$ and let $\theta_n(\cdot)$ be the restriction of $\theta(\cdot)$ to the set X_n. The set $Q_1 := \theta_0^{-1}(X_1)$ is the set of points in $X_0 = Q_0$ that map into X_1. Since $X_1 \subset \theta(X_0)$,

$$Q_1 = \theta_0^{-1}(X_1) \subset \theta_0^{-1}(\theta(X_0)) = X_0 = Q_0.$$

Likewise, let $Q_2 := \theta_0^{-1} \cdot \theta_1^{-1}(X_2)$. Then

$$Q_2 \subset \theta_0^{-1} \cdot \theta_1^{-1}(\theta(X_1)) = \theta_0^{-1}(X_1) = Q_1$$

so $Q_2 \subset Q_1$. Proceeding in this way, a sequence of sets $\{Q_n\}$ can be constructed with $Q_{n+1} \subset Q_n$.[3] Each set Q_n is closed by virtue of the continuity of θ and contained in the compact set X_n so it is compact. It follows from the finite intersection property that

$$Q := \bigcap_{n=0}^{\infty} Q_n$$

is nonempty and compact.[4]

Now consider any $x \in Q$. By construction $x \in Q \subset Q_0 = X_0$. By construction, also, $Q \subset Q_1 = \theta\left(\theta_0^{-1}(X_1)\right) \subset X_1$. Consequently, $\theta(x) \in X_1$. Proceeding recursively one arrives at (7.2).[5] For further reference call this

LEMMA 7.1 *Let $\{\theta, D\}$ be a continuous, viable dynamical system. An itinerary $\{X_n\}$ is admissible if it satisfies (7.2).*

7.1.3 The Existence of Admissible Itineraries

Note that there always exists an admissible itinerary for any continuous dynamical system, namely, $X_n = D$, $n = 0, 1, 2, \ldots$. But this is a trivial example. The fact that there are nontrivial examples is what makes the lemma important. The expansivity conditions (5.10)–(5.11) have this property. To see this, make up a sequence of sets A and B such that any set A is followed by at least one B. Assume that $X_i = B, i = 0, \ldots, k - 1$, that $X_k = A$, and that for any $n > k$ such that $X_n = A$, $X_{n+1} = B$. Then

$$X_n = B \subset \theta(B) = \theta(X_{n-1}), \quad n = 1, \ldots, k - 1,$$

and

$$X_k = A \subset \theta(B) = \theta(X_{k-1}).$$

Moreover,

$$X_{k+1} = B = \theta(A) = \theta(X_k).$$

Therefore, $X_{n+1} \subset \theta(X_n)$ for all n so θ has the nesting property and by Lemma 7.1 the sequence $\{X_n\}$ so constructed is admissible. This gives

LEMMA 7.2 *Suppose $\{\theta, D\}$ is a dynamical system and that D is compact. Suppose also that there exists a compact set A, $B \subset D$ with $B = \theta(A)$ such that*

$$A \cap B = \emptyset, \quad A \cup B \subset \theta(B). \tag{7.3}$$

Let $M := \{X_n\}$ be any sequence of sets A and B such that any A in the sequence is followed by at least one B. That is, if

$$X_n = A \quad \text{then} \quad X_{n+1} = B. \tag{7.4}$$

Then M is admissible.

7.1.4 Existence of Nonperiodic Trajectories

The construction in Lemma 7.2 lets us concoct an immense variety of itineraries that are admissible. We already know from Theorems 5.3 and 5.4 that there are cycles of all orders given the expansivity conditions. In this case there are cyclic itineraries that, using the fixpoint Theorem 5.2, establish the existence of periodic trajectories of all orders. Now we show that there are admissible *nonperiodic* itineraries that contain nonperiodic trajectories and that the number of these is uncountable.[6]

Let $P(M, j)$ be the number of sets A in the first j elements of M, where M is a sequence of sets A and B satisfying (7.3) and (7.4). Let $r \in (0, 1)$. Construct an itinerary $M^r := \{X_0^r, X_1^r, \ldots\}$, satisfying Lemma 7.2, and such that

$$r \cdot j \leq P(M^r, j^2) \leq rj + 1 \quad \text{for all} \quad j \geq J$$

for some sufficiently large number J. Dividing through by j

$$r \le \frac{P(M_j^r j^2)}{j} \le \frac{rj+1}{j} \quad \text{for all} \quad j \ge J,$$

which implies that

$$\lim_{j \to \infty} \frac{P(M^r, j^2)}{j} = r \tag{7.5}$$

and that the map $r \to P(M^r, j^2)$ is one-to-one. Consequently, there is an itinerary for each $r \in (0, 1)$. By construction M^r is admissible so there exists $x \in D$ such that $\theta^t(x) \in X_t^r$, $t = 0, 1, 2, \dots$.

Can the trajectory $\tau(x)$ be eventually periodic? If so, then for some integer $m \ge 0$ and some integer $p \ge 1$, $\theta^{m+np}(x) = \theta^m(x)$ for all $n \in \mathbb{N}^+$. This implies that there must eventually be at least one A in every p elements of M^r, so there must be at least p^2 elements in every p^2 elements of M^r. This implies that

$$\lim_{j \to \infty} \frac{P(M^r, j^2)}{j} = \infty,$$

which contradicts (7.5). We conclude that $\tau(x)$ is nonperiodic.

How many such nonperiodic trajectories are there? Since M^r is admissible for each $r \in (0, 1)$, there is a compact set Q^r such that for each $x^r \in Q^r$, $\theta^n(x^r) \in X_n^r$ for each $x^r \in Q^r$, $n = 0, 1, 2, \dots$. So there is at least one trajectory for each itinerary M^r. But $(0, 1)$ is uncountable, so the number of nonperiodic trajectories is uncountably infinite.

Now for any itinerary M^r under consideration there exists a set of points that map into X_0^r after a finite number of periods. We shall say that such points *eventually exhibit the itinerary M^r*. Let $\bar{Q}^r$ be the union of all those points with Q^r, i.e., let

$$\bar{Q}^r := \{x \mid \theta^m(x) = x^r \in X_0^r \text{ for some finite} m\} \cup Q^r,$$

and define

$$S := \bigcup_{r \in (0,1)} \{\theta^n(\bar{Q}^r), \quad n = 0, 1, \dots\}. \tag{7.6}$$

Certainly, for any $x \in S$, $\theta(x) \in S$, so $\theta(S) \subset S$.

All of this amounts to

PROPOSITION 7.1 *Suppose $\{\theta, D\}$ is a continuous dynamical system, satisfying (7.3)–(7.4). There exists an uncountable set $S \subset D$ with $\theta(S) \subset S$ such that for all $x \in S$, $\tau(x)$ is nonperiodic.*

7.2   Chaos

Next consider the possible stability of trajectories in S.

7.2.1   Sensitivity to Initial Conditions (Path Dependence)

First, it can be shown that not only do nonperiodic trajectories exist given the conditions (7.3)–(7.4), but such trajectories are sensitive to initial conditions (unstable) in the sense of §5.4.1.

Let $x \neq y \in S$. By construction there exist $r \neq s \in (0, 1,)$ and m, n such that $\theta^m(x) = x^r \neq \theta^n(y) = x^s$. Consider the itineraries M^r, M^s. By construction these itineraries are unique with

$$\lim \frac{P(M^r, j^2)}{j} = r, \quad \lim \frac{P(M^s, j^2)}{j} = s$$

so for j large enough, the number of A's in $X^r_{j+1}, \ldots, X^r_{j^2}$ is $r \cdot j$ while the number of A's in $X^s_{j+1}, \ldots, X^s_{j^2}$ is $s \cdot j$. This means that M^r and M^s differ at an infinite number of positions. That is, there exist infinite subsequences $\{X^r_{t_k}\}^\infty_{k=0}$ and $\{X^s_{t_k}\}^\infty_{k=0}$ such that $x^r_{t_k} \neq x^s_{t_k}$ so either $X^r_{t_k} = A$ and $X^s_{t_k} = B$ or vice versa. Since A and $\theta(A)$ are closed and $A \cap \theta(A) = \emptyset$, it must be true that

$$\delta = \inf_{\substack{x \in A \\ y \in \theta(A)}} |x - y| > 0. \tag{7.7}$$

So for $\tau(x^r)$, $\tau(x^s)$ there are infinite subsequences $\{\theta^{t_k}(x^r)\}$, $\{\theta^{t_k}(x^s)\}$ such that $|\theta^{t_k}(x^r) - \theta^{t_k}(x^s)| > 0$ for every element in the subsequence. This implies the following:

PROPOSITION 7.2 *Assume the conditions of Proposition 7.1; then all trajectories in S are unstable with respect to any trajectory in S, that is,*

$$\lim_{t \to \infty} \sup |\theta^t(x) - \theta^t(y)| > 0 \tag{7.8}$$

for all $x, y \in S$.

To put it differently, no trajectory in S converges to any other trajectory in S, and any two trajectories in S always diverge by a finite amount no matter how close they come to one another or how often they do so. Moreover, a small perturbation in a trajectory changes that trajectory forever.

7.2.2 Deceptive Similarity of Nonperiodic Trajectories

Despite the fact that all trajectories in S are unstable, they are bounded because $\theta(D) \subset D$. As a consequence they can't move too far apart, and since they aren't periodic they must wander "among" one another. For maps of the type under investigation (that satisfy (7.3) and (7.4)), this has a perhaps surprising consequence.[7]

PROPOSITION 7.3 *Assume the conditions of Proposition 7.1. Then any trajectory $\tau(x)$ in S approaches close to any other trajectory $\tau(y)$ in S infinitely often, namely, for all $x, y \in S$*

$$\lim_{t \to \infty} \inf \left| \theta^t(x) - \theta^t(y) \right| = 0. \tag{7.9}$$

This means that every point in S is an accumulation point of S. Consequently, nonperiodic trajectories in S will appear to be similar to one another for finite periods of time infinitely often, but because (7.8) also holds, they cannot be similar for very long.

7.2.3 The Li-Yorke Chaos Theorem

Trajectories with the properties found in Proposition 7.2–7.3 are called "chaotic in the sense of Li-Yorke," or "topologically chaotic." I shall just call them *chaotic*.

We shall not call the map $\theta(\cdot)$ chaotic. Instead, we shall say that *it has the chaos properties*. We know from the examples that $\theta(\cdot)$ could be a very simple and regular function that may derive from quite reasonable and regular economic behavior at any given point in time. It is not the dynamic *structure* that we call chaotic but certain of the *histories* it is capable of generating. Although the number of these histories may be uncountable, it may be unlikely to obtain one for initial conditions drawn at random from the domain D even though we are certain to get one if that initial condition is in S. This problem was introduced in chapter 2 and we shall go into it in detail in §8.9.

The fact established in innumerable numerical experiments is, however, that when the expansivity conditions (7.3)–(7.4) prevail, trajectories often emerge that are for all practical purposes chaotic, so we shall investigate them further before tackling the subtle issue of their "chance" of occurrence.

For further reference let us then pull together the properties of nonperiodic behavior described so far. For later reference we shall call it "the chaos theorem." We use the fact that every iterate of a given map generates a higher-order dynamical system.

THEOREM 7.1 (Li-Yorke)   *Let $\{\theta, D\}$ be a continuous dynamical system and suppose there exists a least integer $m \geq 1$ and a nonempty compact set X such that*

$$X \cap \theta^m(X) = \emptyset \qquad (7.10)$$

and

$$X \cup \theta^m(X) \subset \theta^{2m}(X). \qquad (7.11)$$

(i) Then there exists an uncountable set S such that $\theta(S) \subset S$, i.e., S is closed (nonexpanding) under θ, and such that for all $x \in S$ the trajectory $\tau(x)$ is nonperiodic.

(ii) There exists a set P such that for each $p = 1, 2, 3, \ldots$, there is a point of period mp in P.

(iii) Any trajectory in S wanders away from any other trajectory in $S \cup P$, no matter how close it may come.

(iv) All trajectories in S move close to every other one infinitely often.

Proof   Let $A := X$ and $B : \theta^m(X)$. Then use Theorems 5.4 and 7.1–7.3.   ∎

The set S of this theorem is called the *scrambled set*; the set P is called the *periodic set*. Properties (i)–(iv) are the *chaos properties*.

7.3   Constructive Chaos Conditions

7.3.1   The Li-Yorke Overshoot Conditions

With a little practice one can get adept at constructing the conditions of Theorem 7.1 for graphical examples. But such an intuitive technique can be misleading if one is not a very good draftsman. Moreover, it gives us no direct criterion for obtaining analytical results for specific functional forms or for classes of functions that merely satisfy certain properties. Fortunately, simple constructive conditions have already been determined that imply the expansivity condition, namely, the Li-Yorke overshoot conditions (5.12)–(5.13). Using these together with Theorem 7.1, the following is implied:

THEOREM 7.2 (Li-Yorke) *Let $\{\theta, D\}$ be a continuous dynamical system. If there is a point $x \in D$ and an integer m such that*

$$\theta^{3m}(x) \le x < \theta^m(x) < \theta^{2m}(x) \tag{7.12}$$

or

$$\theta^{3m} \ge x > \theta^m(x) > \theta^{2m}(x) \tag{7.13}$$

then the results of Theorem 7.1 hold; that is, θ has the chaos properties.

Note that if $m = 1$ and $a = d$ then "period 3 implies chaos," the title of Li and Yorke's (1975) paper. Of course, these constructive results are subject to numerical round-off error.

The relationship between the local expansivity conditions and the Li-Yorke conditions is illustrated in figure 5.6a.

7.3.2 Example

A simple example is the tent map

$$\theta(x) = \begin{cases} 2x, & 0 \le x \le 1/2 \\ 2(1-x), & 1/2 \le x \le 1. \end{cases} \tag{7.14}$$

Here $D = [0, 1]$. A point satisfying the Li-Yorke overshoot condition is easily obtained; for example, the point $x = \frac{1}{4}$ maps to $\frac{1}{2}$ which maps to 1 and thence to zero. So, $\theta^3(x) < x < \theta(x) < \theta^2(x)$. By Theorem 7.2 there are cycles of every order and an uncountable scrambled set S of nonperiodic trajectories. All trajectories remain in $[0, 1]$, but the cyclic trajectories are all unstable. The nonperiodic ones, therefore, are not eventually periodic or asymptotically periodic but wander through the interval.

In figure 7.1 two trajectories with neighboring initial conditions are shown. Chaotic properties (iii) and (iv) are clearly illustrated.

7.3.3 Stretchable Maps Satisfying the Li-Yorke Conditions

For the general purposes of theoretical analysis, it is convenient to have constructive conditions that are not subject to the round-off error that must be involved in numerical simulations of a given nonlinear map. Fortunately, analytical conditions can be given that provide classes of maps for which the Li-Yorke conditions hold. We give one example here that has proven useful in economic applications as shall be seen elsewhere in this book.

Recall the stretchable maps of §5.5.2 and assume that $\theta_\mu(\cdot)$ is stretchable

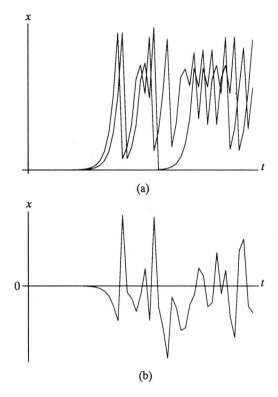

Figure 7.1
Chaotic trajectories. (a) Two trajectories. (b) Difference between trajectory values at time t.

with respect to the parameter μ, i.e., $\theta_\mu(x) = \mu\theta_1(x)$. Define

$$M(\mu) := \max_{x \in I} \theta_\mu(x)$$

$$x^{**}(\mu) := \max\{x \,|\, \theta_\mu(x) = M(\mu)\}.$$

Since $\theta_1(x)$ is continuous and positive on the interior of I, $M(\mu) = \mu M(1)$ exists and is positive for all $\mu > 0$. Moreover, $x^{**}(\mu) = x^{**}(1)$ all μ. Let $\mu'' := x''/M(1)$. Then $M(\mu'') = x''$. Then $\theta(M(\mu'')) = 0$. Let

$$a(\mu) := \max_{x' < x < x^{**}} \{\theta_\mu(x) = x^{**}(\mu)\}$$

and set $b(\mu'') = x^{**}(\mu'')$, $c(\mu') = M(\mu')$. Then $d = 0 < a(\mu'') < b(\mu'') < c(\mu'')$, so the Li-Yorke conditions are satisfied for μ''. But $\theta_\mu(\cdot)$ is continuous with respect to μ, so $a(\mu)$ and $M(\mu)$ are also. Hence, there exists a smallest value of $\mu \leq \mu''$, say μ^c, such that $d(\mu) \leq a(\mu) < b(\mu) < c(\mu)$ for all $\mu > \mu^c$.

PROPOSITION 7.4 (Stretchable Maps) *Let (θ_μ, D) be a continuous compact dynamical system depending on the parameter $\mu \geq 0$. Assume that there exists a nondegenerate open interval $I := (x', x'') \subset D \subset \mathbb{R}^+$ such that*

$$\theta_1(x) > 0 \quad \text{for all} \quad x \in I, \ \theta_1(x') = \theta_1(x'') = 0$$

and assume μ is stretchable, i.e.,

$$\theta_\mu(x) \equiv \mu \theta_1(x) \quad \text{for all} \quad x \in D.$$

Then there exists a value of μ, say μ^c, such that the system has the chaos property for all $\mu > \mu^c$.

The theorem is illustrated in figure 7.2.

7.3.4 A Family of Tent Maps

To illustrate the generic existence of chaos for stretchable maps, consider the family of tent maps

$$\theta_\beta(x) := \begin{cases} 2\beta x, & 0 \leq x < \frac{1}{2} \\ 2\beta(1 - x), & \frac{1}{2} \leq x \leq 1 \end{cases} \tag{7.15}$$

with domain $D := [0, 1]$. Extend the map to $\mathbb{R}$ in the usual way (i.e., define $\theta_\beta(x) = 0$, $x \notin D$). The maximum of $\theta_\beta(x)$ is β and the maximizer is $\frac{1}{2}$. Let

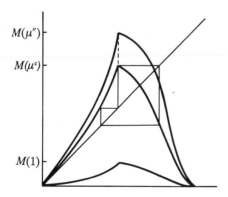

Figure 7.2
Generic existence of the Li-Yorke conditions for stretchable maps

$a(\beta) = \frac{1}{4\beta}$. Then $b(\beta) = \frac{1}{2}$, $c(\beta) = \beta$, and $d(\beta) = 2\beta(1 - \beta)$. If $\beta > \frac{1}{2}$, then $a(\beta) < b(\beta) < c(\beta)$. To get $d(\beta) < a(\beta)$, we must have

$$2\beta(1 - \beta) < \frac{1}{4\beta}. \tag{7.16}$$

There always exist such values.

To see this, consider the left- and right-side expressions as functions of β as shown in figure 7.3. Note that $\frac{1}{4\beta}$ is positive for all β and that $2\beta(1 - \beta)$ is negative for all $\beta > 1$. Moreover, at $\beta = \frac{1}{2}$ the two sides are equal. Consequently, there exists a value of β greater than $\frac{1}{2}$ and less than 1 such that the two sides are equal. (Remember the intermediate value theorem.) Let this be β^c; then we have

$$d(\beta) \le a(\beta) < b(\beta) < c(\beta) \quad \text{for all} \quad \beta > \beta^c.$$

It is not difficult to obtain the value of β^c. It is given by the largest root of the equation

$$8\beta^2(1 - \beta) - 1 = 0, \tag{7.17}$$

which is obtained by rearranging (7.16) but with equality replacing the inequality. We have already observed that $\beta = \frac{1}{2}$ is a root. Dividing (7.22) by $(\beta - \frac{1}{2})$, we get that $8\beta^2(1 - \beta) - 1 = (\beta - \frac{1}{2})(8\beta^2 - 4\beta - 2)$. Therefore,

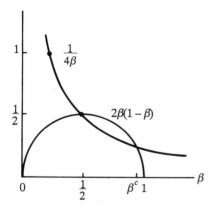

Figure 7.3
Generic existence of the Li-Yorke conditions for the tent map

$$\beta = \frac{1 + \sqrt{5}}{5} \approx .81$$

is the positive root greater than $\frac{1}{2}$. Consequently, β^c is a number close to .81.

7.3.5 Odd Chaos

Various additional useful theorems have been established, using techniques similar to those discussed in §7.2. They are related to the existence of cycles of odd periodicity and to the Švarkovskii Theorem 5.5. Li, Misiurewicz, Pianigiani, and Yorke used a result of Oono based on these facts to weaken the original Li-Yorke existence conditions:

THEOREM 7.3 (LIMPY I) *Let* $\{\theta, D\}$ *be a continuous, compact dynamical system. Suppose there exists a point x and an odd integer $m \geq 3$ such that*

$$\theta^m(x) < x < \theta(x) \tag{7.18}$$

or

$$\theta^m(x) > x > \theta(x), \tag{7.19}$$

then there exists a cycle with odd period k not greater than m such that k divides m, i.e., m/k is an integer ($m \bmod k = 0$). Moreover, by Theorem 7.4 below the chaos properties hold.

We call (7.18)–(7.19) the LIMPY conditions. The use of this theorem is the following. If we generate a finite sequence of points $x_0, x_1, \ldots, x_n$ for a given dynamical system, such that there is a point $x_i \in \{x_0, \ldots, x_n\}$ and an odd integer with $i + m \leq n$ and such that one of the sets of inequalities (7.18)–(7.19) hold, then chaotic trajectories exist. In particular a computer-generated data set of this kind would strongly suggest the potential presence of chaos, although (as before, because of round-off error) it would not constitute a proof.

In a succeeding study the same team of mathematicians established a similar result for even iterates that satisfy (7.18) or (7.19). This result requires the specification of a special "no division" property for a sequence of iterates $\theta^i(x)$, $i = 0, \ldots, n$ in a closed dynamical system $\{\theta, D\}$.

DEFINITION 7.1 *The iterates $\theta^i(x)$, $i = 0, \ldots, n$ are said to have* no division *if there exists no $y \in D$ such that either*

$$x_j < y \quad \text{for all even } j \qquad \text{and} \qquad x_j > y \quad \text{for all odd } j$$

or

$$x_j > y \quad \text{for all even } j \qquad \text{and} \qquad x_j < y \quad \text{for all odd } j. \tag{7.20}$$

Given this definition, we have:

THEOREM 7.4 (LIMPY II) *Let* $\{\theta, D\}$ *be a continuous, compact dynamical system and suppose there exists a sequence* $(\theta^i(x))$, $li = 0, 1, \ldots, n$ *in* D *with no division and such that (7.18) or (7.19) is satisfied. Then there exists a cycle of odd period and the chaos properties hold.*

As examples, consider the illustrations in figure 7.4. In diagram (a), every finite sequence of iterates "has division." In diagram (b), there exist sequences that have no division, hence a scrambled set. In diagram (c), there is always an orbit of period 3, hence cycles of all periods and a scrambled set of nonperiodic orbits.

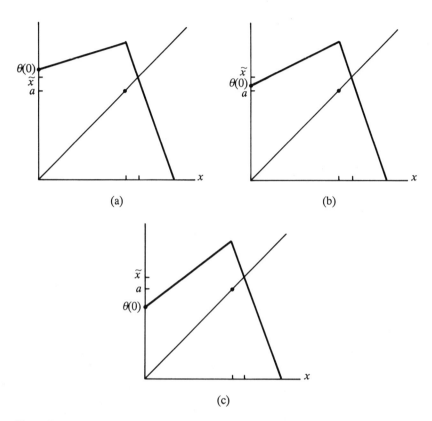

Figure 7.4
Division and no division. (a) Division. (b) No division. (c) No division. The Li-Yorke conditions hold.

8 Statistical Dynamics

Here we may set the problem . . . to determine how the whole number of systems will be distributed among the various conceivable configurations. . . . The changes which take place in the density . . . will depend on the dynamical nature of the systems . . . in special cases the distribution will remain unchanged.
—J. Willard Gibbs, *Elementary Principles in Statistical Mechanics*

In the preceding chapters of this mathematical review, the task of characterizing complex dynamic trajectories was transformed to a study of whole sets of trajectories. Such an idea arose naturally when we considered the existence of epochal evolutions of a multiple-phase dynamical system and then again when we came to consider the existence of nonperiodic, chaotic trajectories. Here we use the idea of measure introduced in §6.2.3 to characterize the behavior of "almost all" trajectories and what can transpire "almost surely."[1]

Chaotic trajectories are unstable, wander in an erratic fashion, and are unpredictable very far into the future. Such behavior suggests the presence of randomness and the idea that chaotic trajectories may have statistical properties like those associated with nondeterministic, stochastic processes.

The benefit of looking at *deterministic* dynamical systems from this viewpoint is that it helps us understand, first, the nature of chaotic behavior; second, how important chaotic behavior is in a given system, that is, how robust it is when initial conditions of the system are changed; and it enables a more precise characterization of multiple-phase dynamics in terms of regime switching and possible phase evolutions.

More than a century ago the physicists Clausius, Boltzmann, and Maxwell, the founders of thermodynamics, realized that an ensemble of interacting particles that obeyed Newton's equations of motion could move in such a complicated way that there was no chance to represent the behavior of any of its individual components. Rather, the distribution of particles and the proportions of time in which given events occur might behave in a coherent way according to stable probabilistic laws. It is interesting to note that these early contributors used the term "chaotic" to describe the seemingly random behavior of deterministic systems.[2] The motivation of statistical dynamics in the present context is, however, very different from that of mechanics. Here we are not dealing with an "ensemble of particles" with complex interactions, but with the generation over time of the behavior of a system characterized by a single state variable. The idea that statistical behavior results from *nonlinearity alone* in *simple* systems is of relatively recent origin.[3]

8.1 An Example

8.1.1 The Tent Map

To set the stage for more general considerations, consider again the family of tent maps dependent on a nonnegative parameter β,

$$\theta_\beta(x) := \begin{cases} 2\beta x, & 0 < x \le \frac{1}{2} \\ 2\beta(1-x), & \frac{1}{2} \le x < 1 \end{cases} \tag{8.1}$$

defined on the domain $D = (0, 1)$, and extend it to the real line in the usual way. Thus, $D = (0, 1)$, $D^0 := (-\infty, 0] \cup [1, \infty)$ and $\theta(x) = 0$, for all $x \in D^0$. We saw in §7.3.4 that the map is "stretchable" and that there was a value, β^c, close to .81 such that for all $\beta > \beta^c$ points satisfying the Li-Yorke conditions exist. Therefore, there are periodic points of all orders and an uncountable scrambled set $S \subset D$ of chaotic trajectories and this result occurs robustly, i.e., for a continuum of values of β. Note that $|\theta'(x)| = 2\beta > 1$ for all $\beta > \frac{1}{2}$, so all the cycles are unstable. (Recall chapter 5.)

Now suppose $\beta > 1$. Let $D^1 := (0, \frac{1}{2})$ and $D^2 := [\frac{1}{2}, 1)$. There exist exactly two points $u \in D_1$, $v \in D_2$ such that $\theta_\beta(u) = \theta_\beta(v) = 1$. These points are

$$u = \frac{1}{2\beta}, \qquad v = 1 - \frac{1}{2\beta}. \tag{8.2}$$

Define

$$E := [u, v]. \tag{8.3}$$

Then $\theta(E) = [1, \beta] \subset D^0$, so $\theta^2[1, \beta] = \{0\}$. Consequently, all trajectories that enter E escape to the null domain, that is, the system "self-destructs." See figure 8.1.

How many such trajectories are there?

8.1.2 The Kickout Time and Escape

To answer this, recall the *Lebesgue measure* $\lambda(\cdot)$ that maps intervals (open, semiopen, or closed) into $\mathbb{R}^+$. (See §6.2.3.) For $\beta \ge 1$, $E = [u, v]$,

$$\lambda(E) = \lambda([u, v]) = \frac{\beta - 1}{\beta}. \tag{8.4}$$

A trajectory that enters E escapes the set $D = (0, 1)$ in one period. In general, the sets

$$E_1 = E, \quad E_2 = \theta^{-1}(E), \dots, E_n = \theta^{1-n}(E)$$

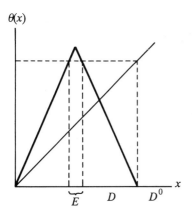

$\theta(x)$

E D D^0 x

Figure 8.1
Escape to the null domain

give the sets of points that escape in $1, 2, \ldots, n$ periods, respectively, and the unstable set

$$U = \bigcup_{n=1}^{\infty} E_n = \bigcup_{n=0}^{\infty} \theta^{-n}(E) \qquad (8.5)$$

gives the set of all points that eventually escape $(0, 1)$. What is the Lebesgue measure of U?

The intervals in the sequence $\{E_n\}$ are disjoint and all belong to $(0, 1)$. Each of their lengths is finite and their sum must be less than the length of D, so

$$0 \leq \lambda(U) \leq 1. \qquad (8.6)$$

The ratio in (8.6) can be given a probabilistic interpretation. Suppose we choose an initial condition at random in D according to a uniform probability distribution. Then

$$\Pr\{x \in U\} = \lambda(U). \qquad (8.7)$$

That is, $\lambda(U)$ gives the chance that a trajectory emanating from a randomly chosen initial condition escapes $(0, 1)$ and enters $]0, 1[$.

Now, define the *escape* or *kickout* time $k_A(x)$. Let A be a set in D. Then $k_A(x)$ is the number of periods the trajectory $\tau(x)$, which begins in A, remains in A before escaping. Precisely,

$$k_A(x) = 1 + \max\{n \mid \theta^k(x) \in A \quad \text{all } 0 \leq k \leq n\}. \qquad (8.8)$$

Obviously, $k_E(x) = 1$. In general, $k_{E_n}(x) = n$ for $x \in E_n = \theta^{1-n}(E)$. The function

$$P_A(N) := \Pr(k_A(x) \le N | x \in A) \tag{8.9}$$

gives the probability that a trajectory with initial condition x chosen randomly in A will escape within N periods.

We should like to know the conditions for which trajectories will escape almost surely, i.e., when $\lambda(U) = \lim_{N \to \infty} P_D(N) = 1$. We should also like to know the conditions for which trajectories remain in D almost surely, i.e., when $\lambda(U) = 0$.

8.1.3 The Probability of Escape

To answer these questions for the example under consideration, we have first to construct the sequence of escape intervals $\{E_n = \theta^{1-n}(E)\}_{n=1}^{\infty}$. Each interval in D has two preimages, one in D_1 and one in D_2. These are obtained from the restriction of $\theta^{-1}(\cdot)$ to the sets D_1 and D_2. We find that

$$E_2 = \theta^{-1}(E_1) = \left(\frac{u}{2\beta}, \frac{v}{2\beta}\right) \cup \left(1 - \frac{v}{2\beta}, 1 - \frac{u}{2\beta}\right)$$

so

$$\lambda(E_2) = \frac{1}{\beta} \cdot \frac{\beta - 1}{\beta}.$$

In turn each of the two intervals comprising E_2 has two preimages, one in D_1 and one in D_2, so $\theta^{-1}(E_2)$ has 2^2 intervals in all, each of Lebesgue measure $\left(\frac{1}{2\beta}\right)^2 \lambda([u, v])$. Therefore,

$$\lambda(E_3) = \lambda(\theta^{-1}(E_2)) = \theta^{-2}(E) = \frac{1}{\beta^2}\lambda(E) = \frac{1}{\beta^2} \cdot \frac{\beta - 1}{\beta}.$$

In general, the inverse image $E_n = \theta^{1-n}(E)$ is the union of 2^n intervals, each of length $\lambda(E)/(2\beta)^n$, so

$$\lambda(E_i) = 2^i \cdot \lambda(E)/(2\beta)^i = \left(\frac{1}{\beta^i}\right)\left(\frac{\beta - 1}{\beta}\right), \quad i = 0, 1, \ldots \tag{8.10}$$

Therefore, the probability of escape in not more than N periods is

$$P_D(N) = \frac{\beta - 1}{\beta}\sum_{n=0}^{N}\frac{1}{\beta^n} = 1 - \frac{1}{\beta^{N+1}}.$$

Consequently,

$$\lambda(U) = \lim_{N \to \infty} P_D(N) = 1.$$

To summarize, for the tent map (8.1) with $\beta > 1$, almost all trajectories (in the sense of Lebesgue measure) are eventually stationary at zero.

Consider the tent map as defined in (8.1) but with domain $D := (0, \beta)$ and with $\theta_\beta(x) \equiv 0$ for all $x \in [1, \beta]$. The null domain $D^0 =]0, \beta[$. Now $\theta(D) \subset D$ so the map satisfies the Li-Yorke Theorem 7.1. Let S and P be the scrambled and eventually periodic sets, respectively. By the preceding argument, we know that almost all trajectories map into $[1, \beta]$. This implies that

$$\lambda(S \cup P) = 0.$$

This means that we should not expect to be able to compute a nonperiodic trajectory for the tent map $\theta_\beta(\cdot)$ with $\beta > 1$. Almost all histories will converge to zero even though in principle there exists an uncountable number of nonperiodic trajectories.

8.1.4   Nonperiodicity Almost Surely

Now consider the case where $\beta = 1$. In this case $E = \{\frac{1}{2}\}$ and $m(E) = 0$. Hence, the probability of escape is 0 even though any trajectory that hits $\frac{1}{2}$ escapes D and becomes stationary at zero. Moreover, all the cycles are unstable (the set of all periodic points in P) and they are also countable in number. Since Lebesgue measure is zero on points, $\lambda(P) = 0$. Therefore, nonperiodic trajectories occur almost surely. More about this later.

When $\frac{1}{2} < \beta < 1$, the result is similar. In this case $\max_{x \in D} \theta(x) = \beta < 1$. Moreover, $\theta(\beta) = 2\beta(1 - \beta)$. Since $\beta > \frac{1}{2}$, it is easy to show that $2\beta(1 - \beta) < \beta$. Therefore, for all initial conditions $x \in [0, 1]$ trajectories must enter the interval $I = [2\beta(1 - \beta), \beta] \subset D$. But $E = \emptyset$. Escape is impossible, and I is a *trapping set*.

Let $D_1 = [2\beta(1 - \beta), \frac{1}{2}), D_2 = [\frac{1}{2}, \beta]$. Then it is easy to see that every orbit that enters D_1 escapes and enters D_2, and vice versa. Moreover, $|\theta'(x)| = 2\beta > 1$ for all $\beta > \frac{1}{2}$ so all periodic trajectories are unstable. It would be reasonable to suppose therefore that almost all trajectories are nonperiodic. We'll be able to give a precise answer in due course.

8.2   Measure and Recurrence

There are many maps—ones that arise naturally in economics—where the scrambled set exists but with a zero measure for some parameter values and positive measure for others. We need to know how to characterize these situations. In order to consider this question we shall use the more general concepts of measure already introduced in chapter 6. Recall Definitions 6.1–6.3.

8.2.1   Measures and Dynamical Systems

Let (θ, D) be a viable dynamical system. Then $\theta^n(X) \subset D$ for all $X \subset D$ and all $n \in \mathbb{N}$. The complement $D\backslash X$ obviously belongs to D and the union of any countable collection of such sets likewise. The collection of all subsets of D generated in this way therefore forms a σ-algebra, which may be denoted (D, Σ_θ). If $\mu(\cdot)$ is a measure defined on this σ-algebra, then (D, Σ_θ, μ) is a measure space and the dynamical system (D, θ) is said to be μ-measurable.

This means that the measure of all potential finite histories that lead into a given set and the measure of all potential trajectories emanating from initial conditions within a given set is determined.

DEFINITION 8.1   *Suppose* (θ, D) *is* μ-*measurable. Then* $\theta(\cdot)$ *is called* measure preserving *and* μ *is called* invariant *with respect to* θ *if*

$$\mu\left(\theta^{-1}(X)\right) = \mu(X) \quad \text{for all} \quad X \in \Sigma_\theta. \tag{8.11}$$

Consider the tent map again. Let $X = [a, b] \subset [0, 1]$. Then $\theta^{-1}(X)$ consists of two disjoint sets

$$\theta_1^{-1}([a, b]) = \left[\tfrac{1}{2\beta}a, \tfrac{1}{2\beta}b\right], \qquad \theta_2^{-1}([a, b]) = \left[1 - \tfrac{b}{2\beta}, \ 1 - \tfrac{a}{2\beta}\right].$$

Therefore,

$$\lambda\left(\theta^{-1}[a, b]\right) = \theta_1^{-1}([a, b]) \cup \theta_2^{-1}([a, b]) = \tfrac{1}{\beta}\lambda[a, b].$$

If $\beta \neq 1$, the tent map (8.1) is not Lebesgue measure preserving. If $\beta = 1$, it is. We conclude that the tent map (8.1) is Lebesgue measure preserving (i.e., Lebesgue measure is invariant with respect to the tent map) if and only if $\beta = 1$. This result is illustrated in figure 8.2.

8.2.2   The Recurrence Theorem

To see how an invariant measure for a dynamical system can be used to determine qualitative properties of trajectories, consider a μ-measurable dynamical

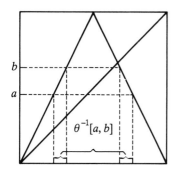

Figure 8.2
A measure-preserving tent map ($\beta = 1$)

system (θ, Σ) for which μ is invariant. Let A be a set in Σ with positive measure.

Consider the set of points A_k that are eventually mapped into A after at least k periods for any $k \geq 0$, that is,

$$A_k := \left\{ x \mid \text{there exists an } n \geq k \text{ such that } \theta^n(x) \in A \right\},$$

or, equivalently,

$$A_k = \bigcup_{n=k}^{\infty} \theta^{-n}(A).$$

Of course, A_0 is the set of all points eventually mapped into A, which obviously includes A. Notice that $\theta^{-1}(A_k)$ is the set of points that map into the set A_k, which themselves map into A after k periods. Therefore,

$$A_{k+1} = \theta^{-1}(A_k),$$

and

$$A_0 \supset A_1 \supset \cdots \supset A_n \cdots.$$

Let

$$A_* = \bigcap_{k=0}^{\infty} A_k.$$

Obviously,

$$A_* \subset A_0.$$

By assumption μ is invariant with respect to θ. Therefore,

$$\mu(A_k) = \mu\left(\theta^{-1}(A_k)\right) = \mu(A_{k+1})$$

for all k. This implies that

$$\mu(A_*) = \mu(A_0).$$

But

$$0 < \mu(A) = \mu(A \cap A_0) \leq \mu(A_0) = \mu(A_*)$$

and

$$\mu(A_* \cap A) = \mu(A_0 \cap A) = \mu(A) > 0.$$

This means that the set of points that both belong to A and eventually "return" to A has positive measure. This result is known as the Poincaré Recurrence Theorem.

THEOREM 8.1 (Poincaré Recurrence Theorem) *Let (X, Σ, μ) be a probability space and let the measure $\mu(\cdot)$ be invariant under θ. Let A be any set of positive measure. Then almost all points of A return to A infinitely often. That is, for almost all $x \in A$*

$$\lim_{N \to \infty} \sum_{n=1}^{N} \chi_A \left(\theta^n(x)\right) = \infty. \tag{8.12}$$

As the tent map is Lebesgue measure preserving for $\beta = 1$, the dynamical system based on it provides an example of this result.

8.3 Limit Sets and Asymptotic Stability

In chapter 5 the asymptotically stable periodic trajectories were considered. The limit points of such trajectories are just the elements of the periodic orbit to which trajectories converge. That is, suppose $\gamma(x)$ is a p-periodic orbit through a point x and let $y \in \gamma(x)$. Then for all z close enough to y, $\lim_{n \to \infty} \theta^{pn}(z) = y$. In chapter 7 it was seen that nonperiodic trajectories must also be considered. For this purpose a more general limit set concept is needed.

DEFINITION 8.2 (Limit Sets and Attractors) *The* limit set $\omega(x)$ *of the trajectory $\tau(x)$ is defined to be the set of all limit points of $\tau(x)$, i.e.,*

$$\omega(x) := \bigcap_{n=1}^{\infty} c\ell\gamma\left(\theta^n(x)\right)$$

where $c\ell(S)$ means the closure of the set S and $\gamma(y)$ is the orbit from y.

An attractor *for θ is a closed set $L \subset D$ such that $\omega(x) = L$ for x in a set B of positive Lebesgue measure. The set B is called the* basin of attraction *of L.*

Note that $\omega(x)$ is closed and $\theta(\omega(x)) = \omega(x)$. Obviously, $L \subset B$ and $\theta(L) = L$.

We can now define asymptotic stability with respect to these concepts. A periodic point y and the corresponding periodic orbit $\gamma(y)$ are called *asymptotically stable* if there is a nondegenerate interval V containing y such that $\omega(x) = \gamma(y)$ for all $x \in V$. In chapter 5 it was shown that it is not unusual for a map to have many, perhaps an infinite number of periodic points and that none of the periodic points need be asymptotically stable. It is in this situation that the theory of statistical dynamics can be used to describe the asymptotic behavior of trajectories.

8.4 Ergodic Dynamical Systems

8.4.1 Ergodicity

Suppose that there exists $X \in \Sigma$ such that $\theta^{-1}(X) = X$ (and hence $\theta^{-1}(D \setminus X) = D \setminus X$). Then the dynamics is split into two separate parts; in fact, if $x \in X$, then $x \in \theta^{-1}(X)$, which implies $\theta(x) \in X$ and the trajectory of x will stay in X forever. Likewise for $D \setminus X$. This motivates the concept of ergodicity.

DEFINITION 8.3 *Let (D, Σ, μ) be a probability space. The dynamical system (θ, D) is μ-ergodic if the measure of every invariant set is either 0 or 1, i.e., if $X \in \Sigma$, then $\theta^{-1}(X) = X$ implies either that $\mu(X) = 0$ or that $\mu(X) = 1$.*

Ergodicity means that μ-almost all trajectories that start in D enter a unique invariant set and remain there, and this set cannot be decomposed into parts with a similar property. This property is also called *metric intransitivity*.

8.4.2 The Tent Map Is Ergodic for $\beta = 1$ and Its Trajectories Are Nonperiodic λ-Almost Surely

To see exactly what is meant by "μ-almost every" in the definition, consider the tent map (8.1) with $\beta = 1$. The domain D is invariant (i.e., $\theta^{-1}(D) = D$), a property that follows from the continuity of θ and the fact that its maximum is one. Lebesgue measure $\lambda(D) = 1$. But D contains a countable set of periodic points, which is an invariant set. The set of points that eventually map into each of these periodic points is also countable. But countable sets have Lebesgue measure zero. These points all belong to D. But D has full measure, so the Lebesgue measure of the set of eventually periodic points must be zero. Moreover, these points are unstable. Therefore, for the tent map (8.1) with $\beta = 1$, almost all trajectories in the sense of Lebesgue measure are nonperiodic and do not converge to periodic orbits. Indeed, almost all trajectories are attracted to the interval [0,1] in the sense of Definition 8.2.

8.4.3   The Mean Ergodic Theorem

The concept of ergodicity plays a key role in establishing a connection between the statistical properties of trajectories and the measure of a dynamical system. The basic statistic to be considered is the mean value of a function. We can think of the map θ as a mechanism for recursively generating a sample from the domain D from a "seed" or initial condition $x \in D$. This sample is just a finite history $\tau_n(x) = \{x, \ldots, \theta^n(x)\}$. If $g(\cdot)$ is some function $g : D \to \mathbb{R}$ that describes some relevant attribute of the state variable x, we may ask what its average or mean value is. This "sample mean" is just

$$\frac{1}{n} \sum_{t=0}^{n-1} g(\theta^t(x)).$$

The measure is a cumulative distribution of the values of almost all trajectories over the domain or "space" of possible states. Consequently, the "population mean" of g is

$$E(g) = \int_D g d\mu.$$

The following famous result establishes the connection between these two mean values:

THEOREM 8.2 (The Birkhoff–von Neuman Mean Ergodic Theorem)[4]   *Let* (D, Σ, μ) *be a probability space and let* θ *be measure preserving and ergodic. Let* $g(\cdot)$ *be an integrable function. Then*

$$\lim_{n \to \infty} \frac{1}{n} \sum_{i=0}^{n-1} g\left(\theta^i(x)\right) = \int_D g d\mu \quad \text{for almost all} \quad x \in D. \tag{8.13}$$

The left side of (8.13) is the average value of $g(\cdot)$ evaluated along the trajectory $\tau(x)$. The right side is the mean value or expected value of $g(\cdot)$ evaluated on the space D. Thus, the theorem asserts that "the time average equals the space average."

Let $A \in \Sigma$ be any set with $\mu(A) > 0$ and consider any trajectory that begins in D. How much time does this trajectory spend in A? Recall that the characteristic function of points in the trajectory given a set A is

$$\chi_A \left(\theta^t(x) \right) = \begin{cases} 1, & \theta^t(x) \in A \\ 0, & \theta^t(x) \notin A. \end{cases}$$

Summed over points in the trajectory we get the number of times the trajectory "enters" the set A. According to Theorem 8.1, we expect this to be infinite if $\mu(A) > 0$. However, the *average* time spent can be finite. Indeed, the Birkoff ergodic theorem says that the time average,

$$\lim_{n \to \infty} \frac{1}{n} \sum_{i=0}^{n-1} \chi_A \left(\theta^i(x) \right) = \mu(A) \tag{8.14}$$

for almost all x in X. To see this we let $g(x) := \chi_A(x)$. This gives the left side of (8.14). Then $\int_D g(x)d\mu = \int_D \chi_A(x)d\mu = \int_A d\mu = \mu(A)$. This implies:

COROLLARY 8.1   *Let (D, Σ, μ) be a probability space and let θ be measure preserving and ergodic on D. Then for μ-almost all x in D, $\tau(x)$ will visit every measurable set proportionally to its measure.*

For ergodic systems, therefore, the concept of measure has the potential to be used to give a qualitatively important, statistical characterization of the long-run (or asymptotic) behavior of typical trajectories of the system.

Unfortunately, however, by itself the concept of ergodicity is of limited utility. This is because ergodic systems may possess atomic or discontinuous measures. Thus, let $\gamma(x)$ be a periodic orbit through x with period p for a dynamical system (θ, D). Then $(\gamma(x), \Sigma, \mu)$ where $\mu(y) := \frac{1}{p}$ for each $y \in \gamma(x)$ is an ergodic dynamical system. But $\mu(\cdot)$ gives no information about the nonperiodic trajectories, or any of the other periodic ones either. Because it is atomic, all the measure is concentrated on just the p points of the particular p-periodic cycle.

8.5   Distributions for Dynamical Systems

8.5.1   Continuous Measures

A step toward a stronger kind of measure is:

DEFINITION 8.4   *A measure μ is called* continuous or nonatomic *if $\mu\{x\} = 0$ for all singletons $\{x\}$.*

A sufficient condition for the existence of a continuous invariant measure is given in:

THEOREM 8.3 (Lasota and Pianigiani 1977))   *Let X be a topological space and let $\theta : X \to X$ be continuous. Let θ satisfy the following "expansivity" condition: there are two compact disjoint sets A and B such that*

$$\theta(A) \cap \theta(B) \supset A \cup B. \tag{8.15}$$

Then there exists a continuous invariant ergodic measure.

It follows that a set of points having positive continuous measure is uncountable.

It can be shown that if there exists a Li-Yorke point, then condition (8.15) holds for θ^3 substituted for θ. Consequently, we have:

COROLLARY 8.2   *Let $\{\theta, D\}$ be a continuous dynamical system. If there exists a Li-Yorke point, then there exists a continuous invariant ergodic measure μ.*

This tells us, for example, that the tent map (8.1) for $\beta > 1$ possesses a continuous (nonatomic) measure μ such that $\mu(S) > 0$ where S is the scrambled set. But if the Lebesgue measure $\lambda(S) = 0$, then S can't be all that "big." What we need is a still stronger regularity concept of measure than mere continuity.

For another example, consider the quadratic mapping $\theta x = Ax(1 - x)$ defined on the interval $[0, 1]$. For a value of A near 3.83, it can be shown that $\theta^3(\frac{1}{2}) = \frac{1}{2}$. As this is a point of period 3, by the Li-Yorke Theorem there exists an uncountable set in which we have chaotic dynamics and there exists a continuous measure μ such that $\mu(S) > 0$. On the other hand, the orbit of $\frac{1}{2}$ is asymptotically stable (the derivative of θ^3 in the orbit is equal to zero) and it is possible to show that it attracts λ-almost all points of $[0, 1]$. Hence, we have chaos with positive, continuous measure but with Lebesgue measure zero just as in the tent map for $\beta > 1$.

We want a concept of measure that avoids such a paradoxical situation.

8.5.2 Absolute Continuity: Density and Distribution

Especially desirable would be measures representable by distributions or density functions of the kind used in statistics and probability theory. Such measures are called absolutely continuous and are defined formally in the following:

DEFINITION 8.5 *A measure is said to be* absolutely continuous *with respect to Lebesgue measure if there exists an integrable function f, called the* density *of μ, such that*

$$\mu(X) := \int_X f(x)\,dx \qquad (8.16)$$

for all $X \in \Sigma$.

Such measures are differentiable λ-almost everywhere, that is,

$$d\mu = f\,d\lambda = f\,dx \quad \text{for almost all} \quad x \in D \qquad (8.17)$$

and for any interval $[a, b]$ in $\mathbb{R}$,

$$\mu([a, b]) = \int_a^b f(x)\,dx. \qquad (8.18)$$

Obviously,

$$\int_X f(x)\,dx / \int_D f(x)\,dx \qquad (8.19)$$

is a probability measure. The integrability of f means that it is continuous λ-almost everywhere, i.e., except for a set of Lebesgue measure zero. The implication is that for every set A with positive measure the density is positive ($f(x) > 0$) λ-almost everywhere on the union of a set of closed intervals.

DEFINITION 8.6 (Strongly ergodic dynamical systems) *A dynamical system (θ, D) that is ergodic with respect to an absolutely continuous measure μ defined on $\mathbb{R}$ will be called* strongly ergodic. *For a strongly ergodic system with density f the measure is equivalent to the cumulative distribution function (c.d.f.)*

$$F(x) := \mu([a, x]) = \int_a^x f(u)\,du, \qquad (8.20)$$

where $a = \inf D$.

If we extend θ to $\mathbb{R}$ in the usual way, then we can write $F(x) = \int_{-\infty}^x f(u)\,du$.

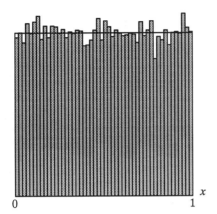

Figure 8.3
Strongly ergodic behavior for the tent map ($\beta = 1$)

8.5.3   Example

We have seen that the tent map preserves Lebesgue measure when $\beta = 1$ and that the corresponding dynamical system is ergodic on $[0, 1]$. Lebesgue measure is also absolutely continuous with

$$f(\cdot) \equiv 1, \ d\lambda = dx \quad \text{and} \quad F(x) \equiv x, \ x \in [0, 1].$$

Consequently, the tent map with $\beta = 1$ is strongly ergodic; the fraction of the time any trajectory spends in any interval $(a, b) \subset [0, 1]$ with $a \leq b$ is just $b - a$.

This result is reflected in the numerical example shown in figure 8.3, which gives the histogram obtained from 10,000 iterates of (8.1) for $\beta = 1$ on intervals of width $1/100$. We see that the theoretical result is closely approximated. The fact that the approximation is not exact is due to the fact that the numerical histogram has not converged to the uniform distribution even after 10,000 iterations. Remember, the concepts employed here are asymptotic results derived from limiting arguments.

8.5.4   Existence of Absolutely Continuous Invariant Measures: Expansive Maps

An early result establishing the existence of an absolutely continuous invariant measure is due to Lasota and Yorke. It applies to the class of piecewise twice differentiable (C^2) mappings. A mapping θ, defined on an interval D with $cl\,D = [a_0, a_n]$, is piecewise C^2 if there exists a sequence $a_0 < a_1 < a_2 < \cdots < a_n$ such that θ restricted to each (a_i, a_{i+1}) is a C^2 function that is extendable as a C^2 function to the closed interval $[a_i, a_{i+1}]$.

THEOREM 8.4 (Lasota-Yorke 1973)   *Let $\theta : D \to D$ be piecewise C^2 where D is an interval. If*

$$|\theta'(x)| \geq \delta > 1, \quad \lambda\text{-almost everywhere in } D, \tag{8.21}$$

then there exists an absolutely continuous invariant measure.

We recall from Theorem 5.10 that inequalities (8.21) imply that all periodic orbits are unstable. Such a map is called *expansive*.

8.5.5   Examples: The Tent and Check Maps

According to Theorem 8.4, the tent map possesses an absolutely continuous measure for $\frac{1}{2} < \beta \leq 1$. We know already that Lebesgue measure is an absolutely continuous measure for $\beta = 1$. For $\frac{1}{2} < \beta < 1$ we know one exists but not its form. Later in this book measures will be constructed for examples in this range.

As another example, consider the "check" map shown in figure 8.4,

$$\theta(x) = \begin{cases} \theta_1(x) := N(1 - x), & x \in [0, 1) \\ \theta_2(x) := x - 1, & x \in [1, \infty), \end{cases} \tag{8.22}$$

where N is an integer. Observe that $\theta(1) = 0$, $\theta(0) = N$ and $\theta(x) < x$ for all $x > 1$. Consequently, all trajectories enter $[0, N]$ after a finite number of periods and cannot leave. What happens in this set determines the long-run dynamics of the process. Let us therefore define $D := [0, N]$. Theorem 8.4 can't be exploited directly because $\theta_2(\cdot)$ is not expansive. Indeed, if $N = 1$, $\theta_1(\cdot)$ is not expansive either. Then any point in $[0, 1]$ is a neutrally stable 2-cycle.

Note that the points $\{0, 1, \ldots, N\}$ are $N + 1$-cyclic. When $N = 2$ the point $x = 2$ is a Li-Yorke point, so there are cycles of all orders. Even though (8.21) does not hold, these must all be unstable. This can be seen by considering the sequence of cyclic points $y, \theta(y), \ldots, \theta^p(y) = y$ where y is p-cyclic. Of the p points, $q \geq 1$ lie in the interval $(0, 1]$ and $p - q \geq 1$ in the interval $(1, N]$. The derivative of $\theta^p(x)$ evaluated at any cyclic point is therefore $(N)^q \geq N \geq 2$.

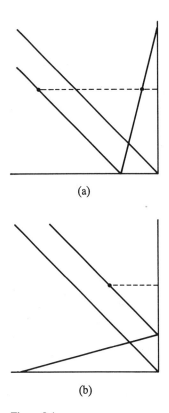

(a)

(b)

Figure 8.4
A check map. (a) The check map. (b) The inverse map.

In particular, suppose $N = 2$. Then $y = 1$ is 3-cyclic because $\theta^3(1) = 1$. But $\frac{d\theta^3(y)}{dy}|_{y=1} = 2$ so $y = 1$ is unstable.

In general, for $N \geq 2$ the iterated map $\theta^N(p)$ for θ given by (8.22) is expansive because $d\theta^N(p)/dp \geq N$. Consequently, by the Lasota-Yorke Theorem an absolutely continuous measure exists that is invariant for θ^N.

8.5.6   The Number of Absolutely Continuous Invariant Ergodic Measures

The theorem does not say how many measures exist or if they are ergodic. We should also like to know how measures are related to the limit sets and whether or not the latter are attractors.[5] These questions are answered for a class of expansive, piecewise strictly monotonic C^2 functions:

THEOREM 8.5   *Let (θ, D) be a dynamical system where D is an interval and the map θ is piecewise strictly monotonic on each piece of the partition D of interval pieces $D_i, i = 1, \ldots n$. Assume that for each $i = 1, \ldots, n$, θ_i restricted to the interior of D_i is continuously differentiable and expansive. Then there exists a finite collection of sets $L_1, \ldots, L_m$ where each $L_i, i = 1, \ldots, m$ is a finite union of closed intervals and there exists a set of absolutely continuous probability measures $\mu_1, \ldots, \mu_m$ invariant under θ such that*

(i) each L_i contains at least one turning point of θ in its interior (which implies that $m \leq n - 1$);

(ii) $\mu_i(L_i) = 1, i = 1, \ldots, m$, i.e., each μ_i is ergodic with respect to L_i, hence $d\mu_i$ is positive almost everywhere there;

(iii) every measure invariant under θ can be written as a linear combination of the μ_i. (That is, the μ_i form a basis in the space of invariant measures.)

Because each turning point of θ is a local maximum or minimum of θ, two distinct ergodic sets cannot have a turning point in common. Therefore, we have:

COROLLARY 8.3   *Given the hypotheses of Theorem 8.5, there exists a partition $\{B_i, i = 1, \ldots, m\}$ such that*

• *each B_i is a finite union of intervals;*

• *$B_i \supset L_i, i = 1, \ldots, m$;*

• *each B_i is the basin of attraction for L_i, i.e., $\omega(x) = L_i$ for λ-almost all $x \in B_i$.*

If $n = 2$ there can be only one turning point of the map θ, so we get:

COROLLARY 8.4   *Given the hypotheses of Theorem 8.5, if $n = 2$ there exists a unique, ergodic absolutely continuous invariant measure with a unique attractor that is the union of closed intervals for λ-almost all $x \in I$.*

The tent system for $\frac{1}{2} < \beta \leq 1$ is the easiest example of a dynamical system with a unique ergodic absolutely continuous invariant measure. The more general piecewise linear map with n pieces gives an example of a system with at most $n - 1$ absolutely continuous ergodic invariant measures.

How about the check map? We know already that an absolutely continuous measure exists. It is also the case that the trapping set $[0, N]$ cannot be decomposed because every point in $(1, N]$ enters $[0, 1)$ after no more than $N - 1$

periods and every point that enters $[0, 1)$ must eventually escape to $[1, N]$. Consequently, there can be only one absolutely continuous invariant ergodic measure on $[0, N]$.

It is easy to verify that if $\mu_p(\cdot)$ is an ergodic measure invariant for θ^p, then $\mu(\cdot) := \frac{1}{p}\sum_{i=0}^{p-1}\mu_p\left(\theta^{-i}(\cdot)\right)$ is an ergodic measure invariant for θ. Consequently, we have:

COROLLARY 8.5 *If a map $\theta(\cdot)$ does not satisfy the assumptions of Theorem 8.5 but there exists an integer, say p, such that the map $\theta^p(\cdot)$ satisfies them, then the theorem holds.*

8.5.7   The Mean and Variance of a Trajectory

For an absolutely continuous invariant ergodic measure the mean ergodic theorem becomes:

COROLLARY 8.6 *Suppose (θ, D) satisfies the assumptions of Theorem 8.5 and let $\{B_i, i = 1, \ldots, m\}$ be the partition of D into basins of attraction as in Corollary 8.2. Moreover, let $f_i = d\mu_i$ for each absolutely continuous invariant ergodic measure μ_i. Then for all $x \in B_i$,*

$$\lim_{n\to\infty} \frac{1}{n}\sum_{j=1}^{n} g\left(\theta^j(x)\right) = \int_D g(u)f_i(u)du.$$

In particular, for all $x \in B_i$, the expected or mean value of states in the trajectory is

$$\bar{x}_i = \lim_{n\to\infty} \frac{1}{n}\sum_{j=1}^{n}\theta^j(x) = \int_D uf_i(u)du$$

and the variance of states in the trajectory is

$$\sigma_i^2 = \lim_{n\to\infty} \frac{1}{n}\sum_{j=1}^{n}[\theta^i(x) - \bar{x}]^2 = \int_D (u - \bar{x})^2 f_i(u)du.$$

8.6   Constructing Densities

The existence of densities for trajectories is an important fact, but it would be nice if such densities could be constructed, for, obviously, they could then be used to derive various specific properties using the Mean Ergodic Theorem. This section summarizes and illustrates this problem.

8.6.1 The Frobenius-Perron Operator

Given a dynamical system (θ, D), where D is a finite interval $[a, b]$, suppose we know that

(i) there exists an invariant probability measure μ;

(ii) μ is ergodic; and

(iii) μ is absolutely continuous (with density f).

Then by invariance we know that

$$\mu(\theta^{-1}(X)) = \mu(X) \quad \text{for all} \quad X \in \Sigma. \tag{8.23}$$

In particular,

$$\mu\left(\theta^{-1}[a, x]\right) = \mu([a, x]) \quad \text{for all} \quad x \in [a, b]. \tag{8.24}$$

By absolute continuity this translates into

$$\int_{\theta^{-1}[a,x]} f(u)\, du = \int_a^x f(u)\, du. \tag{8.25}$$

Differentiating both sides, we get

$$\frac{d}{dx} \int_{\theta^{-1}[a,x]} f(u)\, du = \frac{d}{dx} \int_a^x f(u)\, du = f(x). \tag{8.26}$$

The expression on the left is a particularly convenient expression that will be seen to make possible the construction of closed-form expressions (explicit formulae) for the density $f(\cdot)$ for certain dynamical systems. It is therefore given a name, the *Frobenius-Perron Operator*, and denoted by

$$Pf(x) = \frac{d}{dx} \int_{\theta^{-1}[a,x]} f\, dm. \tag{8.27}$$

From (8.26) we therefore get

$$Pf(x) = f(x), \quad \text{for all} \quad x \in D. \tag{8.28}$$

Thus $f(\cdot)$ is a fixpoint in function space of the map P.

To illustrate, consider the tent map with $\beta = 1$. Recall that Lebesgue measure for this map is invariant and that the associated dynamical system is ergodic. Moreover, Lebesgue measure is absolutely continuous with density $f \equiv 1$. Noting that

$$\theta^{-1}[0, x] = [0, \tfrac{1}{2}x] \cup [1 - \tfrac{1}{2}x, 1]$$

and substituting $f \equiv 1$ into the left side of (8.25), we get

$$\int_{\theta^{-1}[0,x]} Pf(u) \, du = \int_0^{\frac{1}{2}x} du + \int_{1-\frac{1}{2}x}^1 du = x = \int_0^x du.$$

Or, substituting into the left side of (8.26), we get

$$\frac{d}{dx} \int_{\theta^{-1}[0,x]} Pf(u) du = \frac{d}{dx} \left[\int_0^{\frac{1}{2}x} du + \int_{1-\frac{1}{2}-x}^1 du \right] = 1$$

$$= \frac{d}{dx} [x] = 1 \equiv f.$$

8.6.2 Properties of P

The foregoing discussion illustrates several properties of P that are summarized in the following:

PROPOSITION 8.1 (Properties of P)

(i) $P : L^1 \rightarrow L^1$ is linear (where L^1 is the space of integrable functions);

(ii) $Pf \geq 0$ if $f \geq 0$;

(iii) $\int Pf \, dm = \int f \, dm$;

(iv) $Pf = f$ if and only if the measure μ defined by $\mu(E) = \int_E f \, dm$ for all E is invariant under θ.

8.6.3 The Frobenius-Perron Operator for Piecewise Monotonic Systems

Consider a piecewise, strictly monotonic map θ on an interval $D := [a_0, a_n]$, with the restriction of θ to each piece $D_i = [a_{i-1}, a_i]$ denoted by θ_i. As each θ_i is strictly monotonic on D_i, it is "invertible," that is, its inverse $\theta_i^{-1}(\cdot)$ is single-valued (and monotonic) on $\theta_i(D_i) = [\theta_i(a_{i-1}), \theta_i(a_i)]$. This fact is illustrated in figure 8.5 for a map with three monotonic pieces. Note that θ_i^{-1} is not defined outside the interval $[\theta_i(a_{i-1}), \theta_i(a_i)]$.

To deal with this inconvenience we can extend each θ_i to D by defining $\theta_i(x) := x$ for all $x \in]a_i, a_{i-1}[, i = 1, \ldots, n - 1$. Then each θ_i is continuously differentiable almost everywhere (except at a_i, a_{i-1}) where both one-sided derivations exist, and $\theta_i^{-1}(y) = y$ for all $y \notin D_i$.

With these conventions we get

$$\theta^{-1}[a_0, x] = \bigcup_{i=1}^n \theta_i^{-1}[a_0, x] \cdot \chi_{[\theta(a_{i-1}),\theta(a_i)]}(x).$$

Therefore, (8.28) can be rewritten as:

$$Pf(x) = \frac{d}{dx} \sum_{i=1}^{n} \int_{\theta_i^{-1}[a_0,x]\chi_{[\theta(a_{i-1}),\theta(a_i)]}(x)} f(u)d(u). \tag{8.29}$$

Because θ_i is strictly monotonic, $\frac{d\theta_i^{-1}(x)}{dx}$ is either positive or negative throughout D. If the latter, the order of integration between $\theta^{-1}(a_{i-1})$ and $\theta^{-1}(a_i)$ is reversed. Taking this into account, (8.29) simplifies after taking derivatives.

PROPOSITION 8.2   *Let θ be a piecewise, strictly monotonic map satisfying Theorem 8.4. Let L_i be an attractor. Then the absolutely continuous invariant ergodic measure μ_i has a unique density function $f(x)$ that satisfies*

$$Pf(x) = \sum_{i=1}^{n} f(\theta_i^{-1}(x)) \cdot \left| \frac{d\theta_i^{-1}(x)}{dx} \right| \cdot \chi_{[\theta(a_{i-1}),\theta(a_i)]}(x). \tag{8.30}$$

8.6.4   Examples

Using the definition, it is easy to show that $f(x) \equiv 1$ for the tent map for $\mu = 1$. This is in effect what was done at the beginning of §8.6.1.

As a second example, return to the check map (8.22). Even though it is not expansive, we used the Lasota-Yorke Theorem to show that an absolutely

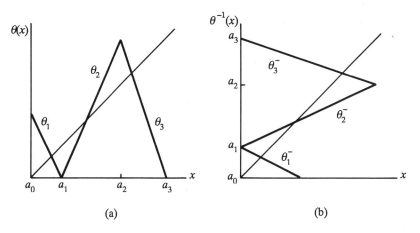

Figure 8.5
A piecewise monotonic map and its inverse. (a) The map. (b) Its inverse.

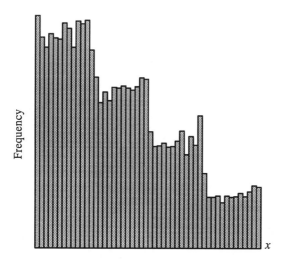

Figure 8.6
Numerical histogram for the check map

continuous invariant ergodic probability measure exists. Using (8.30), we can construct it.

The inverse $\theta^{-1}(\cdot)$ is

$$\theta^{-1}(x) = \begin{cases} \theta_1^{-1}(x) := 1 - \frac{1}{n}x, & x \in (0, N-1) \\ \theta_2^{-1}(x) := 1 + x, & x \in (0, N). \end{cases}$$

Carrying through the differentiation and substituting into (8.31), we get

$$\begin{aligned} f(x) = [f(1+x) + \tfrac{1}{n}f(1 - \tfrac{1}{n}x)]\chi_{[0,N-1]}(x) \\ + \tfrac{1}{n}f(1 - \tfrac{1}{n}x)\chi_{[N-1,N]}(x). \end{aligned} \tag{8.31}$$

To get a clue about what we are looking for, a numerical simulation is shown in figure 8.6. It looks suspiciously like a step function with constant steps on the intervals $(i-1, i)$, $i = 1, \ldots, N$. Assuming that this is the case, let $f(x) = \alpha_i$, $x \in [i-1, i]$; noting that $f(1 - \frac{1}{n}x) = \alpha_1$ for all $x \in [0, N]$, we obtain from (8.31) the equations

$$\alpha_i = \alpha_{i+1} + \frac{1}{N}\alpha_1, \quad i = 1, \ldots, N-1$$

$$\alpha_N = \frac{1}{N}\alpha_1.$$

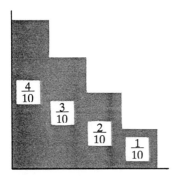

Figure 8.7
Theoretical density for the check map with $N = 4$

Setting $\alpha_N = \alpha$ and solving in terms of α, we find

$$\alpha_i = (N - i + 1)\alpha, \quad i = 1, \dots, N.$$

As the α_i's must add up to one, we get $1 = \Sigma_i \alpha_i = \alpha(N + 1)N/2$. So

$$\alpha = \frac{2}{N(N + 1)}.$$

Consequently,

$$\alpha_i = \frac{2(N + 1 - i)}{N(N + 1)}, i = 1, \dots, n. \tag{8.32}$$

The density function that characterizes the long-run statistical behavior of trajectories is therefore the step function illustrated in figure 8.7.

8.7   Existence of Absolutely Continuous Invariant Measures: Nonexpansive Maps

Consider the smooth quadratic map

$$\theta_A(x) = Ax(1 - x), \quad x \in [0, 1]. \tag{8.33}$$

As this map is not expansive, the Lasota-Yorke Theorem does not apply. However, let us consider it from the point of view of the Frobenius-Perron operator. For $A = 4$ we have $\theta_4^{-1}(0, x) = (0, \frac{1}{2} - \frac{1}{2}\sqrt{1 - x}) \cup (\frac{1}{2} + \frac{1}{2}\sqrt{1 - x}, 1)$, and the Frobenius-Perron operator is

$$Pf(x) = \frac{1}{4\sqrt{1-x}} \left[f\left(\frac{1}{2} - \frac{1}{2}\sqrt{1-x}\right) + f\left(\frac{1}{2} + \frac{1}{2}\sqrt{1-x}\right) \right].$$

We have $P(1) = \frac{1}{2\sqrt{1-x}}$ so that the Lebesgue measure is not invariant. However, it is possible to prove that $P^n(1)$ converges to

$$f(x) = \frac{1}{\pi\sqrt{x(1-x)}} \qquad (8.34)$$

and it is easily seen that $P(f) = f$ so that (8.34) is the density of the invariant measure.[6]

   In general it is extremely difficult to construct the densities for smooth maps, but existence can be established for a large class of them. Indeed, a companion to Theorem 8.5 for nonexpansive maps was established by Misiurewicz (1981) for a class of nonconstant, piecewise functions that are strictly monotonic and C^3 on pieces and that satisfy certain properties that replace the expansivity condition. This class includes the quadratic map as a special case.

THEOREM 8.6 (Misiurewicz)   *Let θ, I be piecewise strictly monotonic on an interval I with an interval partition of pieces $c\ell I_i = [a_{i-1}, a_i], i = 1, \dots, n$. Let $A := \{a_i, i = 0, \dots, n\}$ be the set of endpoints of the intervals. Assume that*

(i) any cyclic point in I is unstable;

(ii) trajectories through any endpoint are eventually cyclic, or they move outside a small enough neighborhood of any endpoint; that is, there is a neighborhood N_A of A such that

$$\gamma(y^i) \subset A \cup (I \setminus N_A).$$

Moreover, assume that in the interior of each set $I_i, i = 1, \dots, n$,

(iii) θ_i is continuously differentiable; and

(iv) $|\theta_i'(x)|^{-\frac{1}{2}}$ is a convex function.

Then the results of Theorem 8.5 and Corollaries 8.2–8.6 hold.

8.8   Divergence from Periodic Trajectories and the Appearance of Deceptive Order

The tent and check maps possesses a property that has interesting interpretations in various economic contexts. The dynamical systems they generate have absolutely continuous invariant ergodic measures on the intervals $[0, 1]$ and $[0, N]$, respectively. When the Li-Yorke Theorem is satisfied (for $\beta > \approx .81$ in the tent map and for $N \geq 2$ for the check map), cycles of all orders exist in their domain. But we have shown that absolutely continuous ergodic measures exist on these domains. This means that nonperiodic trajectories approach cycles of every order infinitely often, indicating that chaotic trajectories contain finite sequences that give the deceptive appearance of cyclic order.

The general result corresponding to these examples is:

THEOREM 8.7   *Let $\{\theta, D\}$ be a continuous dynamical system that satisfies the assumptions of either Theorem 8.5 or Theorem 8.6. Then for each invariant ergodic set L_i, there exists a denumerably infinite set of cyclic points of odd order above some odd integer, say m, and every even integer order. Let P_i be this set of cyclic points in L_i. Then for all $y \in P_i$ and μ_i-almost all $x \in B_i$,*

$$\liminf |\theta^n(x) - \theta^n(y)| = 0 \tag{8.35}$$

$$\limsup |\theta^n(x) - \theta^n(y)| > 0. \tag{8.36}$$

A proof can be developed along the following lines:

Consider the case where $L = [a, b]$ is a single interval with a single interior turning point. Without loss of generality, assume θ is single-peaked in L. (If θ is single-troughed, the argument is analogous.) Since L is an attractor, $\theta(L) = L$. If $\theta(a) < a$, then trajectories that entered L in the neighborhood of a would decline and exit L. If $\theta(b) < a$, the same would be true. If $\theta(b) > a$, then all trajectories would have to become trapped in $[\theta(b), b]$. These possibilities contradict $\theta(L) = L$. Therefore, $\theta(a) \geq a$ and $\theta(b) = a$. Moreover, the turning point, say x^{**}, maps into the maximum value of θ on L, that is, $M = \theta(x^{**})$. If $\theta(M) < a$ trajectories in L could exit, or if $\theta(M) > a$, they would get trapped in $(\theta(M), M)$. Therefore, $M = b$.

Now suppose $\theta(a) < x^{**}$. Then $\theta^{-1}(x^{**})$ contains two elements. Let y be the smaller of these. Then y is a Li-Yorke point. So cycles of all orders exist in L.

Suppose $x^{**} < \theta(a) < \tilde{x}$. Then there exists a sequence of preimages of x^{**} that converge to $\tilde{x}$ and that alternate in value above and below $\tilde{x}$. Eventually, there must exist a preiterate in this sequence that lies above $\theta(a)$. Suppose it is y; then y has a preimage in $[\theta(a), \tilde{x}]$ such that the sequence of $k + 1$ points $y, \theta(y), \ldots, \theta^k(y)$, where k is odd, has the following order:

$$\theta^k(y) = a, \quad y, \quad \theta^{k-2}(y), \ldots, \quad \theta^3(y), \quad \theta(y),$$

$$\theta^2(y), \quad \theta^4(y), \ldots, \quad \theta^{k-3}(y) = x^{**}, \quad \theta^{k-1}(y) = M.$$

This sequence has no division by construction. Therefore, by Theorem 7.6 there is an odd cycle. Hence, by Theorem 7.6 cycles of all odd order greater than k and cycles of every even order exist.

Finally, suppose $\theta(a) > \tilde{x}$. Then it can be shown, using Rolle's Theorem, that there is a point in $[a, x^{**}]$, say y, where $\theta'(y) = \frac{M - \theta(a)}{x^{**} - a} < 1$. So θ could not be expansive as assumed.

To complete the theorem we note that as any nondegenerate interval in L has positive measure, every small neighborhood of any cyclic point will be visited infinitely often, but that every trajectory that enters such an interval must escape.

8.9   Chaos Almost Everywhere

The similar argument can be used to show that for the kind of dynamical system discussed in Theorems 8.5 and 8.6, almost all trajectories are essentially chaotic. We draw on the ideas introduced in chapter 6 concerning the existence of trajectories that exhibit a certain episodic evolution. Thus, consider the finite history

$$\tau_0^n(x) := \{\theta^t(x)\}_{t=0}^n.$$

If $N_\epsilon(x)$ is an epsilon neighborhood of x, define

Tube $\tau_0^n(x) := \{N_\epsilon\left(\theta^t(x)\right)\}_0^n.$

We are interested in showing that almost all trajectories will pass through this tube.

Consider $N_\epsilon(\theta^n(x))$. A point in $N_\epsilon(\theta^{n-1}(x))$ may not map into this set. In fact, only if

$$y \in \theta^{-1}(N_\epsilon(\theta^n(x)) \cap N_\epsilon\left(\theta^{n-1}(x)\right)$$

will it do so.

Similarly, if $y \in N_\epsilon(\theta^{n-2}(x))$, $\theta^2(y)$ will enter $N_\epsilon(\theta^n(x))$ only if

$$y \in \theta^{-1}\left(\theta^{-1}(N_\epsilon(\theta^n(x)) \cap N_\epsilon\left(\theta^{n-1}(x)\right) \cap N_\epsilon\left(\theta^{n-2}(x)\right).$$

Proceeding by backward recursion we find that for a finite history

$$\tau_0^n(y) \in \text{Tube } \tau_0^n(x)$$

we must have

$$y \in \theta^{-1}\left(\cdots \left(\theta^{-1}\left(N_\epsilon(\theta^n(x)) \right) \right) \cap N_\epsilon\left(\theta^{n-1}(x) \right) \cap N_\epsilon \theta^{n-2}(x) \right)$$
$$\cdots \right) \cap \theta^{-1}\left(N_\epsilon(x) \right).$$

The set on the right contains an interval—perhaps a very small one—but as the dynamical system has an absolutely continuous invariant ergodic measure, its measure is positive. This means that a finite history of any trajectory contained in a basin of attraction will be approximated sooner or later by almost any trajectory that starts in that basin.

In particular let S be the scrambled set and choose $x \in S$. Then $\tau_0^n(x)$ is a finite segment of a chaotic trajectory. By the above argument, for any $x \in S$, $\epsilon > 0, n > 0$ there exists a $\delta < \epsilon$ such that for all $y \in N_\delta(x)$,

$$\tau_0^n(y) \in \text{Tube } \tau_0^n(x)$$

and $N_\delta(x)$ has positive measure.

We summarize this as follows:

THEOREM 8.8   *Let (θ, D) be a dynamical system that satisfies the assumptions of either Theorem 8.5 or Theorem 8.6. Let B_i be the basin of attraction for the attractor L_i. Then almost any trajectory in B_i will for a finite period of time approximate periodic cycles of all even orders and all odd orders above some odd integer and will also approximate finite segments of any trajectory in the scrambled set.*

8.10   Laws of Large Numbers

8.10.1   "Sample" Moments

A dynamical system that generates a chaotic trajectory is not a stochastic process. Indeed, for any given value x_t, the succeeding value x_{t+1} is exactly determined and, likewise, for any given initial condition $x \in X$ the entire trajectory $\tau(x)$ is in principle exactly determined. Nonetheless, trajectories do have certain properties like stochastic processes. From the point of view of these properties, a trajectory appears to be like the realization of a stochastic process yielding a series of independent, identically distributed random variables, even though the values in a trajectory are not drawn at random and are not independent. In particular, the trajectories satisfy certain standard laws of large numbers and a central limit theorem.[7]

Consider our familiar check map (8.22). If $x_0 \in R_2$ we could say that $x_1 \in [N-2, N-1], \ldots, x_{n-1} \in [0, 1]$, but we could not say for sure where x_n lies unless we knew in which of the sets $[0, 1] \cap \theta^{-1}(i-1, i), i = 1, \ldots, N$ the point x_{n-1} lies. As t gets large, however, we know that

$$\Pr(x_t \in [i-1, i]) \cong \mu[i-1, i] = \int_{[i-1,i]} f(u)du = \alpha_i, i = 1, \ldots, N.$$

Though we could not make long-run predictions for x, we could give the probability that it would lie in any given interval.

Think now of a finite sequence $\tau_0^n(x) = \{x_t = \theta^t(x)\}_0^{N-1}$ as a "sample" of the trajectory. From the mean ergodic theorem (letting $g(y) \equiv y$ we get

$$\lim_{N \to \infty} \bar{x}(N) = \lim_{N \to \infty} \frac{1}{N} \sum_{n=0}^{N-1} \theta^n(x) = \int_D uf(u)du = E(x), \tag{8.37}$$

so the "sample mean" converges to the mean of the distribution. Likewise, the sample variance

$$\sigma_x^2(N) := \frac{1}{N} \sum_{n=b}^{N-1} [\theta^n(x) - E(x)]^2$$

converges to the variance σ^2 of the density $f(\cdot)$, which is seen by setting $g(y) = (y-m)^2$ and using the mean ergodic theorem to get

$$\lim_{N \to \infty} \sigma^2(N) = \int_x (u - E(x))^2 f(u)du. \tag{8.38}$$

8.10.2 Examples

For the tent map with $\beta = 1$, the mean value of states in any trajectory is

$$\bar{x} = \int_0^1 udu = \tfrac{1}{2}$$

with variance

$$\sigma^2 = \int_0^1 (u - \tfrac{1}{2})^2 du = \tfrac{1}{12}$$

and standard deviation $\frac{1}{2\sqrt{3}}$.

For the check map (8.22) the mean value of states[8] in any trajectory is

$$\bar{x} = \int_0^N u f(u)\, du = \sum_{i=1}^N \frac{2(N+1-i)}{N(N+1)} \int_{i-1}^i u\, du$$

$$= \sum_{i=1}^N \frac{(N+1-i)}{N(N+1)} (2i-1)$$

$$= \frac{2N-1}{6}.$$

The variance is

$$\sigma^2 = \int_0^N [u - \bar{x}]^2 f(u)\, du$$

$$= \sum_{i=1}^N \frac{2(N+1-i)}{N(N+1)} \int_{i-1}^i [u - \bar{x}]^2\, du$$

$$= \frac{1}{3} \sum_{i=1}^N \frac{1(N+1-i)}{N(N+1)} \cdot [3i^2 - (1+2\bar{x})i + (1+3\bar{x}+3\bar{x}^2)]$$

$$= \frac{2N^2 + 2N - 1}{36}.$$

8.10.3   The Central Limit Theorem

In addition to these laws of large numbers, a still more remarkable property holds. Consider the "sample means" obtained by averaging values in the trajectory, then the subsequent values and so on. Denote these by

$$\bar{x}^p(N) = \frac{1}{N} \sum_{t=pN}^{(p+1)N-1} \theta^t(x), \quad p = 0, 1, 2, 3, \ldots, P. \tag{8.39}$$

Then the following has been established:

THEOREM 8.9 (Central Limit Theorem)[9]   *Let θ satisfy the assumptions of Theorem 8.5 or 8.6. Let μ_i be the absolutely continuous invariant ergodic measure with corresponding support $L_i, i = 1, \ldots, k$. Then for almost all x the time averages converge in distribution to a normal distribution $N(m_i, \sigma_i^2)$ with mean m_i and variance σ_i^2, or, alternatively, the normalized averages*

$$\sqrt{N} \left(\frac{\bar{x}^p(N) - m_i}{\sigma_i} \right) \tag{8.40}$$

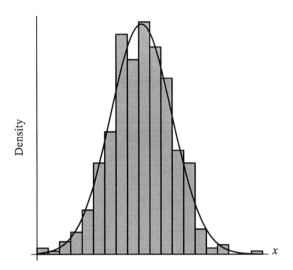

Figure 8.8
Numerical histograms of time averages

converge in distribution to the standard normal $N(0, 1)$ for some i when $P \rightarrow$
∞ and $N \rightarrow \infty$.

In figure 8.8, numerical histograms are given for the sample means of 1,000 consecutive sequences of 100 iterates for the tent and check maps, respectively. The graph of the associated normal distribution is superimposed.

8.11   Escape and Conditional Invariance

In §8.1, we considered trajectories for the tent map that "escape" [0, 1] when $\beta > 1$. We are now in a position to give this idea a more general treatment.

DEFINITION 8.7 (Strongly Expansive and Conditional Invariance) *Let θ :*
$D \rightarrow \mathbb{R}$. We say that a measure μ is conditionally invariant with respect to
θ if there exists a constant α, $1 > \alpha > 0$ such that $\mu(\theta^{-1}S) = \alpha\mu(S)$ for all
measurable S. Of course, if $\alpha = 1$ the measure μ is invariant.

Consider the family of piecewise monotonic maps defined in Theorem 8.6.
Let $W = D \setminus A$ where $A = \{a^0, a^1, \ldots, a^{k+1}\}$ is the set of endpoints defining
the pieces. W is just the union of the interiors of all the sets defining the pieces
of θ. Assume the following additional conditions:

(i) $\theta(W) \supset\supset W$. ($\theta$ maps an open interval of points in W outside of W.)

(ii) $\theta(a^i) \notin W$. (Turning points map either outside D or into the set of turning points.)

(iii) θ is expansive.

(iv) θ is transitive on components. That is, for all $D^i := (a^i, a^{i+1})$ and for all D^i there exists an integer n that depends on i and j such that

$$D^i \cap \theta^n(D^j) \neq \emptyset,$$

that is, the system is indecomposable.

Piecewise monotonic maps that satisfy (i)–(iv) will be called strongly expansive.

THEOREM 8.10 (Pianigiani and Yorke 1979)[10]   Let θ be a piecewise C^2 transformation as defined in Theorem 8.6. If θ is strongly expansive, then there exists an absolutely continuous measure conditionally invariant with respect to the Lebesgue measure.

Define the kickout time function n_θ by

$$n_\theta(x) = \max\{n : \theta^k(x) \in D \quad k = 1, \ldots, n\}.$$

It is easily seen that if μ is the conditionally invariant measure, then

$$\mu\{x : n_\theta(x) \geq k\} = \mu\theta^{-k}(D) = \left(\mu\theta^{-1}(D)\right)^k = \alpha^k,$$

which means that the system decays in an exponential way.

Return to the tent map with $\beta > 1$. It is easy to see that this map is strongly expansive, and that $\lambda\left(\theta^{-1}(X)\right) = \frac{1}{\beta}\lambda(X)$ for all λ-measurable sets in $[0, 1]$. Therefore, Lebesgue measure is conditionally invariant with $\alpha = \frac{1}{\beta}$ for the tent map with $\beta \geq 1$. By Theorem 8.10 the probabilities of escape in periods $k = 1, \ldots$ are just

$$\lambda(E), \ \tfrac{1}{\beta}\lambda(E), \ \tfrac{1}{\beta^2}\lambda(E), \ \ldots = \tfrac{\beta-1}{\beta}, \tfrac{1}{\beta} \cdot \tfrac{\beta-1}{\beta}, \ldots, \tfrac{1}{\beta^t} \cdot \tfrac{\beta-1}{\beta}, \ldots,$$

so

$$\lambda(U) = \frac{\beta - 1}{\beta} \sum_{t=0}^{\infty} \left(\frac{1}{\beta}\right)^n = 1.$$

This verifies the result obtained in §8.1.

9 Multiple-Phase Dynamics II: Further Analysis

The model to be developed here . . . contains several 'regimes' and it views the economic evolution as shifting at times from one regime to another.
—Edmond Malinvaud, *Profitability and Unemployment*

We are now in a position to consider qualitative aspects of multiple-phase dynamics in more detail. In particular we study regime switching, probable evolution, and qualitative histories for a special class of dynamical systems.

9.1 Ergodic Multiple-Phase Systems

9.1.1 Frequency in Phase

Recall that a multiple-phase dynamical system is a set of regimes $\{\mathcal{R}_p := (\theta_p, D^p), \ p \in \mathcal{P}\}$ where θ_p is the pth phase structure and D^p the phase domain. In order to simplify the exposition, it will be assumed in this chapter that

$$D^p = (a_{p-1}, a_p], \quad p = 1, \ldots, n \le \infty, \tag{9.1}$$

with

$$0 \le a_0 < a_1 < \cdots < a_p < \cdots, \tag{9.2}$$

that

$$D^0 = (-\infty, a_0] \cup [a_n, \infty), \tag{9.3}$$

and that each θ_p is bitonic on D^p. During each of the various sojourns in an epochal evolution, the trajectory $\tau(x)$ is *governed* by a particular regime. The *relative frequency* or "*probability*" of any regime is the proportion of time the trajectory is governed by that regime as time passes.

As a direct consequence of the Poincaré Recurrence Theorem 8.1 and the Birkhoff Ergodic Theorem 8.2, we have:

PROPOSITION 9.1   *If (θ, D) is a multiple-phase dynamical system with invariant ergodic probability measure μ, and if B is the basin of attraction for the attractor $\operatorname{supp}\mu$, then in the limit, for any $x \in B$, the relative frequency of states in regime i is $\mu(D^i)$.*

9.1.2 Example: The Check Map

An example is given by the check map defined in (8.22). If we let $D^1 := (0, 1)$ and $D^2 := [1, \infty)$, then from equation (8.32) it is seen that

$$\mu(D^1) = \frac{2}{n+1} \quad \text{and} \quad \mu(D^2) = \frac{n-1}{n+1}.$$

Thus, trajectories that begin in $(0, \infty)$ almost surely spend the fraction $\frac{2}{n+1}$ of time in $\mathcal{R}_1$ and $\frac{n-1}{n+1}$ of time in $\mathcal{R}_2$. In particular, if $n = 2$, then 2/3 of the time the trajectory is governed by $\mathcal{R}_1$ where it fluctuates in expanding two-period oscillations, and 1/3 of the time in $\mathcal{R}_2$ where it declines monotonically.

Note that the point 1 maps into zero so $E = \{1\}$. Now consider trajectories in $U := \bigcup_{n=0}^{\infty} \theta^{-1}(E)$. Any trajectory in $U \cap D^2$ must begin with at most two points in D^2 and terminates at zero after a finite number of expanding two-period fluctuations. Any trajectory that begins in $U \cap D^1$ involves an expanding two-period fluctuation that jumps to E in D^1 after a finite number of fluctuations. These trajectories are infinite in number, but $\mu(U) = 0$.

9.2   Transitional Events

In the check map just considered, the transition from one regime to another can occur in various ways that display various qualitative modes of behavior. Thus, almost surely, evolutions are phase cyclic with regimes $\mathcal{R}_1$ and $\mathcal{R}_2$ alternating in each episode. On the other hand, collapse (the reversion of $\mathcal{R}_2$ to the null regime $\mathcal{R}_0$) can occur either from a two-period decay in D^2 and reversion to D^0 or from a one- or two-period decay in D^2 followed by a reversion to D^1 and then a reversion to D^0 after a finite sequence of expanding two-period fluctuations. (Recall that $D^0 = (-\infty, 0]$.) These possibilities of collapse occur with zero measure in this example, but they suggest that many possible combinations of phase transitions and qualitative behavioral modes are possible.

These qualitative aspects of epochal evolution are going to be studied in this chapter.

9.2.1   Transition Modes and Transition Events

Consider the various possibilities for transitions from one regime to another. If an episode has finite duration, it is terminated when the trajectory *jumps* to a regime with a higher index, or *reverts* to a regime with a lower index. If the trajectory is *trapped* within the regime, the episode continues indefinitely. We shall denote these transitional modes by J, R, and T, respectively. The transition zones J^i, R^i, and T^i form a partition of D^i for, obviously, all trajectories are either trapped or they escape, and in the latter case they can only jump or revert. A reversion into the null regime is called a *collapse*.

Recall from §6.2.2 that the unstable set of a given regime i is defined by

$$U^i = \bigcup_{k=0}^{\infty} \theta_i^{-k}(E^i)$$

so that the *stable set* is

$$S^i = D^i \setminus U^i.$$

Recall also that the set E^{ij} is the switching set in E^i whose points map into D^j, and that the transition set is defined by $U^{ij} = \bigcup_{k=0}^{\infty} \theta_i^{-k}(E^{ij})$. Then the *jumping set* in D^j can be defined by

$$J^i = \bigcup_{j>i}^{n} U^{ij}$$

and the *reversion set* in D^j by

$$R^i = \bigcup_{j=0}^{i-1} U^{ij}.$$

Also, define E_J to be those points in E that jump and E_R those points that revert. Then $E_J^i = \bigcup_{j>i} E^{ij}$ and $E_R^i = \bigcup_{j<i} E^{ij}$. Of course, $E^i = E_J^i \cup E_R^i$. Note that the unstable set is $U = J \cup R$ and the stable set $S = T$.

If the dynamical system is ergodic on D, the *conditional probabilities* $p_i(A) = \mu(A)/\mu(D^i)$ are defined where A is any subset in D^i. We can refer to $p_i(J^i)$, $p_i(R^i)$, or $p_i(T^i)$ as the conditional "probabilities" that a trajectory in the basin B that enters the ith regime jumps, reverts, or is trapped respectively.

9.2.2 The Trapping Mode

The trapping mode is the simplest to consider, as shown in figure 9.1. Two cases are shown. In (a) monotonic growth or decay occurs with trajectories converging to a stationary state within the phase domain. In (b) fluctuations emerge after a possible period of growth or decay, respectively. These could be cyclic or nonperiodic, depending on the profile of θ_i.

If $\theta_i(D^i) \subset D^i$, then D^i traps all trajectories that enter and the regime is stable. If in addition $\mu(D^i) > 0$, then supp $\mu \subset D^i$ and trajectories that start in B are trapped in D^i μ-almost surely. If D^i is an interval and θ_i continuous on

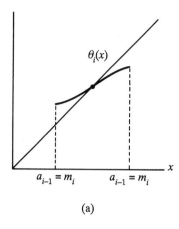
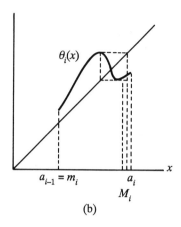

(a)   (b)

Figure 9.1
The trapping mode

D^i, let

$$m_i := \inf_{D^i} \theta_i$$

$$M_i := \sup_{D^i} \theta_i.$$

Then we have the obvious

PROPOSITION 9.2   *A sufficient condition for a trajectory that enters D^i to be trapped in D^i is that*

$$a_{i-1} \leq m_i < M_i \leq a_i. \tag{9.4}$$

If in addition to (9.4) there exists an invariant ergodic measure μ on D and $\mu(D^i) > 0$, then $\operatorname{supp}\mu(D) \subset D^i$ and trajectories are trapped μ-almost surely in D^i.

9.2.3   The Escape Mode

A trajectory that enters a regime $\mathcal{R}_i$ may escape if and only if there exist states in D^i that map outside the domain; that is, $\theta_i(D^i) \cap \setminus D^i \neq \emptyset$. This can happen if either

$$m_i < a_{i-1} \tag{9.5}$$

or

$$M_i > a_i. \tag{9.6}$$

Escape can occur in many different ways. The simplest possibilities occur when

$$\theta_i(x) > x \quad \text{for all} \quad x \in D^i, \tag{9.7}$$

as in figure 9.2a, or when

$$\theta_i(x) < x \quad \text{for all} \quad x \in D^i, \tag{9.8}$$

as in figure 9.2b. Or it can happen when θ_i is monotonic and *both* (9.5) and (9.6) occur, as in figure 9.2c. In (a) and (b) *any* trajectory that enters D^i must escape surely and in (c) almost surely, there being the one exception when the trajectory enters exactly at the stationary state $\tilde{x}^i$. Thus, $J^i = D^i$ when (9.7) holds; $R^i = D^i$ when (9.8) holds; and $R^i = (a_{i-1}, \tilde{x})$, $J^i = (\tilde{x}, a_i)$, and $T^i = \{\tilde{x}^i\}$ when θ_i is monotonic and both (9.5) and (9.6) hold.

The possibilities can be more complicated, as can be seen in figure 9.3. The escape set consists of three intervals. Any trajectory that enters the middle one must jump to a higher regime; any trajectory that enters the lower and upper escape intervals must revert to a lower regime. The unstable set consists of a set of intervals contained in D^i of shrinking length. The Lebesgue measure of E is positive, so $\lambda(U^i) > 0$.

This does not tell us anything about the dynamics of any trajectory as a whole. We can at least say the following:

PROPOSITION 9.3   *If (9.5) holds, then $\lambda(R^i) > 0$; if (9.6) holds, then $\lambda(J^i) > 0$; if there exists an invariant ergodic measure μ on D and $\text{supp}_{D^i} \mu \cap U^i \neq \emptyset$, then trajectories enter and escape D^i almost surely (and infinitely often). In this case, they enter and jump with frequency in proportion to $\mu(J^i)$; they enter and revert with frequency in proportion to $\mu(R^i)$; and they are trapped with measure zero.*

Note in figure 9.3 that trajectories that enter the set F fluctuate. Some of these can enter E^m and jump. Some can enter G where they grow; some can enter D where they decline; those that decline can enter E^u or E^l where they revert. Trajectories that enter G grow and can enter E^m and jump, or they can enter E^l and revert. Some trajectories that enter G or F enter E^u and revert directly.

The upshot of all this is that

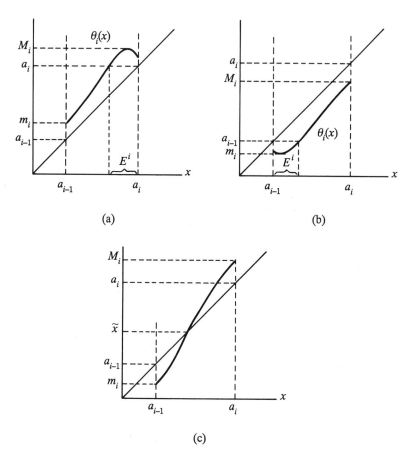

(a)   (b)

(c)

Figure 9.2
Unstable regimes. (a) Growth and escape surely. (b) Decline and escape surely. (c) Decline and escape or growth and escape almost surely.

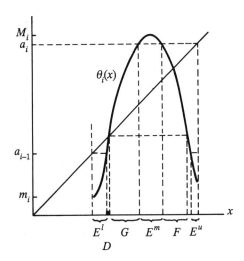

Figure 9.3
Jumps and reversions

$$F \cap J \neq \emptyset$$
$$G \cap J \neq \emptyset$$
$$F \cap R \neq \emptyset$$
$$G \cap R \neq \emptyset,$$

which raises the question, can trajectories that enter a regime where (9.5) or (9.6) occur be trapped with positive probability? Or must they escape with probability 1?

9.2.4   Local Phase Stability

In considering these questions, note that the upper stationary state in figure 9.3 is not asymptotically stable and that the map θ is expansive on points in D^i that are outside the escape intervals. If, on the contrary, that stationary state had been asymptotically stable, then there would exist a locally stable trapping set containing it: some fluctuations would have to converge and could not escape. Thus, suppose $\tilde{x}$ is an asymptotically stationary state in D^i. Then $|\theta'(\tilde{x})| < 1$ and by continuity there exists a $\delta > 0$ such that $|\theta'(x)| < 1$ for all $x \in \tilde{\Delta}$, where $\tilde{\Delta} := (\tilde{x} - \delta, \tilde{x} + \delta)$. Clearly, then, all trajectories that enter the set

$$\bigcup_{n=0}^{\infty} \theta_i^{-n}(\tilde{\Delta})$$

converge to the stationary state, which implies that the trapping set T^i is nonempty and has positive Lebesgue measure of at least 2δ. See figure 9.4.

A similar argument can be used for an asymptotically stable cycle in D^i.

PROPOSITION 9.4 *Suppose there exists an asymptotically stable point $\tilde{x}^p$ of period $p \geq 1$ whose orbit belongs to D^i. Then $\lambda(T^i) > 0$. If (9.4) holds, then $\lambda(U^i) = 0$. If instead (9.5) and/or (9.6) hold, then $\mathcal{R}_i$ is both locally unstable and locally stable. However, if $\mathrm{supp}_{D^i} \mu \cap U^i \neq \emptyset$, then trajectories enter and escape almost surely.*

9.2.5 Escape Almost Surely

Now return to figure 9.3. The fact that, as it is drawn, the map θ is expansive outside the escape set E suggests that we can use the escape Theorem 8.10. Consider the map θ_i as shown in figure 9.5. Note that θ_i has two monotonic

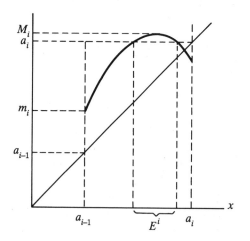

Figure 9.4
Local stability and local instability

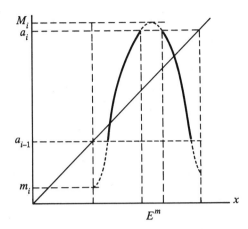

Figure 9.5
Escape almost surely

pieces, say, $I_1 = [a_{i-1}, u_i]$ and $I_2 = [v_i, a_i]$ with $\theta(I_1) \supset I_2$ and $\theta(I_2) \supset I_1$. This means that θ_i restricted to $I_1 \cup I_2$ is transitive on components. Note also that $\theta_i(I_1) \cap E^i \neq \emptyset$ and $\theta_i(I_2) \cap E^i \neq \emptyset$. The map θ_i restricted to $I_1 \cup I_2$ is therefore strongly expansive so that Theorem 8.10 applies. Using this argument, we can assert the following:

THEOREM 9.1 (Escape) *Suppose (9.5) or (9.6) hold and let $I^i := D^i \setminus E^i$. Suppose that θ_i restricted to I^i is strongly expansive. Then there exists a conditionally invariant probability measure μ_i, absolutely continuous with respect to Lebesgue measure, such that any trajectory that enters D^i escapes almost surely. The duration n of any episode in D^i declines exponentially with n. If $m_i < a_{i-1}$, then reversion occurs with positive probability; if $M_i > a$, then jumps occur with positive probability. If there exists an ergodic, absolutely continuous, invariant measure μ on D, then $\mu(R^i) + \mu(J^i) = \mu(D^i)$.*

9.3 Evolutionary Scenarios

9.3.1 Structural Growth, Structural Fluctuations, and Structural Evolution

We are now in a position to say something about possible *evolutionary scenarios*. By this term shall be meant an epochal evolution that has some specified

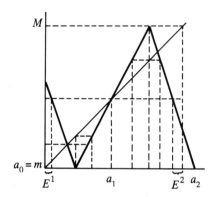

Figure 9.6
Structural fluctuations almost surely

qualitative character in terms of structural change. Let us consider the following.

Structural growth is a finite sequence of jumping transitions. Such a scenario can exhibit episodes of monotonic growth interspersed with irregular fluctuations that are followed by a jump to a higher phase zone where growth and/or fluctuations occur again.

Structural fluctuation is a finite sequence of jumping and reversion transitions where any run of jumping (reversion) transitions is followed by at least one reversion (jumping) transition. This implies that in addition to fluctuations within regimes, fluctuations among regimes can occur through sequences of jumps and reversions in different regimes.

A *structural evolution* is a finite sequence of transitions in which any regime is eventually succeeded by a jump to a regime with higher index, unless it is the last one in a finite sequence or is stable. Such a scenario may exhibit structural growth and structural fluctuations, but *it has a positive trend in the sense that no matter what reversions occur, higher regimes are eventually reached.*

9.3.2   Example: Structural Fluctuations

Consider the system in figure 9.6. It has two regimes. The first is single-troughed and the second single-peaked. It is derived from economic considerations that will be discussed in chapters 10 and 11, where we talk about market adjustments.

Assume that $a_0 \leq m$ and $M \leq a_2$, where m and M are the minimum and maximum values of θ on D, respectively, and θ is expansive on $[m, M]$. The map has two turning points. By Theorem 8.5 there exist at most two absolutely continuous invariant ergodic measures for the dynamical system (θ, D). Suppose $\theta(m) > a_1$ and $\theta(M) < a_1$. Then θ_1 restricted to D^1 is strongly expansive and trajectories that enter D^1 jump to D^2 almost surely. A similar argument shows that trajectories that enter D^2 revert to D^1 almost surely. We know, therefore, that the system is not decomposable and that there is only one absolutely continuous invariant ergodic measure μ on $[m, M]$. The relative frequency of the two regimes is therefore $\mu(D^1)$ and $\mu(D^2)$, respectively, giving an example of structural fluctuations.

We shall study this map rather extensively in chapter 11 in its economic context.

9.3.3 Example: Structural Growth and Structural Evolution

Consider the map illustrated in figure 9.7. There are three regimes; the system is continuous and piecewise bitonic, each regime being single-peaked.

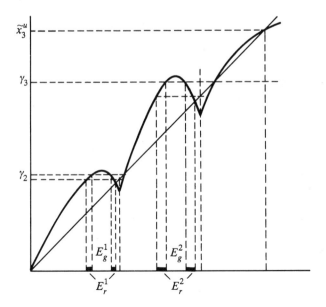

Figure 9.7
Evolution almost surely

Regime 1 has an escape set that is comprised of two subsets. One is an interval of points E_g^1 that map above γ_2 in phase zone 2. The other subset consists of two intervals whose points also map into phase zone 2 but below γ_2. Points that map into E_g^1 jump and grow in phase 2. Those that map into E_r jump but decay and revert. They could fluctuate in expanding two-period oscillations until they enter E_g^1 or E_r^1. Evidently, many qualitatively distinct paths are possible.

If θ restricted to $D^1 \backslash (E_r^1 \cup E_g^1)$ is strongly expansive, then trajectories jump into the second regime and grow almost surely.

A similar argument can readily be constructed for the possibilities of jumping from regime 2 to regime 3. Trajectories that jump but below γ^3 decay and revert to regime 2. Those that enter above γ^3 grow and, in this example, converge to the higher of the two stationary states in D^3. Noticing that θ restricted to $[\gamma_2, \gamma_3] \backslash E^2$ is strongly expansive, we know that *all* trajectories—no matter where they start in D—must converge to $\tilde{x}_3^\mu$.

Moreover, it is also evident that trajectories can occur that grow monotonically in D^1, jump to D^2, grow monotonically in D^2, and jump to D^3, where they converge to a stationary state. Structural evolution can also occur with trajectories that grow in D^1, fluctuate between D^1 and D^2, then grow in D^2 and either jump immediately to D^3 or fluctuate between D^2 and D^3 prior to resuming growth and converging to $\tilde{x}_3^\mu$. Thus, growth eventually takes place but its path is interspersed with periods of fluctuation, reversion, and fluctuation among regimes.

Notice in this example that there is only the trivial invariant measure with all its mass concentrated at the larger stationary state in D^3. Nonetheless, two conditionally invariant measures exist, and these make it possible to assert that structural evolution must occur almost surely.

9.3.4   Probable Evolutions

The argument used in the last example can be extended to a class of maps derived from the theory of economic development to be discussed in volume II. These are maps satisfying (9.1)–(9.3), that are single-peaked on phase domains D^i, and that satisfy certain expansivity conditions.

In order to introduce the basic idea without going into all possible types of evolutionary scenarios, some additional assumptions will be made. Define the growth threshold γ_k in the kth regime by

$$\gamma_k := \begin{cases} a_{k-1} & \text{if } \theta(a_{k-1}) \geq a_{k-1} \\ \tilde{x}_k & \text{if only one fixpoint } \tilde{x}_p \text{ exists in } D^k \\ \tilde{x}_k^l & \text{if two fixpoints } \tilde{x}^l, \tilde{x}^u \text{ exist in } D^k \\ \infty & \text{if } \theta(x) < x \text{ for all } x \in D^k. \end{cases} \qquad (9.9)$$

The set of points that jump from the kth regime into a higher regime (and hence grow for at least one period) is

$$E_g^k := \theta_k^{-1}\left(\theta(D^k) \cap [\gamma_{k+1}, \infty)\right).$$

If

$$M_k > \gamma_{k+1}, \qquad (9.10)$$

then $E_g^k \neq \emptyset$ (by continuity of θ) and the set of points in D^k that eventually jump to a higher regime and therefore grow in $\mathcal{R}_1$ for at least one period is

$$J_g^k := \cup_{n=0}^{\infty}\theta_k^{-n}(E_g^k).$$

It is the union of a set of nondegenerate intervals in D^k with positive Lebesgue measure.

Let $\mathcal{E} := \{p_1, \ldots, p_m\}$ define a conditional evolution. If a trajectory follows this conditional evolution, (6.13) holds; that is, we will write $\tau(x) \sim \mathcal{E}$. Assume that (9.10) holds for every $k \in \mathcal{E}$ except p_m. By continuity, the set of points in each phase zone D^{p_i} that grow and jump into $D^{p_{i+1}}$ is nonempty with positive Lebesgue measure. Call this set $E_g^{p_i, p_{i+1}}$. Of course, $E_g^{p_i, p_{i+1}} \subset E^{p_i, p_{i+1}}$. The transition set $U_g^{p_i, p_{i+1}} := \cup_{n=0}^{\infty}\theta^{-n}(E_g^{p_i, p_{i+1}})$ is therefore nonempty with positive Lebesgue measure. By Proposition 6.2, if μ is a probability measure on D^{p_1}, then $\text{Prob}\{\tau(x) \sim \mathcal{E}\} = \mu(U_g^{p_1, \ldots, p_m}) > 0$.

PROPOSITION 9.5   Let $\mathcal{E} = \{p_1, \ldots, p_m\}$ be a conditional evolution. Assume that (9.10) holds for every $k \in \mathcal{E}$ except the last. Let $\mu(\cdot)$ be a probability measure on D^{p_1}. If an unknown initial condition belongs to a set $S \subset D^1$, then structural growth occurs with probability

$$\mu(S \cap U_g^{p_1, \ldots, p_m}).$$

Many other scenarios can be considered with the help of some additional nomenclature that enable specific sequences of transitions to occur that are followed by specific characteristics of growth, fluctuations, or decline.

9.4 Qualitative History

The preceding diagrams show that various distinct qualitative modes of behavior can precede a transition. For example, in figure 9.3 it is seen that either a jump or a reversion can be preceded by monotonic growth or by fluctuation. Contrastingly, in figure 9.4 a jump can be preceded only by growth, but growth can also turn into trapping fluctuations. Reversion is not possible.

9.4.1 Elemental Events

In order to discuss all the possibilities, some additional nomenclature is needed. An *elemental event* is an episode characterized by a *qualitative mode* and a *transitional mode*, as shown in table 9.1. The symbols identify nine elemental events. The several separate cases can be grouped across the rows to give jumping, reverting, and trapping events, respectively, and down the column giving growing, fluctuating, and decline events, respectively. In general we shall refer to a given elemental event by its qualitative property first, then its transition type. Thus, for example, F_J denotes the fluctuate and jump event. A generic elemental event will be denoted Z; that is, Z is a variable that takes on entries in table 9.1.

9.4.2 Event Zones

Elemental events can be related one for one with the subsets of the phase zone in which they occur. Thus, an *elemental event zone* Z^i is a subset of the phase zone D^i such that any trajectory that enters Z^i exhibits only one elemental event. The event zones will be indexed by the phase zone in which they occur. Thus, Z^i is an element of the set $\{G_J^i, F_J^i, G_R^i, \text{etc.}\}$. With a slight abuse of

Table 9.1
Elemental Events

Transition Mode	Qualitative Mode		
	Grow G	Fluctuate F	Decline or Shrink S
Jump J	G_J	F_J	S_J
Revert R	G_R	F_R	S_R
Trap T	G_T	F_T	S_T

notation, we can now interpret the expression

$$Z^i \subset J^i$$

as meaning that Z^i is one of the event zones in the jumping zone, J^i, etc.

9.4.3 Qualitative History

A *qualitative history* is a sequence of episodes where each episode is characterized by a given qualitative mode of behavior and by a given mode of transition. Synonymously, a qualitative history, $\mathcal{H}$, is a sequence of elemental events

$$\mathcal{H} = (Z^{i_1}, Z^{i_2}, \dots, Z^{i_k}, \dots, Z^{i_m}), \quad m \leq \infty.$$

If a trajectory has an epochal evolution through the sequence of phase domains

$$(D^{i_1}, D^{i_2}, \dots)$$

such that $Z^{i_k} \subset D^{i_k}$, $k = 1, 2, \dots$, we shall say that it exhibits the qualitative history $\mathcal{H}$ and denote this by $\tau(x) \sim \mathcal{H}$. This means that $\tau(x) \sim \mathcal{H}$ if and only if $\theta^t(x) \in Z^{i_k}$, $t \in T_k, k = 1, \dots, m$.

Given this characterization, there are dual existence problems of interest. First, given a trajectory $\tau(x)$, what is the qualitative history $\mathcal{H}$ that it follows? Second, do there exist trajectories that follow a given qualitative history $\mathcal{H}$?

Given a computable system (θ, D), an answer to the first question can be obtained by recursive computation, but an answer to the second must involve a global analysis of the dynamical system and its various regimes. Using concepts analogous to those discussed above, the chance of any given qualitative history occurring can be derived just on the basis of the maximum and minimum state values M_i, m_i of the phase structure θ_i on the phase domain D^i, the thresholds of the regime a_{i-1}, a_i, and the values that the regime assumes at these thresholds. This tedious process will not be pursued in detail here, but the general procedure can be sketched.[1]

9.4.4 Compound Events

To undertake an analysis of the existence of trajectories that exhibit a given history, the scenario $\mathcal{H}$ must be broken down into its pairs of neighboring events $(Z^{i_k}, Z^{i_{k+1}})$. We could ask whether, given that a trajectory kicks into Z^{i_k}, it can subsequently escape and enter $Z^{i_{k+1}}$ next. Even if the answer is yes, this would not guarantee that it will subsequently enter $Z^{i_{k+2}}$. As we know from the general discussion of chapter 6, to make sure a given epochal evolution is followed, we have to go to the last episode and proceed backward. This means that a general solution to the existence problem for specified qualitative histories can only be given for a finite sequence of episodes. This leads to the ideas of conditional qualitative histories or a compound event.

A *compound event* is a finite sequence of two or more elemental events. Given the association of elemental events and elemental event zones, a compound event can be represented by a sequence

$$Z^{i_k}, Z^{i_{k+1}}, \ldots \quad k = 1, \ldots, m - 1.$$

Obviously, any number of distinct compound events can be composed from elemental events.

9.4.5 Existence of Conditional Qualitative Histories

Consider an arbitrary conditional history or

$$^{i_1} \mathcal{Z}^{i_m} := (Z^{i_1}, \ldots, Z^{i_m})$$

and define the compound events

$$^{i_k} \mathcal{Z}^{i_m} := (Z^{i_k}, \ldots, Z^{i_m}), \quad k = 1, \ldots, m - 1.$$

Note that $^{i_m} \mathcal{Z}^{i_m} = Z^{i_m}$ and that $^{i_1} \mathcal{Z}^{i_m}$ is just a conditional history.

Consider a trajectory $\tau(x)$. We shall say that *this trajectory follows the conditional history* $^{i_1} \mathcal{Z}^{i_m}$ if and only if there exists an entry time for each episode such that $\theta^{s_1(x)}(x) \in Z^{i_1}$, $\theta^{s_{k+1}(x)}(x) \in Z^{i_2}, \ldots, \theta^{s_{m-1}(x)}(x) \in Z^{i_m}$. We denote this by

$$\tau(x) \sim {}^{i_1} \mathcal{Z}^{i_m}.$$

The situation is the same as the description of epochal evolutions in chapter 6, except that here episodes are characterized not only by the regime that governs them but by the qualitative mode of behavior they exhibit in that regime. Existence is, therefore, described analogously.

To do so formally, define $Z^{i_{m-1}, i_m} \subset D^{i_{m-1}}$ to be the zone of escape from event $Z^{i_{m-1}}$ to event Z^{i_m}. The compound event $^{i_{m-1}} \mathcal{Z}^{i_m}$ is possible, therefore, if and only if

$$Z^{i_{m-1}, i_m} := Z^{i_{m-1}} \cap \theta^{-1}(Z^{i_m}) \neq \emptyset.$$

This says that the set of all points in episode $m - 1$ that exhibit qualitative behavior described by $Z^{i_{m-1}}$, that eventually enter regime i_m, *and* that exhibit qualitative behavior described by Z^{i_m} must be nonempty.

Now consider $^{m-2}\mathcal{Z}^m$. It is not enough just to consider the binary event $(Z^{i_{m-2}}, Z^{i_{m-1}})$, because all points in $Z^{i_{m-2}}$ that enter Z^{m-1} may not necessarily map eventually into Z^{i_m}. Only those that map into Z^{i_{m-1},i_m} do that. So we must limit attention to the set

$$Z^{i_{m-2},i_m} := Z^{i_{m-2}} \cap \theta^{-1}(Z^{i_{m-1},i_m}).$$

These are the points in event $Z^{i_{m-2}}$ that eventually escape to $Z^{i_{m-1}}$ and that subsequently enter Z^{i_m}. Any trajectory that enters this set exhibits the conditional history $^{m-2}\mathcal{Z}^m$.

In this way we can proceed recursively to define the sets

$$Z^{i_{m-k},i_m} := Z^{i_{m-k}} \cap \theta^{-1}\left(Z^{i_{m-k+1},i_m}\right), \quad k = 1, \ldots, m-1.$$

Then

$$Z^{i_1,i_m} = Z^{i_1} \cap \theta^{-1}\left(Z^{i_{m-2}} \cap \cdots \theta^{-1}\left(Z^{i_{m-2}} \cap \theta^{-1}\left(Z^{m-1} \cap \theta^{-1}(Z^{i_m})\right)\right)\cdots\right).$$

Any trajectory that enters Z^{i_1,i_m} exhibits the conditional history $^k\mathcal{Z}^m$. For purposes of reference, state this fact as:

PROPOSITION 9.6   *The compound event* $^{i_1}Z^{i_m} = (Z^{i_1}, \ldots, Z^{i_m})$ *is a possible conditional history if and only if* $Z^{i_1,i_m} \neq \emptyset$. *Moreover, if* $\mu(\cdot)$ *is a probability measure on* D^{i_1}, *then for initial conditions drawn at random in* D^i *with probability given by* μ,

$$\text{Prob}\{\tau(x) \sim {}^{i_1}Z^{i_m}\} = \mu(Z^{i_1,i_m}).$$

Although concepts developed in this chapter will be most useful for the discussion in volume II of economic business cycles, growth, and, especially, development, they arise naturally in models of market mechanisms that are discussed in the next three chapters.

III MARKET MECHANISMS

supply
unforeseen
demand
adjusting price
wandering
fortunes
flow

10 Tatonnement

. . . groping takes place naturally in the market under a system of free competition since under such a system the price of services rises when demand exceeds offer and falls when offer exceeds demand.
—Léon Walras, *Elements of Pure Economics or the Theory of Social Wealth*

It has sometimes been said that everything in economics boils down to demand and supply. Certainly, the forces of demand and supply are fundamental. Understanding the dynamic behavior of price and quantity adjustments in individual competitive markets is, therefore, a natural starting point for a study of economic dynamics.

The classical concept of a competitive market is one in which individual firms and households, none of which possess monopoly power, will supply and demand commodities in response to current and expected prices according to their individual best interests. If supply and demand are out of balance, then competition will bring about price adjustments until a balance is established and markets clear. Exactly how these adjustments take place was not spelled out in much detail by early expositors.

Walras put the theory on an explicit footing. He formulated *tatonnement* or "market groping" (literally, "groping in the dark") as an abstract analog of an "auctioneer" who adjusts price in response to excess supply or demand.[1] Much later Samuelson gave the model an explicitly mathematical treatment. We shall first look at the form in which he cast the process.[2] Linear supply and demand functions are considered first, then nonlinear ones. The simplest standard example of the general equilibrium pure exchange economy is examined next. In each of the cases studied, market equilibrium and convergent processes are part of the story but complex dynamics arises naturally and generically.

The original version of tatonnement can involve very large absolute price changes even when relatively small changes in excess demand occur. It would be natural to guess that this could be the source of the complex price behavior. To eliminate this source of instability, a *relative tatonnement* process is formulated based on percentage price adjustments in response to percentage changes in excess demand. Although this changes the nature of the nonlinearities, it does not eliminate the possibility of generic price instability.

The analysis of tatonnement in this chapter is instructive not only because it illustrates methods of dynamic analysis, but also because tatonnement is seen to be deficient as a model of real-world markets. Steps toward removing this deficiency are taken in the succeeding two chapters. In chapter 11 explicit market mediation or "middlemen" are introduced into the price adjustment process and the dynamics of a specific market, that for corporate equities, investigated. In chapter 12 the cobweb model of competitive markets with production lags is reconsidered and then modified to make possible an investigation of competitive market adjustments when financial feedback matters. These two chapters constitute an introduction to the theory of how firms and markets work when market-clearing prices have not emerged and when expectations are not fulfilled so that supply and demand decisions are not perfectly coordinated. The microeconomic components are standard and equilibrium plays an important role in the theory, but possibilities enter the picture other than that of living happily ever after. Fluctuating profit and loss, outage and bankruptcy enter the picture as an intrinsic part of the theory—just as they do in the world of economic experience.

10.1   Samuelson Tatonnement

10.1.1   Price Adjustments

Let $S(p)$, $D(p)$ be the supply and demand for a given commodity where p is the commodity's price. The *excess demand* is defined to be the difference between these two functions $e(p) = D(p) - S(p)$.

Samuelson tatonnement specifies that prices change as a monotonically increasing function of excess demand as shown in figure 10.1. In discrete time this means that $p_{t+1} = p_t + g[e(p_t)]$, where $g(\cdot)$ is a monotonically increasing function. The simplest version of this relationship is obtained by assuming that $g[e(p)] := \lambda e(p)$, where λ is a positive constant called the *speed of adjustment*.

In the course of the analysis we will want to consider classes of demand and supply functions generated by a shift parameter μ. Denote these functions as $D_\mu(p) = \mu D(p)$ and $S_\mu(p) = \mu S(p)$ where $D(\cdot)$ and $S(\cdot)$ are the original functions. Excess demand, denoted $e_\mu(p)$, is then

$$e_\mu(p) = \mu e(p). \tag{10.1}$$

We can think of μ as the market "strength" or the "extent of the market" relative to the "base" situation when $\mu = 1$. To make sure price is not negative, the price adjustment equation is given the form

$$p_{t+1} = \theta_\mu(p_t) = \max\{0, p_t + \lambda \mu e(p_t)\}. \tag{10.2}$$

This can introduce a nonlinearity because a kink must occur in $\theta_\mu(\cdot)$ if $p +$

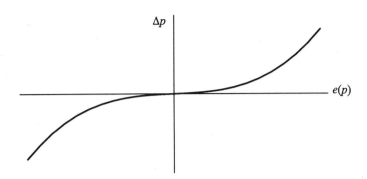

Figure 10.1
Excess demand and price adjustment

$\lambda\mu e(p)$ becomes negative. Note that λ and μ enter as a product so that a strengthening of demand and supply is equivalent to an increase in the speed of adjustment. For purposes of interpretation it is useful to incorporate them both explicitly, and when relative tatonnement is taken up, the distinction is central.

10.1.2   Linear Demand and Supply

Start with affine demand and supply functions,

$$D_\mu(p) := \mu(a - bp) \tag{10.3}$$

$$S_\mu(p) := \mu(c + dp). \tag{10.4}$$

Either of these functions could become negative. For the time being, this possibility will be allowed to avoid complications in the analysis. Later (in §10.3.3) and after nonlinear demand and supply functions have been introduced, non-negativity restrictions will be explicitly incorporated. Given (10.3)–(10.4), excess demand is

$$e_\mu(p) := \mu(a - c - (b + d)p). \tag{10.5}$$

The price adjustment process (10.2) becomes the difference equation

$$p_{t+1} = \theta_\mu(p_t) := \max\{0, \lambda\mu(a - c) + [1 - \lambda\mu(b + d)]p_t\}. \tag{10.6}$$

A stationary state for this equation is a *competitive equilibrium* where demand and supply are equal. In this linear model it is unique and positive if

$$\tilde{p} = (a - c)/(b + d) > 0. \tag{10.7}$$

Let us assume this.

In §5.5.1 it was found that exactly seven qualitatively distinct potential histories are possible for a linear difference equation. In the present case this means that prices could exhibit one of the following paths:

(i) monotonic divergence from $\tilde{p}$;

(ii) linear growth or decay;

(iii) monotonic, asymptotic convergence to $\tilde{p}$;

(iv) one-step convergence to $\tilde{p}$;

(v) oscillatory, asymptotic convergence to $\tilde{p}$;

(vi) neutrally stable two-period cycles around $\tilde{p}$;

(vii) oscillatory, explosive divergence from $\tilde{p}$.

If, however, we assume that demand is downward sloping ($b > 0$), that supply is upward-sloping ($d > 0$), and that the demand is greater than supply at zero price ($a > c$), then several cases are eliminated. Assume these "normal" conditions. And, temporarily to avoid some annoying details, also assume $c \geq 0$. Using Theorem 5.7, asymptotic convergence to a competitive equilibrium (iii) and (v) can occur if and only if

$$|\theta_\mu'(\tilde{p})| = |1 - \lambda\mu(b+d)| < 1,$$

but given that b and d are positive, this requires that

$$0 < \lambda\mu(b+d) < 2. \tag{10.8}$$

Case (i) cannot occur because it would require that $b + d < 0$. Case (ii) cannot occur because it would require that $b + d = 0$. However, for any positive b and d and for any μ, if the speed of adjustment λ is small enough, condition (10.8) will be satisfied. Asymptotic stability, therefore, occurs robustly. These results are illustrated in figure 10.2.

From Theorem 5.10 local instability (in the neighborhood of $\tilde{p}$) occurs if

$$|\theta_\mu'(\tilde{p})| = |1 - \lambda\mu(b+d)| > 1.$$

But under our assumptions about demand and supply this can happen if and only if

$$\lambda\mu(b+d) > 2. \tag{10.9}$$

For given demand and supply, too fast a speed of price adjustment λ will destabilize equilibrium. More interestingly, for *any* λ strong enough demand

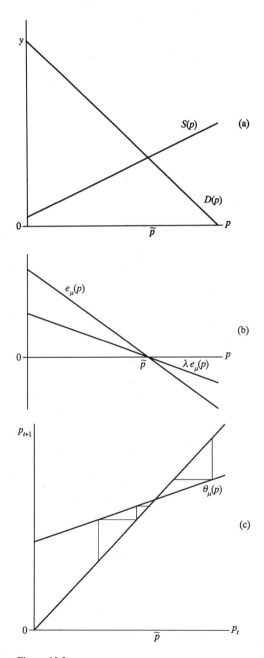

Figure 10.2
Asymptotic tatonnement

and supply will destabilize the equilibrium price. That is, given λ, b, and d, any

$$\mu > \frac{2}{\lambda(b+d)} \tag{10.10}$$

gives locally unstable, expanding cycles in the neighborhood of $\tilde{p}$. These must grow until the linear adjustment component of (10.6) goes negative so that price is set equal to zero. At this point a stable two-period fluctuation occurs with orbit $\{0, \lambda\mu(a - c)\}$. This orbit is an attractor for all trajectories that begin with a nonnegative price. Consequently, the process is globally stable but equilibrium price is unstable; that is, every nonequilibrium trajectory eventually remains a finite distance from equilibrium. These results are illustrated in figure 10.3.

10.1.3 Walras's Graphical Example

In contrast to these linear assumptions, Walras illustrated a supply and demand situation with the nonlinear graph reproduced in figure 10.4a.[3] (Notice that, as before, price is represented by the horizontal axis and supply and demand by the vertical. What appears for Walras as a "downward-bending" supply curve would appear as a "backward-bending" supply curve on the familiar Marshallian diagrams.)

Downward-bending supply functions are not far-fetched. They have been suggested for labor, aggregate farm output, and fishing, so they are more than an idle curiosity. They are based on the supposition that workers, farmers, fishermen, and perhaps people in many work situations would substitute leisure for work (output) in response to an income increase. The assumption is that after having achieved a sufficiently high standard of living, people prefer merely to sustain or to improve only modestly their material standard of living while increasing the time they have to enjoy it.[4] To obtain the graph of excess demand, the Samuelson tatonnement calculates the vertical difference between the two curves as shown in figure 10.4b. To get the graph of the Samuelson tatonnement maps, multiply excess demand by $\lambda\mu$ and add the result to the 45° line through the origin. The result is shown in figure 10.4c for $\lambda\mu = 1$.

Using the usual paper and pencil simulation, you can trace out a path for prices. But you don't need to go to that trouble to see what can happen. Given the scales implicit in the diagrams, it is visually evident that the slope of the map $\theta(\cdot)$ at the stationary price $\tilde{p}$ is less than -1, so $\tilde{p}$ is unstable. Moreover,

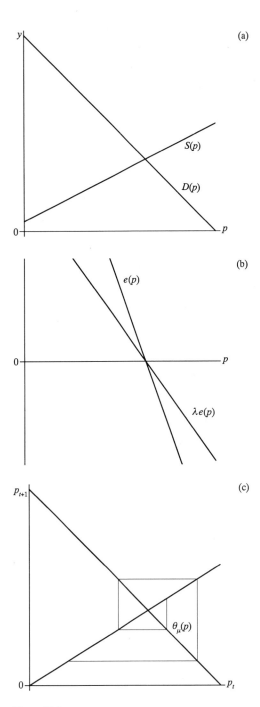

Figure 10.3
Tatonnement is unstable

(a)

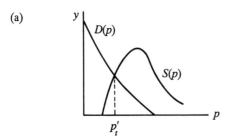

(b)

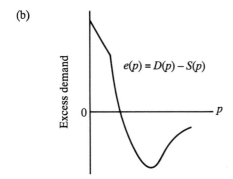

(c)

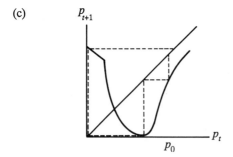

Figure 10.4
Walras's example. (a) Demand and supply. (b) Excess demand. (c) Tatonnement $\lambda = 1$.

you can readily construct a point, say p_0, that satisfies the Li-Yorke overshoot
conditions as shown by the dotted lines on figure 10.4c. Using the Li-Yorke
Chaos Theorem 7.2, we know that price fluctuations persist, that cycles of all
orders exist; and, using Corollary 8.2, that for an uncountable number of initial prices, fluctuations will be nonperiodic with positive continuous measure.
For a smaller value of $\lambda\mu$, say .5, the market would be stable and prices would

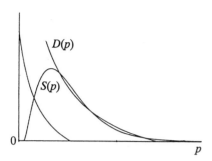

Figure 10.5
Nonlinear demand and supply

converge to a competitive equilibrium where the market clears. This can be seen by multiplying the curve of figure 10.4b by .5 and adding the resulting curve to the 45° line from the origin. Evidently, the Walras example for tatonnement may converge to a stationary solution; but the price trajectory could also be cyclic or chaotic, depending on the speed of price adjustment and the extent of the market.

10.1.4   A Mathematical Analog

Formulas can be found that give supply and demand functions like the ones of Walras. A downward-bending supply function like his is

$$S(p) = \begin{cases} 0, & 0 \le p < p' \\ B(p - p')^\gamma e^{-\delta p}, & p' \le p. \end{cases} \tag{10.11}$$

Supply is nil until the estimated price reaches p'. Above this threshold supply rises steeply, reaches a maximum, and then bends downward, approaching the horizontal axis asymptotically.

A demand function like the one used by Walras is

$$D(p) := \begin{cases} \frac{A}{a+p} - b, & 0 \le p \le p^0 \\ 0, & p^0 < p, \end{cases} \tag{10.12}$$

where $p^0 := A/b - a$ is the price that reduces demand to zero. In between zero and p^0 demand is downward-sloping and convex. Graphs of (10.11) and (10.12) are displayed in figure 10.5. Two demand functions corresponding to different values of A are shown.[5]

Substituting (10.11) and (10.12) into (10.1) to get excess demand and thence into (10.2), the price adjustment process is obtained. Numerical experiments can now be conducted to see how the model behaves. Figure 10.6a shows the phase diagram for an asymptotically stable example. Suppose $\lambda = .5$. By doubling the extent of the market (from $\mu = 1$ to $\mu = 2$) the chaos conditions emerge and an erratic, apparently nonperiodic trajectory results, as shown in figure 10.6b.

In order to see if these possibilities are robust, comparative dynamic experiments are shown in figure 10.7 for the combined parameter $\lambda\mu$. Suppose $\lambda = .5$. Then for μ less than about .86 prices converge asymptotically to the competitive equilibrium. Above this value stable two-period cycles emerge. Above about 1.04 these become unstable and four-period cycles occur, and so on. Between 1.2 or so and 2.0 various fluctuations appear, some stable and cyclic of low or high order and some nonperiodic. If we were to flip the diagram over, it would have the general character of the bifurcation diagram for the quadratic map that arose in the example of §2.3.4 and was illustrated in figure 2.3. This is because the map $\theta(\cdot)$ is single-troughed and, by a simple transformation, single-peaked.

The bifurcation diagram can also be interpreted as giving the comparative dynamics for λ given μ. Thus, suppose $\mu = 1$. If the speed of adjustment is less than .43, then prices converge to the competitive equilibrium. If λ increases above .52, cycles appear, and above roughly .6 high-order fluctuations are interspersed with apparently nonperiodic behavior. Consequently, in this example, for any market scale there is a speed of adjustment that will stabilize or destabilize the process; for any speed of adjustment there is a market strength that will stabilize or destabilize the marketing process. Stable equilibrium and disequilibrium fluctuations occur generically.

In this exercise both demand and supply are shifted when μ changes. In figure 10.5 one can see that an interesting change occurs when supply is held fixed and the demand parameter A is changed. When A is small, there is a single competitive equilibrium that occurs when the supply curve is rising. When A increases, it eventually brings about a situation in which three competitive equilibria exist; then as it increases still more, the equilibrium again becomes unique. This bifurcation in the number of equilibria is related to the results shown in figure 10.8, which gives a bifurcation diagram for changes in A. It has a marvelously intricate pattern, especially within the range of parameter variations $5 \leq A \leq 12$. Outside this range, when A exceeds 12, a jump occurs at the point where the number of stationary states drops from three to one in the manner just described.

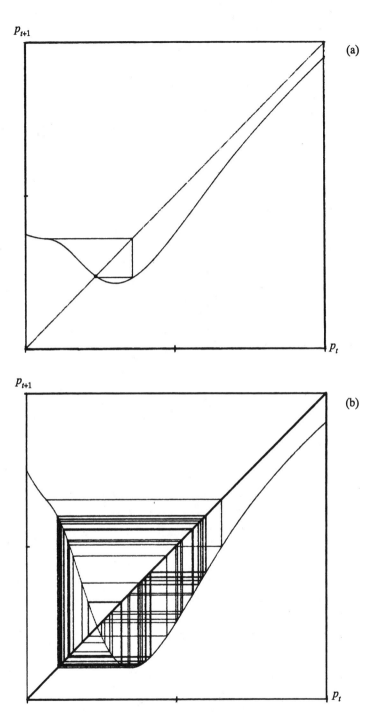

Figure 10.6
Stable and chaotic tatonnement. (a) $\lambda\mu = .5$. (b) $\lambda\mu = 1.0$.

p

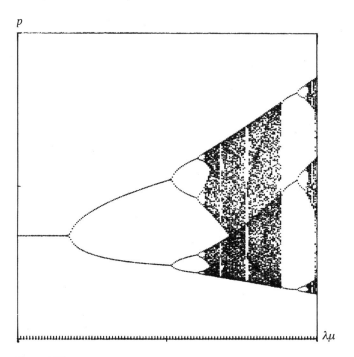

$\lambda\mu$

Figure 10.7
Bifurcation diagram for $\lambda\mu$

Could the chaotic dynamics that occurs when λ, μ, or A are big enough be ergodic and representable by density functions? An affirmative answer is suggested for the two values of A used to obtain figure 10.5b ($A = 7.1$ and $A = 8.85$). Numerical histograms for these cases are shown in figure 10.9 based on 10,000 iterates of the tatonnement process. Perhaps the Walrasian map satisfies the Misiurewicz Theorem 8.6? Unfortunately, simulations alone can't answer this question.

10.2 Examples with Nondecreasing Supply

At this point you might think that the emergence of chaotic price trajectories for tatonnement requires a downward-bending supply function. But this is not the case. In fact, all the dynamic possibilities occur for perfectly normal markets. A series of examples will illustrate this. Then a general class of normal markets can be considered.

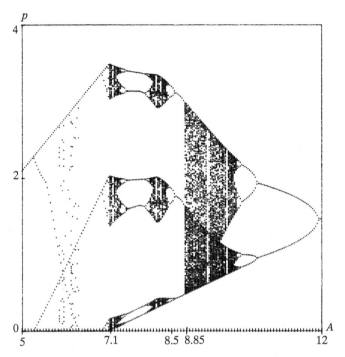

Figure 10.8
Bifurcation diagram for the demand shifter

10.2.1   A Pure Exchange Economy

Consider a pure exchange economy where the demands and supplies of the traders are derived from their underlying preferences for alternative consumption bundles.

Let us suppose that these individual preferences can be represented by a real-valued utility index or function. Suppose there are two consumers (or two types of consumers), Mr. Alpha and Ms. Beta. Consider the consumer's choice of the amounts to purchase x and y of two different goods respectively, and postulate the power (Cobb-Douglas) utility function for Mr. Alpha

$$\psi(x, y) = Ax^{\alpha}y^{1-\alpha}, \tag{10.13}$$

in which α represents the "strength" of preference for good x, $1 - \alpha$ that for good y. Let p and q be the unit prices. Suppose that Mr. Alpha's endowment is an amount $\bar{x} > 0$ of x and zero of y. His most preferred choice can be

Relative frequency

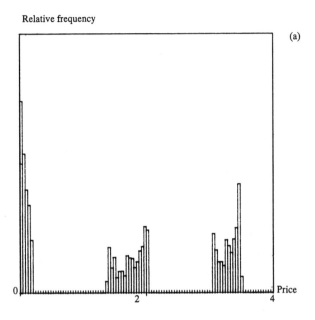

Relative frequency

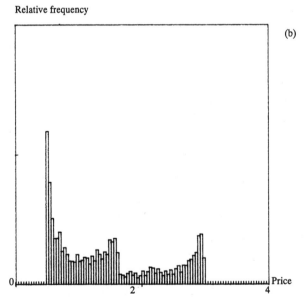

Figure 10.9
Histograms of prices for two levels of demand. (a) $A = 7.1$. (b) $A = 8.85$. (See figure 10.8 for the corresponding places in the bifurcation diagrams.)

represented by maximizing (10.13) subject to the constraints

$$qy \leq p(\bar{x} - x) \quad \text{and} \quad x, y \geq 0. \tag{10.14}$$

Carrying out the required calculations, one finds that the demand functions are

$$\alpha\bar{x} \text{ for } x, \tag{10.15a}$$

$$\frac{(1 - \alpha)p\bar{x}}{q} \text{ for } y. \tag{10.15b}$$

Suppose, now, that Ms. Beta's preferences are also representable by (10.13), but let us denote her utility parameter by β and assume that her endowment is $\bar{y} > 0$ units of y and zero units of x. Her demand functions are then

$$\frac{\beta q\bar{y}}{p} \text{ for } x, \tag{10.16a}$$

$$(1 - \beta)\bar{y} \text{ for } y. \tag{10.16b}$$

Mr. Alpha is therefore a supplier of x in amount $(1 - \alpha)\bar{x}$ and receives the price p for each unit sold. Ms. Beta has to pay p for each unit she purchases. Let good y be the numeraire so that p is calculated in terms of y, that is, $q \equiv 1$. Then the excess demands for x is

$$e(p) = \frac{\beta\bar{y}}{p} - (1 - \alpha)\bar{x}. \tag{10.17}$$

The tatonnement process is

$$p_{t+1} = \theta_\mu(p_t) := \max\{0, \, p_t + \lambda\mu\left[\beta\bar{y}/p_t - (1 - \alpha)\bar{x}\right]\}. \tag{10.18}$$

Demand is unbounded at $p = 0$, so $\theta(p)$ must be positive for small enough p. Moreover,

$$\theta(p) \to p - \lambda\mu(1 - \alpha)\bar{x} \quad \text{for} \quad p \to \infty.$$

Therefore, $\theta_\mu(p) - p$ changes sign as p increases from 0, so a unique competitive equilibrium $\tilde{p}$ exists. It is given by the expression

$$\tilde{p} = \frac{\beta}{1 - \alpha} \cdot \frac{\bar{y}}{\bar{x}}. \tag{10.19}$$

The first derivative of $\theta(p)$ evaluated at $\tilde{p}$ is

$$\theta'(p) = 1 - \lambda\mu\beta\bar{y} \cdot \frac{1}{p^2}. \tag{10.20}$$

This expression changes from $-\infty$ to $+1$ as p increases from 0. If $\theta'(\tilde{p}) < -1$, *and it can be if $\lambda\mu$ is big enough*, then $\tilde{p} < p^*$ where p^* is the minimizer of $\theta(p)$, so $\theta(\cdot)$ has to have a fish hook form. Substituting (10.19) into (10.20) we get

$$\theta'(\tilde{p}) = 1 - \lambda\mu\frac{(1-\alpha)^2\bar{x}^2}{\beta\bar{y}}.$$

Define the stability/instability criterion

$$\kappa := \lambda\mu \cdot \frac{(1-\alpha)^2}{\beta} \cdot \frac{\bar{x}^2}{\bar{y}}. \tag{10.21}$$

The equilibrium $\tilde{p}$ is asymptotically stable if

$$0 < \kappa < 2. \tag{10.22}$$

Given the parameters of demand $\alpha, \beta, \bar{x}, \bar{y}$, a small enough $\lambda\mu$ can stabilize the process so that prices converge to $\tilde{p}$. If, on the other hand, $\lambda\mu$ is large enough, κ will exceed 2 and $\tilde{p}$ will be locally unstable and expanding fluctuations must occur near $\tilde{p}$. It is also clear that increases in Mr. Alpha's endowment $\bar{x}$ or decreases in Ms. Beta's endowment $\bar{y}$ have the same direction of influence on κ as changes in λ or μ.

A possible result of instability is that price could become zero and, as $\theta(0) = \infty$, the model would then be globally unstable. Let p^* minimize $p + \lambda\mu e(p)$. At such a value $\theta'(p^*) = 0$. After a little calculation we find that $p^* = (\lambda\mu\beta\bar{y})^{\frac{1}{2}}$. The condition for global stability is, therefore, $\theta(p^*) = p^* + \lambda e(p^*) > 0$. Substituting for p^* we find after some calculation that this inequality is satisfied for any $\kappa < 4$. Therefore, any combination of parameters such that

$$0 < \kappa < 4 \tag{10.23}$$

is viable. Within the range (2,4), bounded fluctuations are perpetuated. Chaos and ergodic price sequences are possible. One can say, roughly, that in this pure exchange economy, increases in the market strength (μ), the "speed" of price adjustment (λ), the inequality of endowments ($\bar{x}$ relative to $\bar{y}$), all increase the instability of the price adjustment process.

The generic existence of chaos is easily established. Choose a value of κ close to but smaller than 4. Fluctuations must persist but are bounded by the trapping set $[\theta(p^*), \theta^2(p^*)]$. Let p^c be the largest of the two preimage of p^*. By taking κ close enough to 4, p^c will change very little but $\theta^2(p^*) = \theta^3(p^c)$

will get very large. For some κ, then, say κ^c, we must have

$$0 < \theta^2(p^c) < \theta(p^c) = p^* < p^c < \theta^3(p^c),$$

which indeed will be satisfied for all $\kappa > \kappa^c$. Consequently, the chaos overshoot conditions (Theorem 7.2) occur robustly.

Figure 10.10 shows how the price dynamics changes as κ increases.[6] A bifurcation diagram that results from variations of any of the components of κ, given in (10.21), will vary κ. The resulting diagram will look essentially like figure 10.7. Not surprisingly, in the cases where the trajectories seem to fill up an interval the histograms look like that of figure 10.8b.

Can strong chaos occur? That is, can unstable nonperiodic trajectories occur for almost all initial conditions and for a robust range of parameter values? To answer this, consider the Schwartzian condition

$$| \theta'(p) |^{-\frac{1}{2}} = \frac{1}{(1 - \lambda\mu\beta\bar{y}/p^2)^{\frac{1}{2}}}.$$

The function $\theta'(p)$ is shown in figure 10.11a. $1/\theta'(p)$ has the appearance shown in figure 10.11b. Taking the absolute value and the square root gives a curve like figure 10.10c, which is piecewise convex on the intervals $(0, p^*)$ and (p^*, ∞). This gives one of the sufficient conditions for strong ergodicity in the Misiurewicz Theorem 8.6. The simulations suggest that the other conditions are satisfied for many parameter values.

All of this can be summarized as follows: Simple and complex price dynamics exist generically for the pure exchange economy in (10.13)–(10.17) with Samuelson tatonnement. Specifically,

(i) A unique competitive equilibrium exists and is the unique stationary state of the process.

(ii) For κ defined by (10.21), the competitive equilibrium is asymptotically stable for all $0 < \kappa < 2$.

(iii) For all $2 < \kappa < 4$, the process is globally stable.

(iv) For $\kappa > 2$ fluctuations persist almost surely.

(v) For some $\kappa^c \in (2, 4)$, chaotic trajectories exist for all $\kappa \in [\kappa^c, 4]$.

(vi) Given any speed of adjustment λ, these results occur robustly.

(vii) Finally, if the expansivity conditions of Theorem 8.6 are satisfied, then the price dynamics are strongly ergodic.

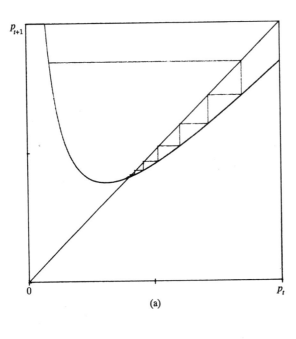

(a)

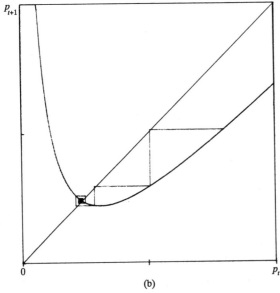

(b)

Figure 10.10
Tatonnement for the pure exchange economy. (a) $\bar{x} = 1.0$. (b) $\bar{x} = 1.65$. (c) $\bar{x} = 1.96$. (d) $\bar{x} = 2.04$. (e) $\bar{x} = 2.05$. (f) $\bar{x} = 2.18$ (scale enlarged).

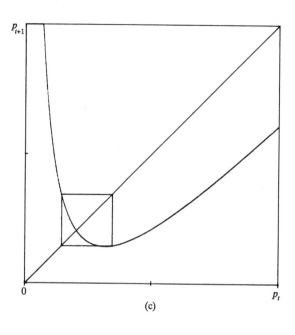

(c)

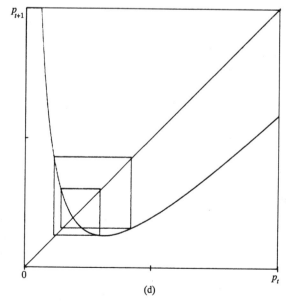

(d)

Figure 10.10 (continued)
Tatonnement for the pure exchange economy. (a) $\bar{x} = 1.0$. (b) $\bar{x} = 1.65$. (c) $\bar{x} = 1.96$. (d) $\bar{x} = 2.04$. (e) $\bar{x} = 2.05$. (f) $\bar{x} = 2.18$ (scale enlarged).

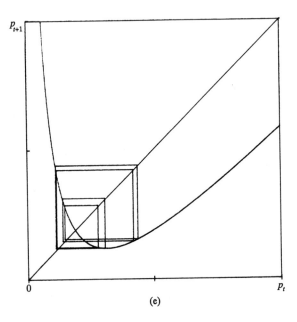

(e)

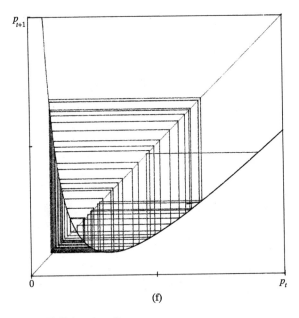

(f)

Figure 10.10 (continued)
Tatonnement for the pure exchange economy. (a) $\bar{x} = 1.0$. (b) $\bar{x} = 1.65$. (c) $\bar{x} = 1.96$. (d) $\bar{x} = 2.04$. (e) $\bar{x} = 2.05$. (f) $\bar{x} = 2.18$ (scale enlarged).

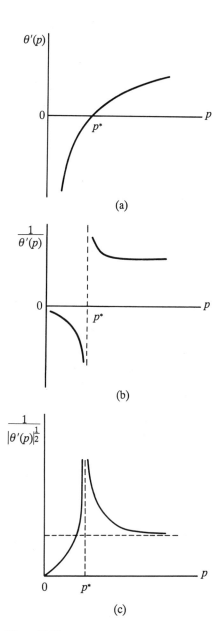

(a)

(b)

(c)

Figure 10.11
The Misiurewicz condition

10.2.2   A Piecewise Linear Economy

A piecewise linear economy provides a convenient heuristic setting to illustrate strongly ergodic price dynamics in a normal market because for certain
special cases density functions can be constructed. Thus, consider the demand
equation

$$D(p) := \begin{cases} a_1, & 0 \le p \le p' \\ a_2 - bp, & p' \le p \le p'' \\ 0, & p'' \le p \end{cases} \tag{10.24}$$

where to preserve continuity $p' = (a_2 - a_1)/b$ and $p'' = a_2/b$. Assume the
supply equation

$$S(p) := \bar{y}, \tag{10.25}$$

where $\bar{y}$ is a positive constant. The Samuelson tatonnement map is

$$\theta(p) := \begin{cases} p + \lambda\mu[a_1 - \bar{y}], & 0 \le p < p' \\ p + \lambda\mu[a_2 - bp - \bar{y}], & p' \le p < p'' \\ p - \lambda\mu\bar{y}, & p'' \le p. \end{cases} \tag{10.26}$$

For illustrative purposes we choose two cases. Both show the same demand,
market strength, and speed of adjustment parameters,

$$a_1 = 3, \quad a_2 = 6, \quad b = 3, \quad p' = 1, \quad p'' = 2, \quad \lambda\mu = 1.$$

But each has a different supply. Thus,

Case I: $\bar{y} = 2$

Case II: $\bar{y} = 1$

The tatonnement process boils down to

$$\text{Case I: } \theta(p) = \begin{cases} 1 + p, & 0 \le p < 1 \\ 2(2 - p), & 1 \le p < 2 \\ p - 2, & 2 \le p \end{cases}$$

$$\text{Case II: } \theta(p) = \begin{cases} 2 + p, & 0 \le p < 1 \\ 5 - 2p, & 1 \le p < 2 \\ p - 1, & 2 \le p \end{cases}$$

You can easily determine that in Case I all trajectories enter the trapping set
[0, 2], and in Case II all trajectories enter the trapping set [1, 3]. These sets are
shown as boxes on the phase diagram in figure 10.12. Case II is a check map
that is isomorphic to the check map example of §8.5.5 (see equation (8.22)),

so we can infer that the density is constant on the intervals $[1, 2]$ and $[2, 3]$ with values respectively of

$$\text{Case II:} \begin{cases} f_1 = \frac{2}{3}, & 1 \le p < 2 \\ f_2 = \frac{1}{3}, & 2 \le p \le 3. \end{cases}$$

Case I is also isomorphic, so we can infer that

$$\text{Case I:} \begin{cases} f_1 = \frac{1}{3}, & 0 \le p < 1 \\ f_2 = \frac{2}{3}, & 1 \le p \le 2. \end{cases}$$

The mean and variances of price trajectories are therefore found to be

Case I: $E(p) = \frac{11}{6}$ $Var = \dfrac{11}{36}$

Case II: $E(p) = \frac{7}{6}$ $Var = \dfrac{11}{36}$

Note that in both cases the Li-Yorke chaos conditions (Theorem 7.2) are satisfied. By Theorem 8.8, almost all trajectories will be chaotic.

Now consider a third case, again with the same parameters as for Cases I and II but with a different supply:

Case III: $\bar{y} = \frac{3}{2}$.

Now

$$\theta(p) = \begin{cases} p + \frac{3}{2}, & 0 \le p < 1 \\ \frac{9}{2} - 2p, & 1 \le p < 2 \\ p - \frac{3}{2}, & 2 \le p \le 3. \end{cases}$$

Here the equilibrium price is $\frac{3}{2}$, but it is unstable since $\theta'(\frac{3}{2}) = -2$. Moreover, every trajectory must enter the interval $S = [\frac{1}{2}, 1]$ or $[2, 2\frac{1}{2}]$. Consider any point, say p in S, $p \in [\frac{1}{2}, 1]$. Then $\theta(p) = p + \frac{3}{2} \in [2, 2\frac{1}{2}]$. Consequently, $\theta(S) = [2, 2\frac{1}{2}]$. But $\theta^2(p) = (p + \frac{3}{2}) - \frac{3}{2} = p$, so $\theta^2(S) = S$. Therefore, every point of S is a fixpoint of $\theta^2(\cdot)$, so every point of S is periodic with period 2. Every trajectory converges in finite time to a two-period cycle.

The measure is atomic. All the long-run density is concentrated on the two cyclic points, each of which occur with relative frequency $\frac{1}{2}$.

Note that the density function is not independent of the initial conditions. Each different initial condition in S (or $\theta(S)$) will lead to a different two-period cycle. The behavior is always cyclic and each cycle is neutrally stable.

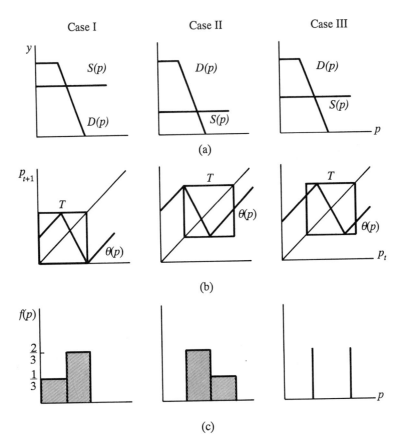

Figure 10.12
Theoretical price densities. (a) Demand and supply. (b) Tatonnement map. (c) Price densities.
Cases I and III are strongly ergodic. Case II is merely ergodic.

No chaos here. This illustrates the great difference between merely ergodic
and strongly ergodic behavior.

Still, the mean and variance can be computed, given convergence to a two-
period cycle with cyclic points x, $x + \frac{3}{2}$.

Case III: $E(p) = x + \frac{3}{4}$, $Var = \frac{9}{16}$.

10.2.2.1 Multiple-Phase Dynamics: Shortages and Gluts

Notice that
these cases all illustrate the phenomenon of multiple-phase dynamics with
phase zones $D^1 = [0, 1)$, $D^2 = [1, 2)$, $D^3 = [2, \infty]$. In D_1 demand is constant,

in D^2 demand is falling, and in D^3 demand is zero. The densities give the fraction of time any trajectory spends in each regime. Think of positive excess demand as a shortage and negative excess demand as a glut. The former occurs for $p < \bar{p}$, the latter for $p > \bar{p}$. Price sequences therefore consist of sequences of shortages and gluts.

The equilibrium prices are

Case I: $\tilde{p} = \frac{4}{3}$,

Case II: $\tilde{p} = \frac{5}{3}$,

Case III: $\tilde{p} = \frac{3}{2}$.

Given the density function derived above, the "chance" of a glut occurring at any future date is

Case I: $\frac{4}{9}$,

Case II: $\frac{5}{9}$,

Case III: $\frac{1}{2}$.

10.3 Normal Markets

The examples in §10.2.2 belong to a general class of normal markets defined by normal demand and supply functions.

10.3.1 Normal Demand and Supply

Demand functions are *normal* that satisfy the following assumptions:

DEFINITION 10.1 *Normal demand functions are those where demand is positive but bounded at zero price, continuous, differentiable for almost all $p > 0$, and monotonically decreasing. Moreover, total revenue touches or approaches zero in the limit. That is,*

$$0 < D(0) < \infty, \tag{10.27a}$$

$$D(p) \geq 0, \ D'(p) \leq 0 \quad \text{for } p \geq 0, \tag{10.27b}$$

$$\lim_{p \to \infty} pD(p) = 0. \tag{10.27c}$$

If all other conditions are satisfied, but $D(0) = \infty$, then demand is called almost normal.

The piecewise linear function (10.24) is an example of normal demand. The demand function in the pure exchange economy (10.15b) and (10.16a) are almost normal.

We call supply functions *normal* that satisfy the following conditions:

DEFINITION 10.2 *Normal supply functions are those where supply is zero below a threshold price $p' \geq 0$. They are continuous, differentiable, and upward-sloping for almost all $p > p'$. Moreover, supply is bounded above. That is,*

$$S(p) = 0, \ 0 \leq p \leq p', \tag{10.28a}$$

$$S'(p) \geq 0, \ p \geq p', \tag{10.28b}$$

$$0 < \sup_{p \geq 0} S(p) = \bar{y} < \infty. \tag{10.28c}$$

If the third condition is not satisfied, then supply is called almost normal.

In both the preceding examples supply was normal.

DEFINITION 10.3 *A commodity with both normal demand and supply functions, such that $D(0) > S(0)$, has a* normal market.

10.3.2 Examples

Examples of functional forms that satisfy the conditions of normal demand and supply are

$$D(p) := \begin{cases} A(a+p)^{-\alpha}(b-p)^{\beta}, & 0 \leq p \leq b \\ 0, & b < p, \end{cases} \tag{10.29}$$

where $0 < \alpha < 1, \beta > 0$, and

$$S(p) := \begin{cases} 0, & 0 \leq p < p' \\ B[1 - e^{-\gamma(p-p')}], & p' \leq p. \end{cases} \tag{10.30}$$

These functions are illustrated in figure 10.13.

Another class of examples is provided by piecewise linear demand and supply. Assume

$$D(p) := \begin{cases} a^i - b^i p, & p^i \leq p < p^{i+1}, \ i = 1, \ldots, m' \\ 0, & p^{m'+1} \leq p \end{cases}$$

with $p^1 = 0$, $p^{m'+1} = a^{m'}/b^{m'}$, and $D(p^{i+1}) = D(p^{i+1})$, so

$$p^{i+1} = \frac{a^{i+1} - a^i}{b^{i+1} - b^i}.$$

Such a market could be composed of market segments, each represented by a linear demand function, or it could be an approximation to a smooth nonlinear curve of the kind given by (10.29) and shown in figure 10.13. Given that each b^i coefficient is positive, demand is strongly downward-sloping, so it is normal but not differentiable at each point p^i.

Suppose supply is also piecewise linear

$$S(p) = \begin{cases} 0, & 0 \le p < q^1, \ i = 0 \\ c^i + d^i p, & q^i \le p < q^{i+1}, \ i = 1, \dots, m'' \\ \bar{y}, & q^{m''+1} \le p \end{cases}$$

with

$$q^{i+1} = -\frac{(c^{i+1} - c^i)}{d^{i+1} - d^i}, \quad i = 1, \dots, m'' - 1$$

and with

$$q^1 = -c^1/d^1 \quad \text{and} \quad q^{m''+1} = (\bar{y} - c^{m''})/d^{m''}.$$

Supply is upward-sloping, except for its first and last segments where the slope is zero. It approximates curves like (10.30) that are illustrated in figure 10.13.

10.3.3 Competitive Equilibrium

In general the conditions for a normal market do not guarantee that the taton-nement map is single-troughed as in the examples shown above. Instead, it can have as many wiggles as there are in the demand and supply curves. In general, the tatonnement map for normal markets can be divided into increasing and decreasing segments in which each increasing segment has a slope

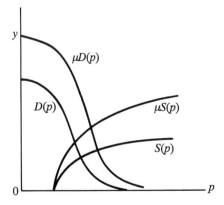

Figure 10.13
Normal markets

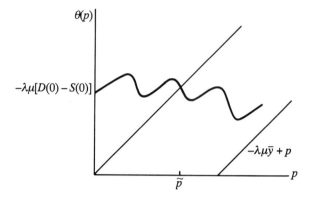

Figure 10.14
General profile for the tatonnement map for normal markets

not greater than 1 and each decreasing segment has a negative slope. Each decreasing segment is followed by an increasing segment and vice versa, except for the last segment which is increasing. The general shape must be like that shown in figure 10.14.

As before, families of demand and supply curves are determined by the market scale parameter μ. Because $D'(p) \leq 0$ and $S'(p) \geq 0$, excess demand is monotonically decreasing, i.e., $e'(p) \leq 0$ wherever the derivative is defined. Moreover, since $D(0) - S(0) > 0$, $\theta_\mu(0) = \lambda\mu[D(0) - S(0)] > 0$. Consequently, $\theta_\mu(p) - p = \lambda\mu e(p)$ begins at a positive value and decreases monotonically. Since $\lim_{p\to\infty} pD(p) = 0$ and $\lim_{p\to\infty} S(p) = \bar{y}$, we get

$$\lim_{p\to\infty} \left[\theta_\mu(p) - p\right] = -\lambda\mu\bar{y}.$$

Therefore, $\theta(p) - p$ changes sign. By Theorem 5.1 there exists a unique competitive equilibrium and stationary state $\tilde{p}$ where $\tilde{p} = \theta_\mu(\tilde{p})$. Multiple equilibria do not occur as in the Walrasian example of §10.1.4.

10.3.4 Stability and Instability

The local stability criterion is

$$-1 < \theta'_\mu(\tilde{p}) = 1 + \lambda\mu\left[D'(\tilde{p}) - S'(\tilde{p})\right] < 1. \tag{10.31}$$

Because demand is downward and supply upward-sloping, the term in brackets is negative, so the local stability criterion reduces to

$$0 < \lambda\mu < \tilde{\sigma} := \frac{-2}{D'(\tilde{p}) - S'(\tilde{p})}. \tag{10.32}$$

For such a $\lambda\mu$, if any price comes close enough to $\tilde{p}$ subsequent prices will converge to the competitive equilibrium. Conversely, if $\lambda\mu$ exceeds σ, $\tilde{p}$ is locally unstable; fluctuations must persist. They are bounded, however, because excess demand is bounded and whenever price becomes large enough, it is adjusted downward. The fluctuations could approach cycles or they could be nonperiodic.

To summarize, we have:

PROPOSITION 10.1   *For Samuelson tatonnement (equation (10.2)) with normal demand and supply functions,*

(i) there exists a unique competitive equilibrium $\tilde{p}$ that is a stationary state of the price adjustment process;

(ii) $\tilde{p}$ is asymptotically stable for all

$$0 \le \lambda\mu < \tilde{\sigma}$$

and unstable for all

$$\lambda\mu > \tilde{\sigma}.$$

In this case fluctuations persist for almost all initial conditions (except those whose orbits end in $\tilde{p}$).

When the competitive equilibrium is unstable and fluctuations persist, various possibilities can occur, including convergence to periodic cycles or nonperiodic fluctuations that are chaotic and strongly ergodic. Let us examine these possibilities.

10.3.5   Chaos

To check for the existence of chaos requires some effort. Assume that $\lambda\mu > \tilde{\sigma}$. Define p^* and p^m by

$$p^m = \theta_\mu(p^*) = \min_{p \ge \tilde{p}} \theta_\mu(p)$$

and note that $p^* > \tilde{p}$. As $\lambda\mu$ gets large, p^m becomes small. For some number σ^0, $p^m = 0$ for $\lambda\mu = \sigma^0$. At this point $\theta(p^m) = \lambda\mu D(0)$. For all $\lambda\mu > \sigma^0$, $p^m = 0$ and p^* is no longer unique but lies in an interval. So as not to introduce extra notation, let p^* be the smallest minimizer of $\theta(p)$.

As $\lambda\mu$ increases above σ^0, p^* approaches $\tilde{p}$ and $\theta(p^m) = \lambda\mu D(0)$ gets large. There are at least two preimages of p^*. There will be at least one below and one above $\tilde{p}$. Choose p^c to be the smallest one greater than $\tilde{p}$. Then as $\lambda\mu$ gets large, $\theta(p^c)$ approaches $\tilde{p}$ from above.

So far we know that $p^m < p^* < p^c$. The Li-Yorke overshoot conditions will be satisfied if $\theta(p^m) = \lambda\mu[D(0) - S(0)] \geq p^c$. Let $\tilde{p}^- = \theta^{-1}(\tilde{p})$ be the smallest preimage of the equilibrium price $\tilde{p}$. Since $p^* \to \tilde{p}$ as $\lambda\mu$ gets large, $p^c \to \tilde{p}^- + \lambda\mu\bar{y}$. Thus, $\theta(p^m) = \lambda\mu[D(0) - S(0)]$ will be greater than p^c if $\lambda\mu D(0) > \tilde{p} + \lambda\mu\bar{y}$. This will be true if $\lambda\mu[D(0) - \bar{y}] > \tilde{p}$ for big enough $\lambda\mu$. But big enough $\lambda\mu$ exist if $D(0) > \bar{y}$. Consequently, the latter is a sufficient condition for chaotic price trajectories in normal markets.

The details of this argument are clarified with the help of the diagrams in figure 10.15. Figure 10.15a shows how the price adjustment function changes as $\lambda\mu$ increases. An example for which the Li-Yorke overshoot conditions are satisfied, but for which chaos exists weakly, is shown in figure 10.15b.

10.3.5.1 Stable Cycles   In general, when $\lambda\mu$ is big enough, all price trajectories must eventually be trapped in the interval $T := \{0, \lambda\mu[D(0) - S(0)]\}$. Suppose 0 and $\lambda\mu[D(0) - S(0)]$ are cyclic as shown in figure 10.15b.

Consider the case for which $\lambda\mu > \mu^c$ and let E be the set of minimizers of θ, that is,

$$E := \{p \mid \theta(p) = 0\}.$$

(Recall that $p^m = 0$ in this case.) This is an interval. Think of it as an escape set E in T. Then the unstable set

$$U = \bigcup_{n=0}^{\infty} \theta^{-n}(E) \cap T$$

has positive Lebesgue measure, which means that prices chosen at random in T must "escape" to the orbit $\omega(0) = \{0, \theta(0), \dots, \}$ with positive probability. Consequently, if p^* is cyclic, then price trajectories with random initial conditions will converge with positive measure to a periodic pattern. Moreover, if there exists a conditionally invariant measure, this result will occur almost surely.

The example of Case III in §10.2.2 illustrates that the local instability of competitive equilibrium does not imply chaos or ergodicity. If there exists a set J for the second iterated map θ^2 on set S with $\theta^{-1}(S) \cap S = \emptyset$ and $J = \theta^{-2}(S) \cap S \neq \emptyset$, such that, for all $p \in J$,

$$|\theta'(p) \cdot \theta'(\theta(p))| < 1,$$

then S must contain an asymptotically stable two-period cycle. If, as in the example of Case III,

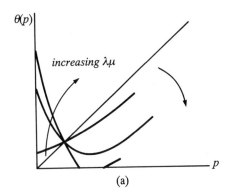

(a)

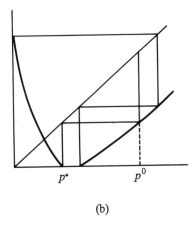

p^* p^0

(b)

Figure 10.15
Changing $\lambda\mu$ in normal markets. (a) Strengthening the market or speeding adjustment. (b) Thin
chaos. Convergence to a 3-cycle almost surely.

$$\left|\theta'(p)\cdot\theta'(\theta(p))\right|=1$$

for all $p\in S$, then all the cycles will be neutrally stable.

In general if there exists a set S for the nth iterated map $\theta^n(\cdot)$ such that for
$k=1,\ldots,n-1$ and

$$\theta^{-k}(S)\cap S=\varnothing \tag{10.33a}$$

$$J=\theta^{-n}(S)\cap S\neq\varnothing. \tag{10.33b}$$

Condition (10.33b) implies that J is an invariant set for the map $\theta^n(\cdot)$ and by the result following Theorem 5.2 contains a fixpoint x that is n-cyclic. Moreover, if

$$\left| \prod_{i=0}^{n-1} \theta'\left(\theta^i(x)\right) \right| < 1, \tag{10.34}$$

this n-cycle (by Theorem 5.8) must be asymptotically stable.

10.3.6 Strongly Ergodic Behavior

We have seen that chaotic trajectories exist but there may exist asymptotically stable cycles, so chaos is "thin" or "weak." For ergodic behavior and strong chaos to exist, an iterate of the Samuelson tatonnement map must be expansive in the sense of Li-Yorke (Theorem 8.4) or, for smooth maps, expansive in the sense of Misiurewicz (Theorem 8.6). We have already presented examples of this kind that satisfy these conditions robustly.

In general the map $\theta(\cdot)$ will be expansive if for almost all $p \in [0, \lambda\mu D(0)]$ there exists a finite m such that $\left|\frac{d\theta^m(p)}{dp}\right| > 1$. Thus, let n be the largest of these values; then $\theta^n(\cdot)$ will be expansive. As we have seen, however, as $\lambda\mu$ increases, this condition will eventually be violated and an "escape set" E will exist. Expansiveness outside E will then guarantee that almost all price trajectories converge to a periodic cycle through zero. The latter case may be far-fetched but could in principle occur, given a fixed tatonnement process.

10.3.7 Summary: Periodic and Nonperiodic Behavior

Without placing much stronger conditions on the demand and supply functions, stronger results than these cannot be given. To summarize, we have:

PROPOSITION 10.2 (Complex Dynamics for Samuelson Tatonnement in Normal Markets)

(i) If $(D(0) - \bar{y}) > 0$, then for some constant $\sigma^c \geq \sigma$ there exist chaotic price adjustment sequences and periodic cycles of all orders for all parameters

$$\lambda\mu \geq \sigma^c.$$

(ii) If for a given value σ^e the price adjustment map satisfies the smooth expansivity conditions of Theorem 8.6 for $\lambda\mu = \sigma^e$, then for all λ and μ such that $\lambda\mu = \sigma^e$, price sequences will be nonperiodic almost surely and strongly ergodic.

(iii) For some large enough constant $\sigma^P > 0$, there will exist a periodic orbit through 0, and for all $\lambda\mu > \sigma^P$, price trajectories with random initial conditions drawn from uniform distribution will be eventually periodic with positive Lebesgue measure.

(iv) If for some $\sigma^e < \sigma^P$ and for some $\delta > 0$ the map $\theta(p)$ satisfies

$$\left| \frac{d\theta^n(p)}{dp} \right| > \delta > 1$$

everywhere except at turning points and

$$p^m = \min_{p \in T} \theta(p) > 0,$$

then Samuelson tatonnement is strongly ergodic generically, i.e., for all $\sigma^e < \lambda\mu < \sigma^P$ relative price frequencies converge to absolutely continuous measures whose densities are continuous almost everywhere.

10.4 Relative Tatonnement

10.4.1 Relative Price Adjustments

In the forms considered so far tatonnement could involve huge absolute price changes in response to rather small percentage changes in excess demand. Such implausible adjustments might be responsible for unstable market dynamics. To eliminate this possibility the price adjustment strategy of the "auctioneer" might make adjustments in percentage terms. Thus, instead of (10.2) he might exploit

$$\frac{p_{t+1} - p_t}{p_t} = \frac{\lambda\mu e(p_t)}{\max\{\mu D(p_t), \mu S(p_t)\}}$$

so that the *proportional change in price* is a multiple of excess demand *as a proportion of the long side of the market*, where the greater of demand and supply is the long side. From this we get the difference equation for the price adjustment process. Taking care to disallow negative prices, it has the form

$$p_{t+1} = \theta(p_t) := \max\left\{ 0, \, p_t + \frac{\lambda e(p_t)p_t}{\max\{D(p_t), S(p_t)\}} \right\}. \tag{10.35}$$

Is this relative tatonnement more or less stable than the "absolute" Samuelson tatonnement?

Notice that the strength of the market parameter, μ, cancels, so proportional changes in demand and supply no longer have an influence. Consider the case of normal supply and demand functions. In this case there is a unique competitive equilibrium $\tilde{p} > 0$, and $D(p) > S(p)$ for $p < \tilde{p}$ and the subsequent price is positive for any price in the interval $[0, \tilde{p})$. Moreover, $D(p) < S(p)$ for $p > \tilde{p}$ and it is for this range that price could become negative. Consequently, the map $\theta(\cdot)$ can be expressed as

$$\theta(p) = \begin{cases} (1 + \lambda)p - \lambda p S(p)/D(p), & p \leq \tilde{p} \\ \max\{0, (1 - \lambda)p + \lambda p D(p)/S(p)\}, & p \geq \tilde{p}. \end{cases} \tag{10.36}$$

10.4.2   The Cone of Price Adjustment

Recall that $S(p) = 0$ for $p \in [0, p']$. Consequently, $\theta(p) = (1 + \lambda)p$ for $p \in [0, p']$. On the interval $[p', \tilde{p}]$, $0 < S(p) \leq D(p)$, so $0 < S(p)/D(p) < 1$. Consequently,

$$(1 + \lambda)p \geq \theta(p) \geq p \quad \text{for } p \in [0, \tilde{p}].$$

Likewise, $1 > D(p)/S(p) > 0$ for $p > \tilde{p}$, and as $\lim_{p \to \infty} pD(p) \to 0$ and $\lim_{p \to \infty} S(p) = \bar{y}$ we have

$$p \geq \theta(p) \geq (1 - \lambda)p, \quad \text{for } p \geq \tilde{p}. \tag{10.37}$$

Moreover,

$$\lim_{p = \infty} \frac{\theta(p)}{p} \to \max\{0, (1 - \lambda)\}. \tag{10.38}$$

Obviously, $\theta(0) = 0$ so the function $\theta(\cdot)$ begins at zero, increases like $(1 + \lambda)p$, but then bends down from this linear relation and crosses the fixpoint $\tilde{p}$ where supply and demand are equal. If $0 < \lambda < 1$, it then approaches the line $(1 - \lambda)p$ asymptotically, or if demand actually touches its bound, reaches $(1 - \lambda)p$ and continues along this line. If $\lambda > 1$, then $\theta(p)$ must eventually reach 0 at some point, say p^0. Then $\theta(p) = 0$ for all $p \geq p^0$.

PROPOSITION 10.3 (The Cone of Relative Price Adjustment)   *Given the relative tatonnement process (10.35), prices belong to the cone of relative price adjustment. That is, prices are bounded by maximum and minimum changes given by*

$$\max\{0, (1 - \lambda)p_t\} \leq \theta(p_t) \leq (1 + \lambda)p_t. \tag{10.39}$$

10.4.3   A Pure Exchange Economy Again

The pure exchange economy used in §10.2.1 offers a good example of the way relative tatonnement modifies the dynamic properties of the price adjustment process in that economy. Given the definition of equations (10.13)–(10.17), the relative tatonnement map is

$$
\theta(p) = \begin{cases} (1+\lambda)p - \lambda\frac{(1-\alpha)\bar{x}}{\beta\bar{y}}p^2, & 0 \le p \le \tilde{p} \\ \max\left\{0, (1-\lambda)p + \lambda\frac{\beta\bar{y}}{(1-\alpha)\bar{x}}\right\}, & p \ge \tilde{p}. \end{cases}
\tag{10.40}
$$

Notice that price cancels in the second term of the second phase structure. Notice also that

$$
\tilde{p} = \frac{\beta\bar{y}}{(1-\alpha)\bar{x}}.
$$

But this term shows up as a coefficient in (10.40). Substituting then, the relative tatonnement process can be written

$$
p_{t+1} = \theta(p_t) := \begin{cases} (1+\lambda)p_t - \frac{\lambda p_t^2}{\tilde{p}}, & 0 \le p_t \le \tilde{p} \\ \max\{0, (1-\lambda)p_t + \lambda\tilde{p}\}, & p_t \ge \tilde{p}. \end{cases}
\tag{10.41}
$$

This simple form results from the facts that the elasticity of supply is zero and the elasticity of demand is -1 and constant everywhere, a direct result of the very special utility function assumed in (10.13).

Evaluated at $\tilde{p}$, we get the stability criterion

$$
\theta'(\tilde{p}) = 1 - \lambda.
$$

Consequently, for $0 < \lambda < 2$, the competitive equilibrium is asymptotically stable. For $0 < \lambda < 1$, prices converge monotonically to $\tilde{p}$. When $1 < \lambda < 2$, they converge cyclically, that is fluctuations emerge near $\tilde{p}$ but dampen out. When $\lambda > 1$, then $\theta(p)$ can fall to zero. Indeed, if the nonnegativity restriction is ignored, negative subsequent prices could occur for any $p > p^0$ where

$$
p^0 = \frac{\lambda}{\lambda - 1}\tilde{p}.
$$

Given this fact, the price adjustment map can be written as

$$
\theta(p) = \begin{cases} (1+\lambda)p - \frac{\lambda p^2}{\tilde{p}}, & 0 \le p \le \tilde{p} \\ (1-\lambda)p + \lambda\tilde{p}, & \tilde{p} \le p \le p^0 \\ 0, & p \ge p^0. \end{cases}
\tag{10.42}
$$

From this we get

$$
\theta'(p) = \begin{cases} 1 + \lambda - 2\lambda p/\tilde{p}, & 0 \le p \le \tilde{p} \\ (1-\lambda)p + \lambda\tilde{p}, & \tilde{p} \le p \le p^0 \\ 0, & p \ge p^0. \end{cases}
\tag{10.43}
$$

For this case, when $\lambda > 1$, the map θ must have a maximum value p^M on the interval $[0, \tilde{p})$. All price trajectories must eventually enter the interval $[q, Q]$ where $q = \theta(p^M)$ and $Q = p^M$. If $p^M \geq p^0$, then $q = 0$.

From (10.43), we find that

$$p^{**} = \frac{1+\lambda}{2\lambda} \tilde{p}$$

and that

$$p^M = \frac{1+\lambda}{2} p^{**} = \frac{(1+\lambda)^2}{4\lambda} \tilde{p}.$$

The value for λ^0 such that $p^M = p_0$ therefore satisfies $(\lambda^0)^3 - 3(\lambda^0)^2 - \lambda^0 - 1 = 0$, or in a convenient form

$$(\lambda^0)^2(\lambda^0 - 3) - (1 + \lambda^0) = 0.$$

From this we conclude that $3 < \lambda^0 < 4$. For any value of $\lambda > \lambda^0$, the Li-Yorke overshoot conditions are satisfied. This can be seen by letting p^c be the smallest of the two preimages of p^{**}. Then $0 = \theta(p^M) < p^c < p^{**} < p^M$. For some $2 < \lambda^c \leq \lambda^0$, they will be true also (by continuity of θ with respect to λ) for all $\lambda > \lambda^c$. Within the range $[\lambda^c, \lambda^0]$ the fluctuations can be strongly or weakly chaotic, depending on λ.

However, when $\lambda > \lambda^0$, there will exist a nonempty escape set E such that $\theta^2(p) = 0$ for all $p \in E$, i.e., for all $p \in E$, $\theta(p)$ belongs to the null domain $D^0 = \backslash(0, p^0)$. As λ increases, the interval E increases and so does $|\theta'(p)|$ for $p \in D \backslash E$. For some large enough λ, say λ^e, $|\theta'(p)| > 1$ for all $p \in D \backslash E$. Therefore, by Theorem 8.8 conditionally invariant measure exists and almost all trajectories converge to zero, although periodic chaotic trajectories and trajectories of all orders exist in principle.

To summarize these findings, for any pure exchange economy ((10.13)–(10.16)), the relative tatonnement process (10.39) can behave in the following ways:

(i) for $0 < \lambda < 1$, monotonic convergence;

(ii) for $1 < \lambda < 2$, fluctuating convergence;

(iii) for $\lambda > 2$, persistent fluctuations (convergent cycles or chaos);

(iv) for some $\lambda^c > 2$, chaotic fluctuations and cycles of all periods exist for all $\lambda > \lambda^c$;

(v) for some $\lambda^0, 3 < \lambda^0 < 4$, trajectories with $p_0 \in [0, p^0]$ converge to zero with positive Lebesgue measure for all $\lambda > \lambda^0$;

(vi) for some $\lambda^e \geq \lambda^0$, trajectories converge to zero almost surely (so fluctuations almost surely disappear and the market self-destructs almost surely).

Although fluctuations, chaos, and self-destruction occur robustly, they occur only when relative price adjustments are more than double the relative excess demand. Thus, for example, a 5 percent change in demand would induce a more than 10 percent change in price. Relative tatonnement is much more stable than absolute tatonnement in this sense. Note that changes in the scale of the market, or variations in endowments, have no influence on the dynamic performance. In short, we could say that, given the very special supply and demand functions implied by power utility functions, stability is "more robust" than instability.

10.4.4   The Piecewise Linear Economy Again

Consider again the example of piecewise linear demand and constant supply in (10.24)–(10.25). With these functions the relative tatonnement process becomes

$$
\theta(p_t) = \begin{cases} [(1+\lambda) - \lambda \bar{y}/a_1] \cdot p_t, & 0 \leq p < p' \\ [(1+\lambda) - \lambda \bar{y}/(a_2 - bp_t)] \cdot p_t, & p' \leq p \leq \tilde{p} \\ [(1-\lambda) + \lambda(a_2 - bp_t)/\bar{y}] \cdot p_t, & \tilde{p} \leq p < p'' \\ \max\{0, (1-\lambda)p_t\}, & p'' \leq p', \end{cases} \tag{10.44}
$$

where $\tilde{p} = [a_2 - \bar{y}]/b$ and $p'' = a_2/b$ (the price at which demand falls to zero). Assume that $a_2 > a_1 > \bar{y} > 0$ and that $p' = (a_2 - a_1)/b$.

The profile of the relative tatonnement map is like that shown in figure 10.16. On the interval $[0, p']$ it is a linear segment. On $[p', \tilde{p}]$ it is a hyperbolic segment, and on $[\tilde{p}, p'']$ it is a quadratic segment. For $p > p''$ it is the linear segment $(1 - \lambda)p$ if $0 < \lambda < 1$, but is identically zero if $\lambda > 1$. The function as specified is continuous and differentiable everywhere (even at $\tilde{p}$) except at p'' where it has a kink.

The derivative of the map $\theta(\cdot)$ is

$$
\theta'(p) = \begin{cases} 1 + \lambda - \lambda \bar{y}/a_1, & 0 \leq p < p' \\ 1 + \lambda - \lambda \bar{y} a_2/(a_2 - bp)^2, & p' \leq p < \tilde{p} \\ 1 - \lambda + \lambda(a_2 - 2bp)/\bar{y}, & \tilde{p} \leq p < p'' \\ \max\{0, 1 - \lambda\}, & p \geq p''. \end{cases} \tag{10.45}
$$

Evaluated at $\tilde{p} = \frac{a_2 - \bar{y}}{b}$,

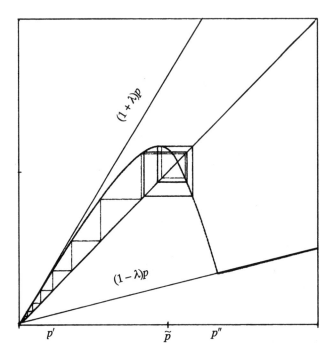

Figure 10.16
Relative tatonnement

$$\theta'(\tilde{p}) = 1 - \lambda \frac{(a_2 - \bar{y})}{\bar{y}}. \tag{10.46}$$

Let $\kappa = \lambda \frac{(a_2 - \bar{y})}{\bar{y}}$. Then competitive equilibrium is asymptotically stable for all

$$0 < \kappa < 2$$

and unstable for all

$$\kappa > 2.$$

Consider the three examples discussed in §10.2.2. Upon calculation we find that

Case I: $\kappa = 2$,

Case II: $\kappa = 5$,

Case III: $\kappa = 3$.

Consequently, competitive equilibrium is unstable in Cases II and III.

An argument along the lines discussed for the pure exchange economy also carries through here. Note that $\theta'(\tilde{p})$ becomes more steeply negative as λ or a_2 increase, or as $\bar{y}$ decreases. One can show also that $\theta'(p')$ becomes steeper and that $\theta(p')$ increases in the same way. The map $\theta(\cdot)$ is concave, which means that the slope of $\theta(p)$ increases as p increases above $\tilde{p}$, which means that p^0 approaches $\tilde{p}$. Indeed, we can show that

$$\theta(p') = \lambda^2(a_2 - a_1)(a_2 - \bar{y} > p^0 = a_1\left[\bar{y} + \lambda(a_1 - \bar{y})\right].$$

It follows that $p^M = \theta(p^{**}) > \theta(p') > p^0$ when a_2 or λ become big enough or $\bar{y}$ small enough. This means that for a big enough a_2 or λ or small enough $\bar{y}$ an escape set exists, such that trajectories converge to zero. By continuity there are smallest such values. (That is, given any two parameters of the three, there is a smallest value of the third with this property.)

In this manner you can show that all the simple and complex dynamics occur. To summarize, for the piecewise linear economy (10.24)–(10.25), the relative tatonnement process (10.42) can behave in the following ways:

(i) for $0 < \kappa < 1$, monotonic convergence to $\tilde{p}$;

(ii) for $1 < \kappa < 2$, dampened fluctuations converging to $\tilde{p}$;

(iii) for $\kappa > 2$, persistent fluctuations or for κ big enough convergence in finite time to $p = 0$.

Suppose $0 < \lambda < 1$. Then for a big enough ratio $a_2/\bar{y}$, there exists a $\kappa^c > 2$ such that

(iv) for all $\kappa > \kappa^c$, chaotic fluctuations and cycles of all order exist; whenever the expansivity conditions of Theorems 8.4 or 8.6 are satisfied, the process will be strongly ergodic.

All of these results can be obtained for absolute tatonnement with piecewise linear demand and supply functions, as can be seen by using a corresponding stability analysis of equation (10.26).

10.4.5 Relative Tatonnement for Normal and for Regular Normal Markets

In general, even for normal markets, the profile of $\theta(\cdot)$ can be very wiggly with upward-sloping intervals (always with $\theta'(p) < 1$) interspersed with downward-sloping ones. (Recall figure 10.14.)

10.4.5.1 Existence, Stability, and Instability of Equilibrium   Nonetheless, given the discussion in §10.4.1, it is clear that a unique competitive equilibrium exists and that its asymptotically stability or instability results can readily be obtained. Thus, we have

$$\theta'(p) = 1 + \lambda - \lambda \frac{S(p)}{D(p)} \left[1 + \eta^S(p) - \eta^D(p) \right],$$ (10.47)

where

$$\eta^D(p) := p \frac{D'(p)}{D(p)} \quad \text{and} \quad \eta^S(p) := p \frac{S'(p)}{S(p)}$$

are the elasticities of demand and supply with respect to price, respectively. Because $D(\tilde{p}) = S(\tilde{p})$,

$$\theta'(\tilde{p}) = 1 - \lambda \left[\eta^S(\tilde{p}) - \eta^D(\tilde{p}) \right].$$ (10.48)

Let $\kappa := \lambda[\eta^S(\tilde{p}) - \eta^D(\tilde{p})]$. When $0 < \kappa < 1$, equilibrium is asymptotically stable, and when $\kappa > 2$ fluctuations persist. Note that for normal demand $\eta^D(p) \leq 0$ for all $p \geq 0$. Thus, for any λ (not necessarily greater than 2) there is a continuum of demand and supply functions for which fluctuations persist, so that asymptotic stability and instability of equilibrium both occur generically. To summarize:

PROPOSITION 10.4   *Relative tatonnement for normal markets exhibits all the forms of simple and complex dynamics: generally, convergence to a unique competitive equilibrium, convergence to periodic cycles, chaos, strong chaos, and self-destruction.*

10.5 Summary

Using the concepts of stability, chaos, and ergodicity, we found that all the basic kinds of simple and complex dynamics occur in the Walrasian formulation of the competitive price adjustment process. For any reasonable demand and supply functions, a sufficiently slow adjustment speed can produce convergence to a competitive equilibrium. But the slower the adjustment speed, the longer it will take for markets to clear even approximately; and the faster the adjustment speed, the more likely is instability. And for *any* adjustment coefficient, no matter how small, there exist perfectly reasonable demand and supply systems that will not converge—in the absolute Samuelson case when the extent of the market is large enough, or in the relative case when the elasticity of either demand or supply or both together is sufficiently large. It is important to note also that even in the convergent case, equilibrium is only approached. In general it is not reached in finite time, it can only be approximated.

Thus, one can say that whenever the tatonnement process begins out of equilibrium, disequilibrium persists indefinitely almost surely, either because convergence does not take place or because it is only asymptotic.

Suppose then that price is not a stationary state. There will be a positive excess demand or supply. Some desired purchases or sales, therefore, cannot be consummated. What happens then to the excess supply? And what happens to individuals who cannot satisfy their demands at going prices? These problems do not arise in equilibrium; they do arise out of it.

The traditional explanation is that participants in a given market adjust their price and quantity offers until an equilibrium occurs and then exchange their goods and money. But as markets almost surely do not clear in finite time, this is a far from satisfactory explanation. Evidently, the original tatonnement mechanism, while capturing the spirit of competitive market adjustments, cannot fully represent an actual marketing process.[7]

Nonetheless, what has been learned from studying its dynamic properties is still of use, for with slight modification of the mechanism itself, the difficulties can be surmounted. This modification is to introduce explicit market mediation.

11 Market Mediation

Price announcements and arrangements for transactions in flex price markets, such as metals, grains or financial assets, are made by trade specialists of some sort, such as brokers, dealers or middlemen.
—Clower and Friedman, "Trade Specialists and Money in an Ongoing Exchange Economy"[1]

In the real world, transactions are rarely made directly between the producers and consumers of goods, and only in special markets are prices arrived at through a bidding process. Instead, transactions are most often mediated by retailers and wholesalers and by merchants, brokers, or trading specialists. Sometimes these "middle men" supply demanders out of inventory at announced prices and then replenish inventories by purchasing from suppliers, again at an announced price. Such *market mediators* adjust prices in response to changes in inventory that reflect excess demand or supply. This is the case with retail stores for most consumer goods, for fuels such as petroleum and coal, for various kinds of tools and machinery used in farming and industry. In such markets inventories are goods on display in stores or available on order through catalogs from wholesale distributors. Suppliers and demanders do not bargain with each other or with the middleman; they simply carry out their desired actions given the current price (and whatever expectations they may have about the future). They then modify their actions in response to whatever prices are announced as time passes. The merchant must, of course, invest in this inventory, earn a wage on his management of it and a reasonable rate of return on the capital invested.[2]

The market mediation process can be given a mathematical form within the tatonnement framework merely by adding a marketing fee in the form of a price markup and by keeping track of the mediator's inventories and wealth to see if outages or bankruptcy occurs. This chapter explores such a model, first in general terms and then for a particular market; one designed to mimic the market for equities, i.e., the "stock market."

One may ask, why will individuals purchase from a mediator at a price above the supply price? The answer lies in the transaction costs associated with exchange, which consist of the time and energy required to identify, bargain, and renegotiate terms with prospective traders, and the opportunity returns if that time and energy were expended on other pursuits. Such costs are generally very high.

The importance of the mediation model is that purchases and sales can occur in real time even though supply and demand are out of balance at prevailing prices; the market can work out of equilibrium period after period, under favorable conditions, indefinitely.

The dynamics of the pricing mechanism is essentially the same as before except for the introduction of a new price markup parameter that can influence the process. Three new considerations are relevant, however. First, is mediation profitable for the mediator and under what conditions of stability and instability? Second, can inventory outages occur, i.e., could excess demand exceed supply plus inventories so that not all desired purchases of demanders could be consummated? Third, could the mediator experience a kind of gambler's ruin; that is, could he go into bankruptcy and could this happen in finite time even if mediation is profitable on average?

11.1 Price Adjustment with a Market Mediator

11.1.1 Mediator Tatonnement

Let us recast the tatonnement model, then, so that it incorporates mediation. There are Demanders and Suppliers as before and now a Mediator. We assume that the Mediator purchases from Suppliers at an announced price and marks this price up by a fraction v for sales to Demanders. Suppliers, therefore, receive p per unit and supply $\mu S(p)$. Demanders pay $(1 + v)p$ and purchase $\mu D_v(p) := \mu D[(1 + v)p]$, where μ is the market strength or extent of the market as before. Demanders and Suppliers belong to separate groups and both demand and supply must be nonnegative. The parameter v is called the *markup* and $(1 + v)p$ the *markup price*. It shall be assumed that v is a constant.

The Mediator's inventory at the beginning of period t is s_t. Sales to Demanders reduce inventory, and purchases from Suppliers increase inventories. Inventories change, therefore, by the amount of excess supply ($= -$ excess demand),

$$s_{t+1} - s_t = -e_v(p_t) = -\mu [D_v(p_t) - S(p_t)]. \tag{11.1}$$

The mediator does not know the demand or supply functions nor does he know the price where they are equated. He adjusts his price in response to the change in inventories, which he does observe. Thus, he sets

$$p_{t+1} = p_t - \lambda(s_{t+1} - s_t). \tag{11.2}$$

Again, taking care that prices cannot be negative, and using (11.1), the price adjustment process is in effect the same as equation (10.2) with $D_v(\cdot)$ replacing $D(\cdot)$. That is,

$$p_{t+1} = \theta(p_t) := \max\{0, p_t + \lambda\mu[D_v(p_t) - S(p_t)]\}. \tag{11.3}$$

I shall call this process *mediator tatonnement*. (If v is zero, the process reduces to the standard Walrasian form.) Recall that λ is a coefficient indicating the "speed" or magnitude of price adjustment.

The stability analysis is changed very little except that the local stability criterion is now

$$\theta'(\tilde{p}) = 1 + \lambda\mu\left[(1+v)D'[(1+v)\tilde{p}] - S'(\tilde{p})\right]. \tag{11.4}$$

If we retain the assumptions that demand and supply are normal, all the arguments of Propositions 10.1 and 10.2 apply.

11.1.2 Relative Mediator Tatonnement

For *relative mediator tatonnement* the adjustment equation is

$$p_{t+1} = \theta(p_t) := \max\left\{0, p_t + \frac{\lambda e_v(p_t)p_t}{\max\{D_v(p_t), S(p_t)\}}\right\} \tag{11.5}$$

with stability criterion

$$\theta'(\tilde{p}) = 1 - \lambda\left[\eta^S(\tilde{p}) - \eta_v^D(\tilde{p})\right], \tag{11.6}$$

where $\tilde{\eta}_v^D = (1+v)\tilde{p}D'\left[(1+v)\tilde{p}\right]/D_v(\tilde{p})$ and $\tilde{\eta}^S = \tilde{p}S'(\tilde{p})/S(\tilde{p})$. Then, *ceteris paribus*, Propositions 10.3–10.4 hold analogously.

11.1.3 Simple and Complex Price Dynamics

In short, anything can happen in the market mediation processes. Prices may converge to a market-clearing equilibrium or they may not. Periodic cycles may emerge or nonperiodic fluctuations. It all depends on the profiles of demand and supply, on the mediator's price markup, and on the strength or speed of his response to inventory changes. Moreover, as parameters of the underlying structural relationships change, those that appear in the supply and demand functions or that govern specialist behavior, the qualitative behavior will also change, perhaps in a complex way.

For the record then, we have:

PROPOSITION 11.1 *For normal demand and supply functions both* mediator tatonnement (11.3) *and* relative mediator tatonnement (11.5) *have the following properties:*

(i) a unique nonnegative stationary state $\bar{p}$ exists;

(ii) for a "robust" range of parameter values, the process converges to a market-clearing equilibrium;

(iii) for a robust range of parameter values, the process exhibits cyclic or chaotic price sequences;

(iv) when the price adjustment map $\theta(\cdot)$ satisfies Theorem 8.4 or Theorem 8.6, then the price adjustment process is strongly chaotic.

All of this suggests the possibility that a part of the explanation for real world market instabilities is the intrinsic working of the market mechanism itself. Additional irregularities may be engendered by changes in other variables. These could come from other markets and prices whose endogenous working interacts with the market under consideration. They could also come from "exogenous" shocks produced by forces "outside" the market system but which impinge on it in some well-defined way, such as by shifting price expectations. The bifurcation diagrams for mediator tatonnement and relative mediator tatonnement would be similar to those given in chapter 10, and give a hint of the kinds of changes such additional variables could cause, not only shifting behavior at any given time, but shifting from one qualitative type to another, sometimes engendering asymptotically stable adjustments, then stimulating a shift to cycles or to chaos.

11.2 Viable Mediation

11.2.1 Inventories

For market mediation to work indefinitely, the mediator must have at any one time a sufficiently large initial inventory to cover the largest excess demand that can occur. Over time, the accumulation of inventories when excess supply occurs must replenish the decumulation that occurs during periods of excess demand. If excess demand exceeds supply plus inventory, then some desired transactions cannot be executed. An *outage* is said to occur.

11.2.1.1 Mediator Tatonnement Consider the mediator tatonnement first. Using (11.2) recursively and taking the sum of the sequence of terms

on both sides, we find that

$$s_{t+1} = s_0 - \frac{1}{\lambda}(p_{t+1} - p_0),$$

or

$$s_t = s_0 - \frac{1}{\lambda}\left(\theta^t(p_0) - p_0\right).$$ (11.7)

The question of concern is, will s_t be nonnegative for all t?

To answer this we recall that the price adjustment process is bounded and that eventually prices will lie in a trapping set given by an interval $[q, Q]$. That is, for any $p_t \geq 0$,

$$\limsup_{t\to\infty} \theta^t(p) = Q$$ (11.8a)

$$\liminf_{t\to\infty} \theta^t(p) = q,$$ (11.8b)

and for any $p \in [q, Q]$, $\theta^t(p) \in [q, Q]$. Consequently,

$$\limsup_{t\to\infty} |\theta^t(p) - p| \leq Q - q.$$

Combining this with (11.7), therefore, we find that for all $p \in [q, Q]$

$$s_0 \geq \frac{1}{\lambda}(Q - q) \text{ implies } s_t \geq 0 \quad \text{for all } t.$$

If $p_0 > Q$, then supply exceeds demand and inventories increase until $[q, Q]$ is entered, so there is no problem. If $p_0 < q$, then demand exceeds supply, but in view of (11.8b), this can only happen for a finite number of periods. Let $p_0 = 0$ and let m be the smallest value of t, such that $\theta^m(0) > q$. Let

$$s^m = \sum_{i=1}^{m} e(p_i).$$ (11.9)

This is the amount of inventory that must be available initially until prices enter the trapping set. Consequently, if

$$s_0 > \frac{1}{\lambda}(Q - q) + s^m,$$

no outage will occur. This implies that the slower the speed of adjustment, the wider the *range* of long-run price variation, and the more prices are perturbed below the range of long-run variations, the greater initial inventories must be to prevent an outage.

11.2.1.2 Relative Mediator Tatonnement   Now consider the same issue for relative mediator tatonnement. Start with the percentage adjustment equation (11.5) in the form

$$\frac{p_{t+1} - p_t}{p_t} = \max \left\{ -1, \frac{\lambda e(p_t)}{\max\{D_v(p_t), S(p_t)\}} \right\}. \tag{11.10}$$

Eventually, after big enough t, $q < p_t < Q$. We shall here confine ourselves only to the case where $0 < \lambda < 1$, so $q > 0$, and so that the system does not self-destruct in the sense that price goes to zero even though demand is positive there. Therefore,

$$\frac{p_{t+1} - p_t}{Q} \leq \frac{p_{t+1} - p_t}{p_t} \leq \frac{p_{t+1} - p_t}{q}. \tag{11.11}$$

Note also that

$$\tilde{y} \leq \max\{D_v(p), S(p)\} \leq \bar{Y} := \max\{D_v(0), \bar{y}\}, \quad \text{for all} \quad p \geq 0.$$

Therefore,

$$\frac{\lambda e(p_t)}{\bar{Y}} \leq \frac{\lambda e(p_t)}{\max\{D_v(p_t), S(p_t)\}} < \frac{\lambda e(p_t)}{\tilde{y}},$$

or, using the definition $s_{t+1} - s_t = -e(p_t)$,

$$\frac{-\lambda(s_{t+1} - s_t)}{\bar{Y}} \leq \frac{-\lambda(s_{t+1} - s_t)}{\max\{D_v(p_t), S(p_t)\}} \leq \frac{-\lambda(s_{t+1} - s_t)}{\tilde{y}}. \tag{11.12}$$

But the middle of this expression equals the middle expression of (11.11). Therefore,

$$-\lambda \frac{(s_{t+1} - s_t)}{\bar{Y}} \leq \frac{p_{t+1} - p_t}{q}.$$

Summing both sides for $t = 0, \dots, n$ and simplifying, we get

$$\frac{-\lambda(s_{n+1} - s_0)}{\bar{Y}} \leq \frac{p_{n+1} - p_0}{q},$$

but as $p_{n+1} - p_0 < Q - q$ for all n, this translates into the inequality

$$s_{n+1} \geq s_0 - \frac{\bar{Y}}{\lambda} \frac{(Q - q)}{q}.$$

Define s^m as in (11.9). Then if

$$s_0 \geq s^m + \frac{\bar{Y}}{\lambda} \frac{(Q - q)}{q},$$

no outage will occur.

In a manner analogous to absolute mediator tatonnement, the slower the speed of adjustment, the wider the *relative* range of long-run price variation, the greater the bounds on demand and supply, and the closer the initial price to zero, then the greater the initial inventory must be to prevent an outage.

11.2.2 Profits and Cash Reserves

The profits of the market mediator, as for any business enterprise, consist of the sales revenues less business costs. For the mediator revenues are a function, say $R_v(p)$, of the price and the markup defined by

$$R_v(p) := (1 + v)p\mu D_v(p).$$

Costs include the expenditure on inventory accumulation, which is given by $\mu p S(p)$ each period, the cost of carrying inventory, and the cost of the mediation process itself. Suppose as a crude approximation that these latter costs do not vary with sales but constitute a fixed overhead cost per period in amount H. Then the total cost of mediation is

$$C(p) := \mu p S(p) + H.$$

Gross profit is then

$$\pi_v(p) := R_v(p) - C(p) \equiv v\mu p D_v(p) + \mu p e(p) - H.$$

See figure 11.1.

Let there be a stationary state $\tilde{p}$ at which supply and demand are equal. Then $e(\tilde{p}) = 0$, so

$$\pi_v(\tilde{p}) = v\mu \tilde{p} D_v(\tilde{p}) - H.$$

Consequently, the mediator makes a profit if and only if $v\mu \tilde{p} D_v(\tilde{p}) \geq H$, which will occur if the extent of the market is great enough, i.e., if and only if

$$\mu \geq H / \left[v\tilde{p} D_v(\tilde{p}) \right]. \tag{11.13}$$

If the market is out of equilibrium but the price converges to $\tilde{p}$, then $\pi(p_t) \to \pi(\tilde{p})$, so if $\pi(\tilde{p}) > 0$, then

$$\lim_{t \to \infty} \inf \pi(p_t) > 0. \tag{11.14}$$

What (11.14) means is that for any p_0, there exists a finite smallest integer, say

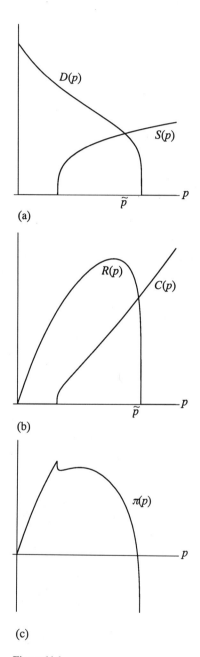

(a)

(b)

(c)

Figure 11.1
Revenue, cost, and profits of mediation. (a) Demand and supply. (b) Revenue and cost. (c) Cost.

m, such that $\pi(p_t) > 0$ for all $t \geq m$ (depending on p_0). That is, profits must eventually be positive.

The cash reserve of the firm, say w_t, is given by

$$w_{t+1} = w_t + \pi(p_t) = w_0 + \sum_{n=0}^{t} \pi(p_n).$$

If the firm's initial reserve is sufficiently great, it will remain nonnegative forever. Indeed, it must eventually grow. If dividends are built into the overhead term, then, as $p_t \to \tilde{p}$, they can be adjusted so that

$$\lim_{t \to \infty} \pi(p_t) = 0,$$

in which case the cash reserve remains at a constant level. To sustain the overhead for any p_0, the initial wealth must be equal to

$$w_0 > - \sum_{t=0}^{m-1} \pi[\theta^n(p_0)],$$

where m is the smallest integer that gives positive profits. Note that w_0 depends on p_0. Consequently, if p_0 is far from equilibrium and the convergence is slow, bankruptcy could occur unless the initial cash reserve is large.

A similar analysis applies for asymptotically stable cycles. Let q be n-cyclic. Then $\gamma(q) = \{q, \theta(q), \ldots, \theta^{n-1}(q)\}$ is an n-period cycle. In general profits will rise and fall over the cycle. The average profit over the cycle is

$$\tilde{\pi}^n := \frac{1}{n} \sum_{i=0}^{n-1} \pi[\theta^i(q)].$$

If the n-period orbit $\gamma(q)$ is asymptotically stable, then

$$\lim_{t \to \infty} \theta^{nt}(p_0) = \theta^i(q)$$

for some $i \in \{0, \ldots, n-1\}$. Then

$$\lim_{t \to \infty} \frac{1}{n} \sum_{i=t}^{t+n-1} \pi(p_i) \to \tilde{\pi}^n.$$

Therefore, for any p_0 there is a smallest nonnegative integer m such that if

$$w_0 > - \sum_{i=0}^{m} \pi(p_i)$$

then

$$w_t > 0 \quad \text{for all} \quad t.$$

For chaotic trajectories the situation is complicated by the fact that prices do not converge to a finite orbit. Nonetheless, a corresponding result exists for any ergodic process. For such processes, the mean profit exists. Thus, suppose

$$E(\pi) = \lim_{t \to \infty} \frac{1}{t} \sum_{i-1}^{t} \pi(p_i) > 0.$$

Consider the cash reserve at any time averaged over t years,

$$\frac{1}{t} w_{t+1} = \frac{1}{t} w_0 + \frac{1}{t} \sum_{i=0}^{t} \pi \left[\theta(p_i) \right].$$

Taking the limit as $t \to \infty$, we find that

$$\lim_{t \to \infty} \frac{1}{t} w_{t+1} = \lim_{t \to \infty} \frac{1}{t} \sum \pi \left[\theta^i(p_0) \right] > 0. \tag{11.15}$$

But this implies that for each p_0 there exists a smallest time T, such that $w_t > 0$ for all $t \geq T$.

The worst capital loss the firm can experience until time T is reached, for any initial p_0 and w_0, is given by

$$w^m = \min_{0 \leq s \leq T} \sum_{i=0}^{s} \pi[\theta^i(p_0)]. \tag{11.16}$$

Consequently, if $w^0 > w^m$, then $w_t > 0$ for all t.

Note that (11.15) implies that the cash reserve grows without bound. However, if dividends are incorporated into overhead and adjusted upward to absorb the accumulated profit, then the cash reserve will be bounded.

To sum up these findings, we can state that if a given price adjustment process is ergodic (which includes convergence to a stationary state or cycle) and if the statistical expectation of profit is positive, then there exists a large enough initial wealth such that the market mediator can sustain his costs and pay a positive dividend indefinitely.

11.2.3 Viability

If a process can work indefinitely, it is *viable*. It is clear that the viability of the mediator or relative mediator framework depends on profitability, cash reserves, and inventory.

To summarize, we have:

PROPOSITION 11.2   *The market mediator or relative mediator tatonnement process is viable if and only if*

(i) it is profitable on average;

(ii) initial cash reserves are large enough;

(iii) initial inventories are large enough.

In the previous chapter examples of strongly ergodic pricing processes were given. With suitable modification some of these can be used to illustrate the findings just obtained. Rather than do this here, we shall develop a rather elaborate example that is designed to mimic salient features of an especially interesting actual marketing process.

11.3   The Stock Market

11.3.1   Some Stylized Facts

Markets for corporate equities, especially the New York Stock Exchange, work something like the mediator tatonnement process.

Individual buyers and sellers of ownership shares do not trade directly with one another. Instead, they place orders with local broker representatives or financial consultants who in turn place orders with a floor trader or licensed broker to buy or sell either at specified prices or at whatever is the current price. These orders are recorded by a specialist who is charged with the responsibility of "maintaining an orderly market" in a particular stock. He adjusts announced prices in response to differences in the amount of purchase and sell orders, buying and selling out of his inventory as necessary so as to prevent excessive changes in price that could be required if it were necessary to clear the market at every moment. This representative-broker-specialist hierarchy constitutes the mediation system, which shall be represented here by a single stylized "market maker."

Stock prices have two striking characteristics that suggest the presence of complex dynamics. First, stock prices fluctuate in a highly irregular manner. Second, they generate alternating regimes called "bull" and "bear" markets that switch from one to the other at irregular intervals. The terms "bull" and "bear" are financial market lingo for periods of trading that can be described as follows. In the bull markets prices move upward for some time accompanied by relatively steep "pullbacks," with higher transaction volumes near the highs. Fluctuations are irregular and can be superimposed on a rising trend. Conversely, in the bear markets prices trend downward with relatively steep "snapups" in price. The fluctuations are generally irregular and can be superimposed on a falling medium-term trend, although over many decades the trend of prices has been positive.

In the remainder of this chapter the theory of mediator tatonnement will be used to generate dynamic behavior like these stylized facts.[3]

11.3.2 A Stylized Market

We shall imagine a "stylized market" for shares of a giant holding company of all corporations that in effect provides shares in the private sector as a whole. The *current fundamental value* of each share of the holding company, say v_t, is the present value of current earnings based on its most recent quarterly report, capitalized at the current interest rate plus risk factor, divided by the number of outstanding shares.[4] Stocks almost never trade at such a value. Instead, they trade at a *current market price*, say p_t, which is set by the specialist. As we shall see, it reflects investors' expectations about the future and the aggregate forces of market supply and demand. The current fundamental value reflects the current profit as determined by the private sector's recent actual performance, which is the result of current business conditions throughout the various production and service sectors of the economy.

In addition to the specialist, our stylized market has two basic types of investor who will be called α- and β-*investors*, each type using a distinct buy/sell strategy. In reality there are a great many strategies used by market participants. Two, however, are sufficient for the purpose of giving a theoretical explanation of the stylized facts summarized above entirely in terms of intrinsic market behavior.

The actual stock market is always in motion. Prices are almost always increasing or decreasing. We shall assume here that both types of investors perceive this reality. Their problem is to take advantage of these price movements to increase their income and wealth. Unfortunately, future prices are not known and are more or less unpredictable. They must decide what to do in a situation of great uncertainty. Each type of investor follows a very different strategy in response to this situation. Consider the two types of investor in turn.

11.3.3 α-Investors

Despite the fact that market prices fluctuate above and below the current fundamental value, α-investors believe that over the long-run the average prices must reflect fundamental values. These future fundamental values, of course, are not known and have to be estimated. With respect to a future horizon of from several quarters to several years, α-investors calculate the *investment value u* of the stock.[5] It is the *stock's worth at present if estimated long-run economic conditions actually came to dominate the future.* If profits and financial conditions are expected to improve, the investment value will be above the current fundamental value; if conditions are expected to deteriorate, investment value will be less than current fundamental value. The estimate of future performance is based on statistical analyses of trends in aggregate economic variables, industry data, individual company performances, and so on. These quantitative estimates are then augmented by judgments based on political and economic opinions expressed in newspaper articles, weekly magazines, business journals, etc., interviews with business managers, direct observations of company operations, general impressions based on travel, various forms of "brain picking," and so on. All of this is used to form an estimate of future earnings and financial conditions so that the "future fundamental value" can be anticipated.

α-Investors attempt to incorporate the most recent information into their estimates of u, which can, of course, change drastically because of technological breakthroughs, inventions, altered political conditions, natural and human disasters, and so forth. Because germane events may occur almost randomly, the investment value is likely to be volatile, perhaps changing even on a daily basis. This volatility depends upon the weight given current events by the individual and is a reflection of the subjective aspect of the process. In contrast to the investment value, the current fundamental value v changes only quarterly. It is what the stock would be worth if its most recent earnings and financial position were used as the basis of the valuation.

We will abstract from these important "external" perturbations and imagine a situation in which the estimate of u is unchanging over time. This will absolve us from describing the process for determining u and enable us to isolate the contribution of internal forces to the overall process.

A comparison between the investment value and the current price serves as the basis of the α-investor's strategy. If market price exceeds the investment value, the stock is "overpriced." Conversely, if investment value exceeds the market price the stock is "underpriced." If p is less than u, a capital gain can be expected. The lower p, the greater is the perceived chance it will rise and the better a bargain is the stock. As it approaches an anticipated *bottoming price* p^B, this subjective or anticipated chance of capital gain approaches certainty.

If the decision to buy is delayed and if the price does subsequently rise, then the investor will miss the opportunity for a high capital gain and—at best— have to settle for a lower one. The situation is reversed if $p > u$. Then it is a capital loss that must be feared. The higher p, the more it is overpriced and the greater the perceived chance of incurring a capital loss if one delays to sell. As it approaches an estimated *topping price* p^T, this chance becomes a certainty. If p is close to u then the chance for gain or loss is perceived to be modest, so there is little to be gained or lost by buying or selling.

Given these considerations, the α-investor strategy is to weight the current "spread," $p - u$, by the chance of capital gain or loss, which is zero when $p = u$ and rises to unity when $p = p^B$ or p^T. I assume that the α-strategy is to buy or sell in proportion to the product of these terms. Denote the α-investor's buy/sell strategy by $\alpha(p)$. Given the description above, $\alpha(p)$ has a constant positive value, say A, for a price below the bottoming price (because a capital gain is expected with certainty); it falls monotonically as p increases and becomes zero at $p = u$. That is, when the current price is just equal to the investment value, α-investors hold their positions. As p increases above u, α-investors sell, so $\alpha(p)$ becomes increasingly negative. At a price above the topping price, sales are constant at A.

To summarize, when the price is below the investment value, investors are net buyers of shares. When price is above, they are net sellers of shares; when market price equals investment value investors simply hold their current stocks and excess demand is zero. Formally, $\alpha(p)$ has the following properties:

$$\alpha(p) = A, \quad \alpha'(p) = 0, \quad p \le p^B, \tag{11.17a}$$

$$\alpha(p) > 0, \quad \alpha'(p) \le 0, \quad p^B < p < u, \tag{11.17b}$$

$$\alpha(u) = 0, \quad \alpha'(u) = 0, \quad p = u, \tag{11.17c}$$

$$\alpha(p) < 0, \quad \alpha'(p) \le 0, \quad u < p < p^T, \tag{11.17d}$$

$$\alpha(p) = -A, \quad \alpha'(p) = 0, \quad p \ge p^T. \tag{11.17e}$$

A function with these properties is shown in figure 11.2.

11.3.3.1 Short- and Long-Term α-Investors

Investors may have very different time horizons that could lead to quite different excess demands. Short-term investors who don't take into account long-run trends but only very near-term conditions are called traders. Their guesses for u might be close to v but be strongly influenced by current shocks. Their anticipated spread between p^B and p^T might be rather narrow. They try to make money from short-

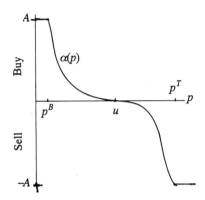

Figure 11.2
The α-investor's strategy

term price changes that take place over a few hours, days, or weeks. They buy and sell frequently, jumping in and out of the market. Long term α-investors take into account longer trends. They anticipate investment values that could be much higher—or lower—than v and think in terms of a very much wider spread between p^B and p^T. They are patient for anticipated price movements to materialize and are content to make money over the long term, usually entering and exiting at infrequent intervals of months or even years.

The sum of all such investors is what we have in mind for the function $\alpha(p)$. It would have a wiggly shape and be downward sloping between upper and lower bounds. To keep our analysis as simple as possible, however, we shall assume that all α-investors are alike, and that $|\alpha(p)|$ is convex and symmetric on the interval $[p^B, p^T]$. This gives a curve that satisfies the properties in (11.17) as illustrated in figure 11.2.

11.3.4 β-Investors

The behavior of α-investors is expensive: it takes time, uses costly information, and requires substantial investment in intellectual and computational capital. Most market participants can't afford to pursue behavior of this kind *and in reality they do not*. The great majority, whom we call β-investors, instead use relatively simple rules and relatively low-cost advice. In particular many investors and many investment advisors (broker representatives and financial consultants) base their expectations on an extrapolation of a current price and fundamental value. For this purpose the spread $p - v$ can be taken as a signal of the future price. When it is positive, the "market" is projecting a rising trend; when it is negative, the "market" is projecting a falling trend. The rule is to buy into a rising (bull) market and sell into a falling (bear) market, which is captured by the β-strategy, denoted by $\beta(p)$ where

$$\beta'(p) > 0 \quad \text{and} \quad \beta(v) = 0. \tag{11.18}$$

Given this form,

$$\beta(p_{t+1}) \cong \beta(p_t) + \beta'(p_t)(p_{t+1} - p_t),$$

where $\beta'(p)$ reflects the relative importance of β-investors and the strength of their response to price signals. This form, which is illustrated in figure 11.3, implies that changes in β-investor demand are positively correlated with changes in price. In the interest of simplicity, we assume that all β-investors are alike and their strategies conform to (11.18).[6]

11.3.5 Market Mediation

As in the abstract model of markets with mediation introduced earlier in this chapter, the market mediator—here, the specialist—sets the price, and at this price supplies demand from inventory and accumulates inventory from supply. His primary function is to dampen excessively volatile price movements. To do this, he must be prepared to mediate transactions out of equilibrium, that is, to "make the market" in financial parlance, when the demand exceeds supply, or vice versa.[7]

In this market the α- and β-investors can be suppliers or demanders, depending on current economic conditions and anticipations. Correspondingly, aggregate excess demand consists of the sum of the buy and sell orders for α- and β-investors,

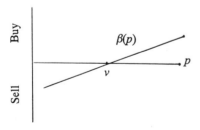

Figure 11.3
The β-investor's strategy

$$e(p) := \alpha(p) + \beta(p).\qquad(11.19)$$

For simplicity, it is assumed that all α-investors are alike and that all β-investors are alike. Also, to simplify the analysis we suppose that the market maker announces a price at fixed intervals of time, say daily or hourly. He then executes orders at that announced price. An excess of orders to buy over orders to sell then appears as a reduction of his inventory. Negative excess demand is the same as positive excess supply and appears as an accumulation of inventory.

To keep inventory in balance is essential because excess buying will exhaust the market maker's financial resources and excess selling will exhaust his inventory. Consequently, he adjusts his price from period to period so as to balance his holdings over time while at the same time moderating his response so as not to destabilize the market excessively in the process. But this is just the mediator tatonnement of §§13.1–13.2 operating in "real" or market time with exchanges occurring out of equilibrium through the facilitating medium of stock inventories and mediator wealth.

The mediator pricing strategy is, therefore,

$$\theta(p) := \max\{0,\, p + \lambda[\alpha(p) + \beta(p)]\},\qquad(11.20)$$

which, taking account of the specifications on $\alpha(\cdot)$ and $\beta(\cdot)$, has the profiles of the types shown in figure 11.4.[8]

11.3.6 Background Assumptions

In addition to the characteristics of α- and β-investors described so far, two additional background assumptions will be made. First, we shall assume that a flow of α-investors exit the market. Their assets are distributed to new β-investors who enter in a steady flow. The latter replace those β-investors who learn how to become α-investors and those who go bankrupt or get discouraged and abandon the stock market permanently. We shall assume these flows are just enough to keep the aggregate market excess demand function at a fixed profile. Second, we shall examine the dynamics of the market when the parameters u and v are constant and equal, and when the parameters p^B and p^T that enter the α-investor's strategy are constant. Given these assumptions, the dynamics of the process are tractable using the tools of analysis in the present volume. Of course, for a complete theory of the market and for empirical work, these assumptions must be relaxed and relationships added to the theory that incorporate other variables. More general studies that move in this

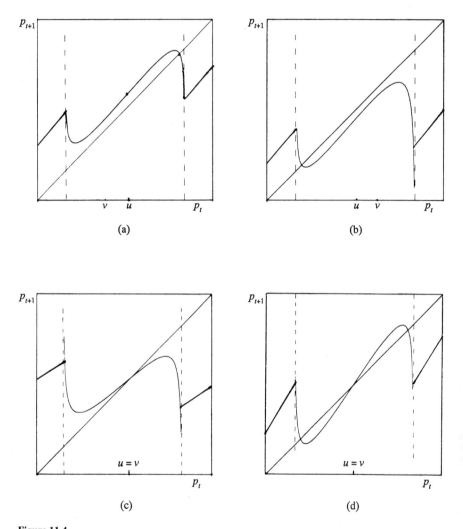

Figure 11.4
The price adjustment function. (a) Bullish market. (b) Bearish market. (c) Efficient market. (d) Churning market.

direction are undertaken elsewhere. Our task here is to see what insights are gained from the simplified framework that falls within the scope of analysis to which this book is limited.

11.4   Numerical Experiments

11.4.1   The Investment Strategies

For illustrative purposes choose the α-strategy to be

$$\alpha(p) := \begin{cases} A^+, & p < p^B \\ a(u-p)k(p-p^B+\epsilon)^{-c}(p^T+\epsilon-p)^{-c}, & p^B \leq p \leq p^T \\ A^-, & p > p^T, \end{cases} \qquad (11.21)$$

where $A^+ = a(u - p^B)k$, $A^- = a(u - p^T)k$, $k = \epsilon^c(p^T - p^B + \epsilon)^c$, and $0 < c < 1$, and let the β-strategy be

$$\beta(p) := b(p - v). \qquad (11.22)$$

The parameters a and b give the strengths of the two types of investors in the market.

These were the functions used for illustration in figures 11.2–11.4.[9]

11.4.2   Simulated Price Trajectories

Figure 11.5 illustrates the mechanics of price adjustment with the parameter values used to construct figures 11.2, 11.3, and 11.4d. In this experiment the initial price, p_0, is just above the fundamental value so β-investors enter what they perceive to be a rising, bull market. They create an excess aggregate demand because α-investors have little fear of a capital loss at this point. The market maker sells from inventory and adjusts the price upward. A sequence of such price increases is driven by the bullish behavior of β-investors until the price gets close enough to p^T that α-investors sell in sufficient amounts to create an excess supply. The market maker is forced to accumulate, so he pulls the price down. The pullback is relatively minor, however, on this first runup. Later runups may be longer (or shorter) and the fallbacks greater or less. Cycles of varying period and amplitude occur as excess demand alternates in sign, generating the characteristics of a bull market as described above. Eventually, however, the price comes very close to the anticipated topping price; α-investors sell in so large an amount that the market mediator is induced to drop the price drastically, thus precipitating a bear market.

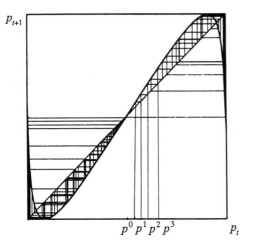

Figure 11.5
Simulated stock price dynamics. Source: Day and Huang (1990, 311).

A time series of prices generated by the model would not look exactly like a typical stock market series, but bear in mind that all of the coefficients have been held constant. In the real world these parameters would actually be variables. In particular, v would change with the business cycle around the general growth trend of the economy as a whole and u would also fluctuate, possibly in a volatile manner in response both to real and monetary changes in the economy and to news events and public opinion bearing on future investment value in the manner explained above. The α-investors would also adjust their values of p^B and p^T and, perhaps, even the coefficients ϵ and c in an effort to take into account the effect of various kinds of news on the behavior of other market participants. You should also keep in mind that in the highly simplified model, the intrinsic forces are exaggerated and stand out more boldly than in the real world, where a myriad of distinctions among individual investors exist and where a complex hierarchy of mediation is at work.

Nonetheless, numerical market simulation exhibits two salient features of real stock market data, namely, irregular fluctuations and randomly switching bear and bull markets.

11.4.3   Statistical Characterizations

Do the data generated by the simulation behave like a stochastic process? To answer this question, it is necessary to view the process over a very long number of periods.

For this purpose the model solution was generated for 10,000 periods. The histogram of prices is shown in figure 11.6. Given the assumed parameters, it would appear to approximate a trimodal density function with modes at the long-run equilibrium, $u = v$, and at the topping and bottoming prices, p^B and p^T. But notice also that prices are distributed throughout the interval $[q, Q]$.

Imagine now that our stylized market is open a total of 240 days per year divided into months of 20 open days. To see what happens to the data when they are averaged over time, we computed 5-, 20-, 60-, and 240-day averages corresponding to stylized market "weeks," "months," "quarters," and "years" and plotted the histograms for each average price series in figure 11.7. As the number of days averaged is increased, the distribution changes drastically. The histogram for 5-day averages has a roughly trimodal shape. The 20-day averages are also roughly trimodal but with very "fat" modes. The 60- and 240-day averages begin to suggest a normal, bell-shaped curve.

As we know from chapters 2 and 8 and from Theorem 8.8, this progression is the kind of thing one expects to obtain from a strongly ergodic process: if you average n data points, each independently sampled from a fixed distribution of whatever shape, and do this m times, the distribution of averages will approach normality as m and n become large. This also is what one expects from a stationary stochastic process. The data used here, however, are not gen-

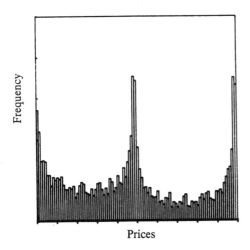

Prices

Figure 11.6
Histogram of simulated prices. Source: Day and Huang (1990, 313).

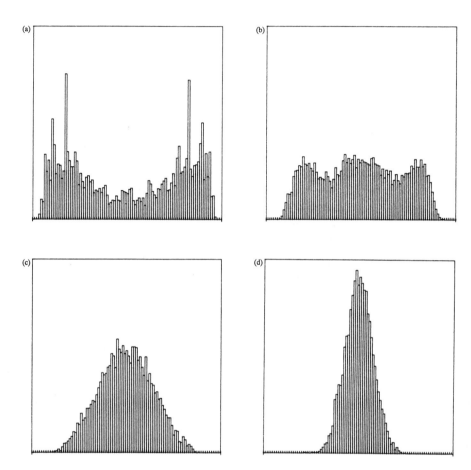

Figure 11.7
Histograms of price averages. (a) 5 days. (b) 20 days. (c) 60 days. (d) 240 days. Source: Day and
Huang (1990, 314–315).

erated by a stationary stochastic process but by a deterministic process given
by equations (11.20)–(11.22).

11.5   Theoretical Analysis

11.5.1   Stationary States and Competitive Equilibria

Suppose that price is stationary at a level p. Then

$$e(p) = \alpha(p) + \beta(p) = 0, \tag{11.23}$$

so that the excess α-investor demand (supply) just equals excess β-investor
supply (demand). If $p \neq v$, then $\beta(p) \neq 0$ so $\alpha(p) \neq 0$. Given (11.18), it
follows that $p \neq u$. In a recurrent market at such a point the stock inventories
of the mediator would be constant. To sustain such a point, the inflow of
β-investors would have to just balance the outflow of α-investors. This is a
kind of steady state, but it is not a true equilibrium because the assumption
that $u \neq p$ is inconsistent with a stationary value of p. Investors are in full
equilibrium only if $\alpha(p) = 0$, which implies that $p = u$. Likewise sheep are
in equilibrium only if $\beta(p) = 0$, which implies that $p = v$. Consequently, we
have:

*A stationary state of mediator tatonnement is a competitive market equilibrium
if and only if the market price = current fundamental value = investment
value, $\tilde{p} = v = u$. Such an equilibrium is unique.*

Given the properties of $\alpha(\cdot)$ listed in (11.17), it is easy to see that there are
at least two other stationary states p^l and p^u, which will be called *artificial
equilibria*, one below v and one above v. These satisfy (11.23) but $p^l \neq v$ and
$p^u \neq v$.

11.5.2   Unstable Fluctuations and Switching Regimes

The local stability criterion at the equilibrium $\tilde{p}$ is

$$\theta'(\tilde{p}) = |1 + \lambda[\alpha'(\tilde{p}) + \beta'(\tilde{p})]|. \tag{11.24}$$

By assumption $\alpha'(\tilde{p}) = 0$ and $\beta'(\tilde{p}) > 0$ so $\theta'(\tilde{p}) = 1 + \beta'(\tilde{p}) > 1$. We therefore have:

*The competitive equilibrium price $\tilde{p}$ is unstable for all positive λ. Moreover,
price increases or decreases monotonically near $\tilde{p}$.*

Denote by p^m and p^M the smallest and largest prices respectively that the mediator will set inside the interval $[p^B, p^T]$. That is, let

$$p^m := \min_{p \in [p^B, v]} \theta(p) \quad \text{and} \quad p^M := \max_{p \in [v, p^T]} \theta(p). \quad (11.25)$$

Assume that

$$\theta(p^m) > p^m \quad \text{and} \quad \theta(p^M) < p^M. \quad (11.26)$$

Then $Z := [p^m, p^M]$ is a trapping set. Once the price enters Z it will stay there indefinitely. Limiting the trapping set in this way insures that the price adjustment process is globally stable. Other possibilities are not without interest, but we shall confine our attention to the globally stable case where the market can "work" indefinitely.

Now let $Z^b := [p^m, v)$ and $Z^B := (v, p^M]$ and call these the *bear* and *bull zones*, respectively. The restriction of θ to these zones, θ_{Z^b} and θ_{Z^B}, gives bear and bull phase structures, while the pairs (θ_{Z^b}, Z^b) and (θ_{Z^B}, Z^B) are *bear* and *bull regimes*. For completeness call $(\theta_{\{v\}}, \{v\})$ the *market equilibrium regime*.

Given our assumptions about Z, we have $Z = Z^b \cup \{v\} \cup Z^B$ and there exist exactly two artificial equilibria $p^l \in Z^b$ and $p^u \in Z^B$. As remarked above, these can't be competitive equilibria. They are technical stationary states of the model, but only in the sense that v and u are held constant for our present purpose of purely theoretical analysis. Moreover, by similar reasoning prices can't remain in either the bear or the bull zone indefinitely because that too would be inconsistent with the assumption that u and v are constant.

To prevent convergence to the artificial equilibria, p^l and p^u must be unstable, that is,

$$\alpha'(p) < -2/\lambda - \beta'(p) \quad \text{for} \quad p = p^l \quad \text{and} \quad p^u \quad (11.27)$$

By assumption, $\alpha'(p) \leq 0$ and $\beta'(p) > 0$, so both sides of these expressions are negative. It is clear that for any λ if $|\alpha'(p)|$ is sufficiently big near p^m or p^M, then p^l and p^u are locally unstable. Moreover, if

$$\alpha'(p) < -\beta(p) \quad \text{for} \quad p = p^l \quad \text{and} \quad p^u \quad (11.28)$$

then for λ large enough, p^l and p^u are unstable. Given these conditions, then, prices can't converge to artificial equilibria.

To make it possible not to get stuck in either bull or bear regimes, there has to exist a price $p \in Z^b$ that jumps into Z^B, and vice versa. This requires that

$$\theta(p^m) > v > \theta(p^M). \quad (11.29)$$

Given these *switching conditions*, there exist nonempty *escape zones*

$$G := \theta^{-1}[v, \theta(p^m)] \subset Z^b, \qquad H := \theta^{-1}[\theta(p^M), v]. \tag{11.30}$$

By construction if $p \in G$ then $\theta(p) \in Z^B$ and if $p \in H$ then $\theta(p) \in Z^b$.

Now construct the sets of all points that map into these escape zones from within them. These are, respectively,

$$\mathcal{G} := \cup_{n=0}^{\infty} \theta_{Z^b}^{-n}(G) \qquad \text{and} \qquad \mathcal{H} := \cup_{n=0}^{\infty} \theta_{Z^B}^{-n}(H). \tag{11.31}$$

The sets $\theta^{-n}(G)$ and $\theta^{-n}(H)$ are the prices within the bear and bull regimes, respectively, that escape in n periods. That is, they give the set of prices in Z^b and Z^B that lead to a switch in regime after n trading periods. Each is the union of disjoint intervals of finite length. Their unions have the same structure, so

$$0 < \frac{\lambda(\mathcal{G})}{|v - p^m|} \leq 1 \qquad \text{and} \qquad 0 < \frac{\lambda(\mathcal{H})}{|v - p^M|} \leq 1, \tag{11.32}$$

where here $\lambda(\cdot)$ means Lebesgue measure. Consequently, for initial conditions drawn at random in Z^b according to a rectangular distribution, the probability of switching to a bull market is $\lambda(\mathcal{G})/(\bar{p} - q)$ while the probability of switching from bull to bear markets given $p \in Z^b$ is $\lambda(\mathcal{H})/(Q - \bar{p})$.

11.5.3   Chaos and Ergodicity

If θ is expansive on $Z^b \setminus G$ and $Z^B \setminus H$, then θ is *conditionally expansive* and, using Theorem 8.9, there exist conditionally invariant measures μ_b and μ_B defined on Z^b and Z^B, such that

$$\mu_b(\mathcal{G}) = 1 = \mu_B(\mathcal{H}), \tag{11.33}$$

that is, switching from bear to bull or bull to bear markets occurs *almost surely* and prices will fluctuate within and between regimes indefinitely.

When the switching conditions (11.29) hold, it is easy to see that the Li-Yorke conditions for chaos hold. Moreover, given the Misiurewicz smooth expansivity conditions of Theorem 8.6, then there exists an absolutely continuous invariant (probability) measure for θ defined on Z and the central limit Theorem 8.9 holds. All this is summarized in the following:

PROPOSITION 11.3   *Given the switching conditions (11.29),*

(i) there exists an uncountable scrambled set $S \subset Z$ (with positive continuous measure) such that for all initial prices $p_0 \in S$ the price trajectories are

chaotic and switch bull and bear regimes at nonperiodic intervals. Moreover, there exist periodic price trajectories of all periodicities;

(ii) if $\theta(\cdot)$ is conditionally expansive on $Z^b \setminus G$ and $Z^B \setminus H$, then for almost all $p_0 \in Z$ regime switching occurs indefinitely;

(iii) if θ satisfies the smooth strong ergodicity conditions on Z as in Theorem 8.6, or if $\theta(\cdot)$ is expansive in the sense of Theorem 8.4, then for almost all initial conditions

(a) the cumulative distribution of prices converges to a unique, absolutely continuous, invariant, ergodic measure $\mu(\cdot)$ such that

$$\mu(S) = \int_S f(p)dp \qquad \text{for all} \qquad S \subset Z,$$

where $f(\cdot)$ is an integrable function, and where $\mu(S)$ gives the relative frequencies of prices in the interval of set S;

(b) price averages obey the central limit theorem;

(c) price trajectories display the appearance of deceptive order, that is, they pass close to cycles of varying periodicities but move away from any such order;

(iv) these results occur generically; that is, for a continuum of parameter values.

The properties of this theorem are all reflected in the numerical experiments of §11.4.

11.6   A Piecewise Linear Example

11.6.1   Model Components

A piecewise linear version of the theory is of interest because it allows for a concrete characterization of the statistical aspects of model behavior. In addition to the parameters already defined, two additional sensitivity thresholds $\underline{p}$ and $\bar{p}$ are specified, such that

$$p^B < \underline{p} < u < \bar{p} < p^T. \tag{11.34}$$

These thresholds determine when α-investors are active or inactive. In the interval $[\underline{p}, \bar{p}]$ α-investors hold their current positions. If $p \in [p^B, \underline{p}]$, they buy; if $p \in [\bar{p}, p^T]$, they sell. As before, the parameters p^B and p^T indicate the prices below and above which prices are expected to rise or fall almost certainly.

Given these parameters, the α-strategy is

$$
\alpha(p) := \begin{cases}
A, & p \le p^B \\
a(\underline{p} - p), & p^B \le p \le \underline{p} \\
0, & \underline{p} \le p \le \bar{p} \\
-a(p - \bar{p}), & \bar{p} \le p \le p^T \\
-A, & p^T \le p,
\end{cases}
\tag{11.35}
$$

where $A = a(\underline{p} - p^B) = a(p^T - \bar{p})$ and where the parameter a is the strength of α-investor demand. Consequently, $\underline{p} - p^B = p^T - \bar{p}$. Also, $a(\underline{p} - u) = a(u - \bar{p})$. Consequently, α-demand is *skew symmetric* about the investment value u, $\alpha(u + q) = -\alpha(u - q)$. Let the β-strategy be the same as in the previous example, i.e., equation (11.21). Substituting into the mediator tatonnement equation (11.10), and remembering that $u = v$, the price adjustment equation becomes

$$
p_{t+1} = \theta(p_t) := \begin{cases}
k_1 + \rho p_t, & p_t \le p^B \\
k_2 - \pi p_t, & p^B < p \le \underline{p} \\
k_3 + \rho p_t, & \underline{p} < p \le \bar{p} \\
k_4 - \pi p_t, & \bar{p} \le p \le p^T \\
k_5 + \rho p_t, & p^T < p,
\end{cases}
\tag{11.36}
$$

where the several coefficients are

$\rho = 1 + \lambda b$

$\pi = \lambda(a - b) - 1$

$k_1 = \lambda(A - bv)$

$k_2 = \lambda(a\underline{p} - bv)$

$k_3 = -\lambda bv$

$k_4 = \lambda(a\bar{p} - bv)$

$k_5 = -\lambda(A + bv).$

These basic model components are illustrated in figure 11.8.

11.6.2   Switching Bear and Bull Regimes and Irregular Price Fluctuations

As in the earlier example, the long-run equilibrium $\tilde{p} = u = v$ is unstable for all $\lambda, b > 0$. Two artificial equilibria also exist:

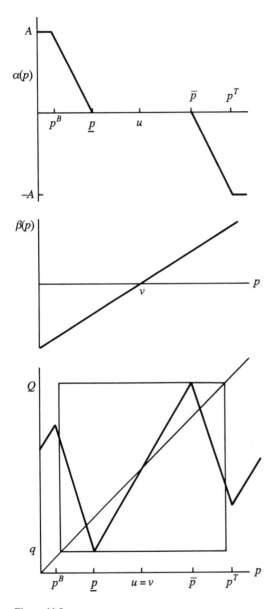

Figure 11.8
The piecewise linear model

$$\tilde{p}^l = \frac{bv - a\underline{p}}{b - a} \quad \text{and} \quad \tilde{p}^u = \frac{bv - a\bar{p}}{b + a}. \tag{11.37}$$

These are unstable if

$$a - b > 2/\lambda. \tag{11.38}$$

To make it possible for both bull and bear regimes to occur, we assume the switching condition (11.29). Also, to preclude interesting but globally unstable cases, assume condition (11.26). Then all price trajectories that begin in the interval $Z = [p^m, p^M]$ remain there, so this interval is a trapping set. But (11.38) implies that θ is expansive on Z, so, by Theorems 8.4, 8.7, and 8.8, this implies:

PROPOSITION 11.4   *Given conditions (11.26) and (11.38), the piecewise linear model (11.34)–(11.36) exhibits all of the properties of Proposition 11.3.*

Figure 11.8c provides a graph of the mediator tatonnement map given by equation(11.36) that satisfies these assumptions. In the diagram the map also satisfies the conditions

$$p^m = \theta(\underline{p}) = q \geq p^B \quad \text{and} \quad p^M = \theta(\bar{p}) = Q \leq p^T. \tag{11.39}$$

11.6.3 Constructing Price Densities

In the discussion of statistical dynamics in chapter 8, piecewise linear dynamical systems were used to illustrate the construction of price densities. Similar examples were given in chapter 10 for Walrasian tatonnement, which we know can apply to mediator tatonnement as well. In these earlier cases crucial use was made of the assumption that the turning points of the map $\theta(\cdot)$ were cyclic. The same technique can be used here. The resulting densities have insightful interpretations, so we shall devote some attention to their derivation.

To simplify this process, assume in addition to (11.26) and (11.38) that conditions (11.39) hold. Assume also that the boundary points q and Q are cycles of period $2m$ where m is a positive integer, such that

$$q = \theta^m(Q), \dots, \theta^2(Q), \theta(Q), \theta(q), \theta^2(q), \dots, \theta^m(q) = Q.$$

Given these assumptions, the trapping set $Z = [q, Q]$ can be divided into $2m$

disjoint intervals $I_i, J_i, i = 1, \ldots, m$ given by

$$
\begin{aligned}
I_1 &= \left[\theta^m(Q), \theta^{m-1}(Q)\right), & J_1 &= \left(\theta^{m-1}(q), \theta^m(q)\right] \\
I_2 &= \left[\theta^{m-1}(Q), \theta^{m-2}(Q)\right), & J_2 &= \left(\theta^{m-2}(q), \theta^{m-1}(q)\right]
\end{aligned}
$$

$$\vdots$$

$$
\begin{aligned}
I_{m-1} &= \left[\theta^2(Q), \theta(Q)\right), & J_{m-1} &= \left(\theta(q), \theta^2(q)\right] \\
I_m &= \left[\theta(Q), v\right), & J_m &= \left(v, \theta(q)\right].
\end{aligned}
$$

Let the width $\lambda(I_i)$ of any interval I_i be denoted ℓ_i. Because θ is skew symmetric around v, we have

$$\lambda(I_i) = \ell_i = \lambda(J_i), \quad i = 1, \ldots, m.$$

It is easy to show that

$$\ell_{i+1} = \frac{1}{\rho}\ell_i, \quad \text{or} \quad \ell_i = \left(\frac{1}{\rho}\right)^{i-1}\ell_1, \quad i = 1, \ldots, m-1. \tag{11.40}$$

Of course,

$$\ell_1 = (\underline{p} - q) \quad \text{and} \quad \ell_m = v - \theta(Q). \tag{11.41}$$

In previous settings where the densities for a dynamical system were constructed, it was surmised that the densities were step functions with constant steps on the intervals determined by the points of the cyclic orbit through the turning points. It is reasonable to suppose in this case that a similar result holds and, in view of the skew symmetry of $\theta(\cdot)$ about v, that the density function $f(p)$ will be symmetric. That is, we guess that

$$f(p) = \phi_i, \quad p \in I_i \cup J_i \tag{11.42}$$

for $i = 1, \ldots, m$. This implies that the unique, absolutely continuous, invariant, ergodic measure $\mu(\cdot)$ has the property that

$$\mu(I_i) = \mu(J_i) = \phi_i \ell_i \tag{11.43}$$

and in view of symmetry that

$$2\sum_{i=1}^m \mu(I_i) = 2\sum_{i=1}^m \phi_i \ell_i = 1. \tag{11.44}$$

The measure $\mu(\cdot)$ whose density function $f(\cdot)$ we are looking for is invariant, which means that

$$\mu(I_i) = \mu\left[\theta^{-1}(I_i)\right], \quad i = 1, \ldots, m.$$

If $\mu(\cdot)$ must be absolutely continuous, then

$$\int_{I_i} f(p)dp = \int_{\theta^{-1}(I_i)} f(p)dp, \quad i = 1, \ldots, m. \tag{11.45}$$

The same can be said for J_i. The sets I_i and J_i are intervals. However, $\theta^{-1}(I_i)$ is comprised of two intervals for $i = 1, \ldots, m-1$ and three intervals for $i = m$. By carefully noting how these intervals are formed, equation (11.45) can be reexpressed in a concrete form.

From (11.43) we get

$$\mu(I_i) = \int_{I_i} f(p)dp = \phi_i \ell_i, \quad i = 1, \ldots, m.$$

Now consider $\theta^{-1}(I_i)$. All the points of I_2 map into I_1, so $\theta^{-1}(I_1) \supset I_2$. An interval of points in I_1 also maps into I_1. The length of I_1 is ℓ_1 and the length of the interval that maps into I_1 must be of length ℓ_1/π. Consequently,

$$\phi_1 \ell_1 = \mu\left[\theta^{-1}(I_1)\right] = \mu\left[\theta^{-1}(I_1)\right] = \phi_2 \ell_2 + \phi_1 \ell_1/\pi.$$

In like manner we find that

$$\phi_i \ell_i = \phi_{i+1}\ell_{i+1} + \phi_1\ell_i/\pi, \quad i = 1, \ldots, m-1. \tag{11.46}$$

In the case of I_m, parts of three intervals I_1, I_m, and J_1 map into I_m. The width of the intervals in I_1 and J_1 is ℓ_m/π. The length of the part of I_m that maps into I_m is ℓ_m/ρ. Consequently,

$$\phi_m \ell_m = \phi_m \ell_m/\rho + 2\phi_1 \ell_m/\phi. \tag{11.47}$$

Substituting $\ell_{i+1} = \frac{1}{\rho}\ell_i$ from equation (11.40) into (1.46) and canceling the lengths ℓ_i, $i = 1, \ldots, m$ in (11.46)–(11.47), we find that

$$\phi_i = \frac{1}{\rho}\phi_{i+1} + \frac{1}{\pi}\phi_1, \quad i = 1, \ldots, m-1 \tag{11.48a}$$

$$\phi_m = \frac{1}{\rho}\phi_m + \frac{1}{\pi}\phi_1, \tag{11.48b}$$

which gives m equations in the m unknowns $\phi_1, \ldots, \phi_m$.

The first $m-1$ of these rearranged gives

$$\phi_{i+1} = \rho[\phi_i - \frac{1}{\pi}\phi_1], \quad i = 1, \ldots, m-1. \tag{11.49}$$

Solving recursively yields

$$\phi_2 = \rho[1 - \frac{1}{\pi}]\phi_1$$

$$\vdots$$

$$\phi_j = \left[\rho^{j-1} - \frac{1}{\pi}\sum_{i=1}^{j-1}\rho^i\right]\phi_1 \tag{11.50}$$

$$\phi_m = \left[\rho^{m-1} - \frac{1}{\pi}\sum_{i=1}^{m-1}\rho^i\right]\phi_1.$$

Substituting these expressions into (11.44) and using (11.40), we find that

$$\phi_1\ell_1 + \sum_{j=1}^{m-1}\left[\rho^{j-1} - \frac{1}{\pi}\sum_{i=1}^{j-1}\rho^i\right]\frac{\ell_1\phi_1}{\rho^{j-1}} = \frac{1}{2},$$

or, rearranging,

$$\phi_1 = \frac{1}{2}\left\{m\ell_1 - \frac{\ell_1}{\pi}\sum_{j=2}^{m-1}\sum_{i=1}^{j-1}\rho^{1+i-j}\right\}^{-1} \cdot \frac{1}{2}, \tag{11.51}$$

where ℓ_1 given by (11.41).

Consequently, the density function is

$$f(p) = \sum_{i=1}^{m}\phi_i\chi_{I_i\cup J_i}(p), \tag{11.52}$$

where the parameters ϕ_i and the intervals I_i and J_i, $i = 1, \ldots, m$ are determined by the parameters of α-demand: $a, \underline{p}, \bar{p}, p^B, p^T, u$; β-demand: a, b; and market maker behavior: λ.

From (11.44) it is clear that

$$\ell_1 > \ell_2 > \cdots > \ell_{m-1}.$$

Moreover, we can show that $\phi_{j+1} > \phi_j$. To see this, first observe that

$$\pi\ell_1 = \sum_{i=1}^{m}\ell_i + \ell_m = \ell_1 + \sum_{i=2}^{m-1}\ell_i + 2\ell_m$$

and that

$$\rho \sum_{i=2}^{m-1} \ell_i = \sum_{i=1}^{m} \ell_i.$$

On rearranging and substituting we find that

$$\rho(\pi - 1)\ell_1 = \rho \sum_{i=2}^{m-1} \ell_i + 2\ell_m$$

$$= \pi\ell_1 + \ell_{m+1}.$$

From this it follows that

$$\rho(1 - \frac{1}{\pi}) > 1.$$

Consequently, from (11.49),

$$\phi_2 > \phi_1.$$

Suppose $\phi_i > \phi_{i-1}$. From (11.48),

$$\phi_{i+1} - \phi_i = \rho(\phi_i - \frac{1}{\pi}\phi_1) - \rho(\phi_{i-1} - \frac{1}{\pi}\phi_1)$$

$$= \rho(\phi_i - \phi_{i-1}) > 0.$$

By induction,

$$\phi_{i+1} > \phi_i, \quad i = 1, \ldots, m - 1.$$

This means that the density function has increasing steps from q to v and decreasing steps from v to Q.

Combining equation (11.48a) and the last equation in (11.50) gives

$$\pi = \rho^{1-m}\left[\frac{2\rho}{\rho - 1} + \sum_{i=1}^{m} \rho^i\right]. \tag{11.53}$$

This restriction applies in this special case where the turning points $\underline{p}$ and $\bar{p}$ are cyclic with period $2m$. It means that given ρ and m, there is a unique value for π that will give $2m$ periodicity for q and Q.

Summing up our findings, we have:

PROPOSITION 11.5   *Given the piecewise linear model described by (11.34)–(11.36) and for any integer $m \geq 1$,*

(i) p and $\bar{p}$ belong to a cyclic orbit of period $2m$ for all values of π and ρ satisfying equation (11.53);

(ii) all the results of Proposition 11.3 hold;

(iii) the absolutely continuous invariant ergodic measure to which the relative frequencies of prices in the trajectory converge almost surely is

$$f(p) := \phi_i, \quad p \in I_i \cup I_j, \ i = 1, \ldots, m,$$

where the intervals I_i and I_j are given in (11.41) and the constants ϕ_i are given by (11.50) and (11.51);

(iv) moreover,

$$\phi_1 < \phi_2 < \cdots < \phi_m$$

and

$$\ell_1 > \ell_2 > \cdots > \ell_{m-1},$$

where $\ell_i = \lambda(I_i) = \lambda(J_i), i = 1, \ldots, m - 1$.

As a corollary, if $m = 1$, then

$$f(p) \equiv \frac{1}{Q - q}, \quad p \in (q, Q),$$

that is, $f(\cdot)$ is the rectangular (uniform) density.

Recalling that $\rho = 1 + \lambda b$ and that $\pi = \lambda(a - b) - 1 = \lambda a - \rho$, equation (11.52) means that given m and given values for any two of $\{a, b, \lambda\}$, there is a unique value of the third that satisfies (11.52). This fact enables you to construct examples satisfying the theorem. In figure 11.9 five cases are shown.

11.7   Viability

11.7.1   The General Case

Although the strategy of β-investors yields a demand for stocks that is non-normal, the results of proposition 11.2 still hold. Consider profitability first. Suppose the mediator charges buyers and sellers a commission consisting of a "bid/ask spread" of ψ "points." This constitutes a positive flow regardless of whether the market is rising or falling and at any time t consists of the amount $\psi[|\alpha(p_t)| + |\beta(p_t)|]$. The value of stock purchases minus the value of stock sales presents a capital gain or loss in amount $p_t e(p_t)$. Supposing that the cost

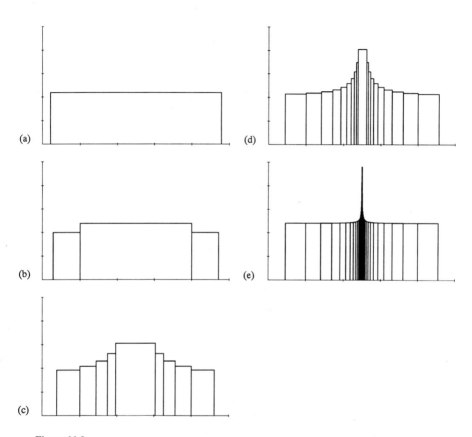

Figure 11.9
Density functions for the stock price adjustment process. (a) $m = 2$; (b) $m = 4$; (c) $m = 10$; (d) $m = 20$; (e) $m = 40$. Source: Gu (1991, 40).

of mediation is a fixed amount (for simplicity), say H, the profit consists of

$$\pi(p_t) = \psi\left[|\alpha(p_t)| + |\beta(p_t)|\right] + p_t e(p_t) - H.$$

If

$$Epe(p) > -\psi E\left[|\alpha(p)| + |\beta(p)|\right] - H,$$

then $E(\pi(p)) > 0$ and mediation is profitable on average. Under these conditions wealth can accumulate. If initial wealth is great enough, the market maker will not experience gambler's ruin.

The argument that inventories will balance out on average is identical to that for the general process discussed in §11.2. Together with the above results, we can assert the following:

PROPOSITION 11.6   *Given that the market maker pricing process is ergodic, it is viable if and only if*

(i) it is profitable on average;

(ii) initial cash reserves are large enough;

(iii) initial inventories are large enough.

11.8 Summary

Market mediation provides a mechanism that—in addition to lowering transaction costs—makes it possible for decentralized exchange to take place out of a competitive equilibrium when demand and supply are not in balance at the current price. The process may or may not be viable, however. If initial inventories are inadequate, an outage may occur. Some orders could not then be filled. Or, if initial cash reserves are insufficient, the mediator can experience gambler's ruin or bankruptcy. He would then not have enough cash to cover costs.

Entrepreneurs know (or find out) that one of the greatest hazards of a venture is undercapitalization, i.e., inadequate physical and financial capital. For the merchant, undercapitalization means inadequate inventory and cash reserves. Experience shows that many firms in reality fail for these reasons. The moral is that effective operation of decentralized exchange through mediators requires adequate capitalization. If outages or bankruptcy occur, new investment must occur to reinitialize the process. Such outages or bankruptcy need not be the result of managerial incompetence, but rather the result of intrinsic market forces of demand and supply.

12 Financial Feedback

The problem that we are about to consider arises from the fact that supply adjusts itself to a given market situation at a slower rate than demand. . . . This results in a zigzag . . . fluctuation of price and quantity.
—Wassily Leontief, "Delayed Adjustment of Supply and Partial Equilibrium"

Leaving turnover of working capital out of a book on economics is like leaving the circulation of the blood out of a treatise on physiology.
—John Burr Williams, *The Current Assets Mechanism: A Financial Theory of the Firm*

In various industries, such as agriculture, fishing, forestry, and construction, there is a lag between the application of production inputs and the flow of production output. This lag requires an investment in variable costs, which can yield a return only with a delay, and this investment must be undertaken without an understanding of how the market works in general and without a knowledge of equilibrium prices in particular. In all of these industries there are strong cyclic tendencies, persistent forecast error, and no evidence of convergence to equilibrium prices.

The archetype of such a situation is the production of crops. The growing season guarantees a finite lag between the time the production decision is made and the time the crop is ready for sale. The producer must base his decision on current and past experience and then hope for the best consequence. This consequence depends not only on what he has done himself, but also on what all other producers have done and on the demand for the crop.

Long before the discovery of complex mathematical dynamics, the "cobweb model" of demand and supply with production lags was invented to mimic this sort of market setting.[1] It is reconsidered briefly in the light of our now more complete understanding of the full range of possible behavior. After that we consider a model with production lags in which a budget constraint plays a central role. This model may be thought of as an introduction to the competitive disequilibrium theory of the firm. Our analysis shows that fluctuations in perpetual disequilibrium may be viable and, from the point of view of long-run average profits, may even be preferable to competitive equilibrium if firms are cautious enough.

12.1   The Cobweb Model

12.1.1   The Production Period, Price Forecasts, and Lagged Response

In the basic cobweb model, within each period supply is fixed, having been determined in the previous period. A market-clearing equilibrium price is determined by the equation of demand with this supply.[2] Supply in the succeeding period is based on a price estimate that is adjusted to take account of recent experience.

Let p_t^e be the price estimated at the beginning of period t, when production is planned. At the end of the period t, output will be sold at the actual market price p_t. In empirical work an adaptive expectations formula

$$p_{t+1}^e = p_t^e + \mu \left[(p_t - p_t^e) \right] \tag{12.1}$$

has been used,[3] but in the theoretical work it has usually been assumed for simplicity that $\mu = 1$ so

$$p_{t+1}^e = p_t, \tag{12.2}$$

that is, the price estimate for the next period is simply the current price. This is called *naive expectations*.

Adaptive expectations in general, and naive ones in particular, have long been objected to on grounds that producers should learn to do better. Price estimates in the model are mistaken in general (just as is so often the case in reality). Evidently, agents do have plenty to learn—if they can. Various alternatives have been proposed, but while some forecasting formulae can claim to give superior estimates, they raise objections of a different kind. In particular most of them assume that agents are well-trained statisticians with accurate data and costless computing capacity, *and that the "real world" is as simple as the model we are using to study it.* None of these assumptions has much empirical validity. The real world is in fact vastly more complicated than our models of it, so methods that are optimal for a simple model are likely to be suboptimal, perhaps badly so, for a more complex world. Add to this objection the information and computational cost of using sophisticated strategies and you find more than ample reason why an adaptive estimate like (12.1) or even a naive estimate like (12.2) could and probably does persist in practice. This supposition is supported by recent evidence from experimental economics.[4] For those reasons the models discussed in this chapter should be of some practical interest. They point in the direction that must be taken in theoretical research if real-world market performance is to be understood.

12.1.2   Production Lags and Market Feedback: The Basic Model

Consider a set of microsupply functions that describe the dependence of supply of a given firm, say y^i_{t+1}, on that firm's expected price, say p^e_{t+1}:

$$y^i_{t+1} = S^i(p^e_{t+1}). \tag{12.3}$$

Each firm is assumed to have exactly the same price expectations, and these have the naive, adaptive form given by equation (12.2). The behavior of the ith firm is given by

$$y^i_{t+1} = S^i\left(D^{-1}(Y_t)\right).$$

Evidently, what each firm does in a given period depends through the market on what the aggregate of firms did in the previous period, although no individual firm takes account of this. Aggregate supply is therefore

$$Y_{t+1} = S(p_t) = \sum_i Y^i_{t+1} = \sum_i S^i(p_t). \tag{12.4}$$

Let demand be $Y = D(p)$. Given supply, a convergent, market-clearing process is assumed that, together with the assumption of regular normal demand, enables market price to be expressed as a function of supply,

$$p_{t+1} = D^{-1}(Y_{t+1}), \tag{12.5}$$

where $D^{-1}(\cdot)$ is the *inverse demand function*.[5] Substituting (12.4) into (12.5), we get the sequence of *temporary equilibrium market prices* given by

$$p_{t+1} = \theta(p_t) := D^{-1}[S(p_t)]. \tag{12.6}$$

12.1.3   Stability Analysis

The stability analysis proceeds in the now familiar way. We have to consider $\theta'(\cdot)$, which in this model is

$$\theta'(p) = D^{-1'}[S(p)]S'(p). \tag{12.7}$$

If demand and supply are affine, it is a straightforward exercise. Only simple dynamics are possible. If the curves are nonlinear, we expect additional possibilities. As always, the causal effect reversal responsible for generating complex dynamics comes about if $\theta(\cdot)$ bends the right way. If demand is downward sloping, (12.8) can change sign *only if the supply function slope changes sign.* If this occurs $\theta(\cdot)$ has a minimum with fishhook profile. Given these facts, it is not difficult to establish two implications.

• If the market is normal, then asymptotically stable and unstable equilibrium and stable and unstable two-period cycles are all possible. Higher-order cycles and complex dynamics cannot occur. Moreover, there must be a two-period cycle of greatest amplitude.

• If demand is normal, a necessary condition for complex dynamics in the basic cobweb model is that supply be downward bending.

12.1.4 Walras's Example Again

If we consider Walras's graphical example of demand and supply, as shown in figure 10.4, but now use the process (12.6), we obtain the picture shown in figure 12.1. Within the degree of accuracy possible with purely graphical means, it would appear (i) that the equilibrium is unstable (because any point close to $\tilde{p}$ moves away), but (ii) that all points nonetheless converge in a finite number of steps to $\tilde{p}$ (because price falls below p', thence to $p_4 = D^{-1}(0)$ and thence to equilibrium).[6] This result is very different from the tatonnement dynamics described in chapter 10.

12.1.5 A Mathematical Analog

A mathematical representation of supply and demand analogous to Walras's diagram was given in equations (10.11) and (10.12). The inverse demand function is

$$p = D^{-1}(\tfrac{1}{\mu}Y^s) = \begin{cases} \frac{A}{b+\frac{1}{\mu}Y^s} - 1, & 0 \le p \le \mu D(0) \\ 0, & \mu D(0) < p. \end{cases} \tag{12.8}$$

Lagging supply in (10.12) and substituting into (12.8), we get the cobweb process for prices

$$p_{t+1} = \theta(p_t) := \begin{cases} \frac{A}{b} - a, & 0 \le p \le p' \\ \frac{A}{b+B(p-p')^\gamma e^{\delta p}} - a, & p' < p \le p^0 \\ 0, & p^0 < p. \end{cases}$$

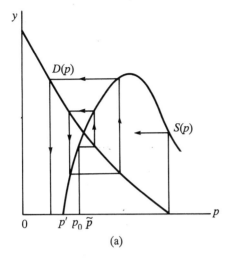

(a)

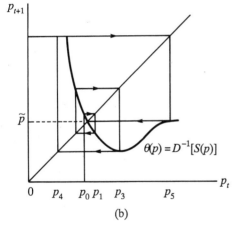

(b)

Figure 12.1
The cobweb interpretation of Walras's example. (a) Walras's demand and supply functions. (b)
The composite map.

The picture is very much like figure 12.1. Causal effect reversal occurs because supply is downward sloping. The reader is by now familiar with the results when the map, θ, can be stretched to have a single-troughed shape. Without going into the details, it can be said that both simple and complex dynamics occur generically. Numerical illustration and an analytical proof can be developed using concepts with which the reader is by now familiar.[7]

12.2 Competitive Disequilibrium with Financial Feedback

12.2.1 Cautious, Adaptive Behavior

Now we are going to consider a model of competitive markets with production lags in which the cobweb principle continues to play a role but in which supply is derived from an explicit microeconomic model of the production decision. In particular, the role of finance is introduced by incorporating a budget constraint that limits supply at any one time but that may grow or decline in response to changes in sales revenue.

Although the ingredients of the analysis are the familiar ones of standard theory, my utilization of them departs from the conventions of static analysis in several crucial ways. The firm is assumed to make a choice in the neighborhood of its immediate experience constrained by a cautionary bound or *flexibility constraint* using a guesstimate of the prospective price and constrained by its inherited "reinvestment" or "working" capital. Its constraints are adjusted to experience period after period in response to market feedback and to its success or failure. This adaptive economizing model represents an agent with imperfect knowledge of market conditions, and involves the kind of trial and error that characterizes business behavior under actual operating conditions.[8]

The key ingredient in the analysis is the "Robertsonian lag": current expenditures must come from previous incomes, which in the present context means that current production costs must be financed from previous sales revenues. As in the standard cobweb model, market prices are determined by the equation of current supply and demand while anticipated prices are assumed to be based on naive, adaptive expectations; that is, upon the market price that emerged in the previous period. Assume as a first approximation (so as to leave banks out of the picture) that firms do not borrow but finance current production entirely from retained earnings. If expected profits are positive, output is determined by the equation:

Current Production Costs = Reinvestment Income,

where

Reinvestment Income = Lagged Total Revenue − Overhead Costs

− (Dividends or Consumption Expenditures).

Of course, in reality firms often finance a part of their investments from borrowing or new equity offerings. To see, however, in the most transparent possible manner how financial feedback can influence the dynamics of supply, we shall use these several simplifying assumptions.

A competitive equilibrium exists and all the standard results apply: output is produced at minimum cost, supply equals demand, and extraordinary profits are zero.

Suppose output is initially very small but sufficient to cover overhead and other deductions so that initial reinvestment income is positive. A period of growth may occur so long as demand is elastic and total revenue increasing. It is possible that output will gradually converge to a stationary state. On the other hand, if supply reaches the inelastic portion of the demand curve, revenues fall, reinvestment income declines, so that output must subsequently be reduced. Later, because market supplies are reduced, prices increase and revenues recover. A sequence of market fluctuations can ensue. If they are perpetuated, as can also be the case, equilibrium is not reached. Instead, a long-run stochastic disequilibrium emerges in which average profits may be positive. If firms are extremely cautious, the variance of these fluctuations will be small but average profits will also be small. If they are more daring, prices and industry output will be more variable but average profits will also be higher. If they are excessively daring, then prices and industrial output will be still higher but average profits will be zero. This suggests the possibility of an optimum level of caution and a link to the theory of optimal decision making under uncertainty.

With the background of previous chapters now at our disposal, we should be prepared for all of these qualitative possibilities: convergence to cycles of various orders, chaos, and ergodic fluctuations. The latter possibilities mean that firms can overexpand or "spoil their market," to use Alfred Marshall's apt phrase. They experience losses and return to a profitable state only after production is cut back in the face of financial duress.

12.2.2   The Behavior of Firms and Industrial Supply

The firms' price expectation, p^e, formed at the beginning of a given period is the estimate of what price will be when output is ready for sale at the end of the period. Let y be the output level to be determined and $C(y)$ the total cost of producing it, where $C(y) = h + c(y)$, h is the fixed cost or overhead, and $c(y)$ the variable cost which changes with the level of output.[9]

The firm would like its actual profits to be as large as possible. Not knowing the price that it will actually receive, it can only choose an output level that makes its estimated profit $\pi^e(y) = p^e y - c(y) - h$ as large as possible. Suppose for simplicity that $c(y) = cy$ so that c is a constant unit cost. Then the firm's objective is

$$\pi^e(y) = (p^e - c)y - h. \tag{12.9}$$

The choice of y is constrained by the firm's financial resources, which will be denoted by F; that is, it can utilize no more cash than it has, so

$$C(y) = h + cy \leq F. \tag{12.10}$$

The maximum output compatible with the supply of working capital F is therefore $C^{-1}(F) = \frac{1}{c}(F - h)$, a term that will play an important role because if it is negative, there is no feasible production level and the firm is bankrupt.[10]

The choice of y is also constrained by the firm's caution in responding to profit opportunities. It must worry that it may invest too much in current production and that it may not recover its investment. A cautious approach is to limit output in any one period and to expand it a step at a time only if current expectations continue to be favorable. Let this *flexibility bound* be denoted by y^u and call the interval $[0, y^u]$ the *zone of flexible response*. (Its determination will be specified below.) It is assumed that output is limited to this zone; that is,

$$y \in [0, y^u]. \tag{12.11}$$

The highest estimated profit level that is both financially attainable and that does not require an output level exceeding the firm's willingness to be flexible, maximizes (12.9) subject to (12.10) and (12.11).[11] The output level that produces this is the firm's supply. It depends on the price estimate p^e, the flexibility bound y^u, and the working capital F and can be written

$$S(p^e, F, y^u) := \arg\max_{y} \{(p^e - c)y \mid C(y) \leq F, \quad y \in [0, y^u]\}. \tag{12.12}$$

How does this supply function behave?

Suppose the estimated gross profit is positive. Then the firm will want to supply the maximum amount it is willing to produce on the basis of caution, that is, in its zone of flexible response—if it can finance that amount. If it can't finance that amount, then it will want to produce all it can finance, namely, $C^{-1}(F)$. But this amount could be negative if $C(0) > F$, which would occur if the amount of working capital is inadequate to cover overhead. This means bankruptcy and zero output. Zero output also is chosen if estimated gross profit is negative. Putting all these considerations together, we have the following characteristic of supply.

Given that production is determined by (12.12), the supply function is given by the following rules:

(i) if production is feasible ($C(0) = h < F$) and

(ii) if a positive gross profit is estimated ($p^e - c \geq 0$),

then

$$y = S(p^e, F, y^u) = \begin{cases} y^u & \text{if } C(y^u) < F \\ C^{-1}(F) & \text{if } C(y^u) \geq F. \end{cases} \tag{12.13}$$

Otherwise,

(iii) if the firm is bankrupt ($C(0) = h > F$) or

(iv) if a gross loss is estimated ($p^e - c < 0$),

then

$$S(p^e, F, y^u) = 0. \tag{12.14}$$

The supply curve is illustrated in figure 12.2 for three different values of unit costs. If $c < c''$, then $S(p) = b^u$ when $p^e \geq c$. Contrastingly, if $c > c''$, then $S(p) = \frac{1}{c}(F - h)$ when $p^e \geq c$. When demand is D' and supply S''', the temporary equilibrium y''' occurs where *finance is constraining*. When unit costs are given by c' or c'', then *caution is constraining*. When demand is D'' and unit cost c''', there is no positive temporary equilibrium, and so on.

The sources of scarcity that limit the firm's output are the budget and flexibility constraints. These constraints have values or shadow prices imputed from profits. Define

$$c^u = \frac{d\pi}{dy^u}, \quad \rho := \frac{d\pi}{dF} = \frac{d\pi}{dh}. \tag{12.15}$$

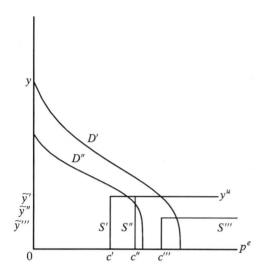

Figure 12.2
The demand and supply curves for the firm

Call c^u the *uncertainty premium* and ρ the *internal rate of return*. From (12.13) and (12.15) it follows that

$$c^u = (p^e - c), \quad \rho = 0 \qquad \text{if } C(y^u) < F \tag{12.16a}$$

$$c^u = 0, \quad \rho = \frac{p^e - c}{c} \qquad \text{if } C(y^u) \geq F \tag{12.16b}$$

From this it follows that

$$p^e = (1 + \rho)c + c^u. \tag{12.17}$$

In standard economic parlance this equation means that the firm produces at an output at which the estimated marginal revenue p^e is equal to the marginal cost of production, which includes the cost of capital, c, evaluated at the internal rate of return ρ plus the risk premium c^u. The risk premium is the *opportunity cost of caution* or, in other terms, the estimated marginal gain in profit that would accrue to a marginal increase in flexibility.

Suppose now that at the beginning of each period t, the firm forms its price expectation for the succeeding period p_t^e, determines the working capital F_t inherited from the previous period, and calculates the production bound within which it is willing to be flexible in allocating its resources. Then its supply for period t is

$$y_t = S(p_t^e, F_t, y_t^u). \tag{12.18}$$

Given n firms, all with identical expectations, unit costs, working capital endowments, and flexibility bounds, aggregate industry supply is

$$Y_t = ny_t = nS(p_t, F_t, y_t^u). \tag{12.19}$$

The industry supply and demand curves are similar to the firm level curves illustrated in figure 12.2, differing only by the output scale.

12.2.3   Market Feedback

12.2.3.1   Demand, Temporary Equilibrium, and Price Estimates   Let us now invoke the assumption of a rapidly convergent, purely competitive market that clears a given aggregate supply of Y_t at a market equilibrium price p_t. Assume that demand, $D(\cdot)$, is normal so that $D^{-1}(\cdot)$ is single-valued. Then

$$p_t = D^{-1}[Y_t] = D^{-1}[ny_t]. \tag{12.20}$$

The market-clearing price is based on the supply forthcoming at the end of period t, which, given (12.19), depends on the price expected at the beginning of that period, the working capital available, and the flexibility bound. The price estimate made at the beginning of the period given (12.2) is[12]

$$p_{t+1}^e = p_t = D^{-1}(ny_t). \tag{12.21}$$

12.2.3.2   Financial Feedback and Transitory Dividends   The firm's sales revenue at the end of period t is $p_t y_t$. This amount constitutes the working capital available for production in the succeeding period under the further assumption that any working capital not invested in production is distributed as extra dividends (in addition to the "fixed" dividend incorporated in h). Thus, let d_t be the *transitory dividends* paid out at the end of period t after the market has cleared. Then

$$d_t = F_t - C(y_t). \tag{12.22}$$

Note that $C(y_t) \leq F_t$ so $d_t \geq 0$. Consequently, transitory dividends will be positive if caution constrains the firm so that the money expended on production is less than that available. But, as the firm does not carry over any cash balance,

$$F_{t+1} = y_t D^{-1}[Y_t] = y_t D^{-1}[ny_t]. \tag{12.23}$$

12.2.3.3 Adaptive Flexibility   The firm's experience determines its willingness to be flexible. Specifically, we assume that if y_t is the most recent production level, then the maximum change contemplated at any one time is

$$\frac{y - y_t}{y_t} \leq \beta, \tag{12.24}$$

where β is called the *flexibility coefficient*. The greater β, the more flexible is the firm; the smaller β, the more cautious.

The flexibility bound is defined adaptively by

$$y_t^u = (1 + \beta)y_t. \tag{12.25}$$

To see the implication of this constraint, suppose that the flexibility constraint has governed the production decision for several periods. Then $y_{t+1} = (1 + \beta)y_t$ and output will have grown exponentially (at the rate β), so the firm will become more and more flexible, i.e., less and less cautious. But this only happens if expected profits—hence, lagged actual profits—have been positive. Thus, continued profitability leads to increasing flexibility and to decreasing caution in the further expansion of output.[13]

12.2.3.4 Adaptive Supply   The dependence of the firm's finance on the past level of output in the firm and industry, and of its flexibility constraint on past production, implies that the horizontal segment of the supply function (as illustrated in figure 12.2) moves up and down over time. The supply curve for a given period is therefore a short-run phenomenon that is adjusted to the firm's experience. When the past output level occurs at a long-run competitive equilibrium, the competitive equilibrium price is estimated, long-run equilibrium output levels will be chosen, and expectations will be fulfilled.

12.3   The Dynamics of Industrial Output

12.3.1   The Multiple-Phase Structure

Equations (12.21) and (12.23) determine the feedback affect through the market of past aggregate behavior on the subsequent behavior of the individual firms. Equation (12.25) determines the affect of the individual production experience on the subsequent degree of caution or equivalently the degree of flexibility in responding to perceived profit opportunity. Putting these together with equation (12.19) for aggregate supply, the dynamics of production for the firm and industry are derived. Because all firms are assumed to be identical, we can write[14]

$$y_{t+1} = \theta(y_t) := S\{D^{-1}(ny_t), C^{-1}[y_t D^{-1}(ny_t)], (1+\beta)y_t\}. \tag{12.26}$$

This rather formidable-looking expression disguises an underlying multiple-phase structure that helps interpret how the industry behaves. To make this explicit, define the following *phase structures*

$$\theta_0(y) := 0 \tag{12.27a}$$

$$\theta_1(y) := (1+\beta)y \tag{12.27b}$$

$$\theta_2(y) := \frac{1}{c}\{[yD^{-1}(ny)] - h\} \tag{12.27c}$$

Also, define the corresponding *phase zones*: Phase zone X^0 is the set of output levels where firms are bankrupt or are estimated to be unprofitable. Subsequent output is zero. Let $y^c = \frac{1}{n}D(c)$. Then the null regime is entered whenever $y_t > y^c$, that is, whenever losses occur. Phase zone X^1 is the set of outputs where subsequent production is increased as much as flexibility allows and within which transitory dividends are paid. Phase zone X^2 is the set of outputs in which transitory dividends are not paid; all earnings are retained and ploughed back into production. Production is limited by the supply of working capital. Formally, these zones are

$$X^0 := \{y|[yD^{-1}(ny) - h] < 0\} \cup \{y|D^{-1}(ny) < c\} \tag{12.28a}$$

$$X^1 := \{y|(1+\beta)y \leq \frac{1}{c}[yD^{-1}(ny) - h]\} \setminus X^0 \tag{12.28b}$$

$$X^2 := \{y|\frac{1}{c}[yD^{-1}(ny) - h] < (1+\beta)u\} \setminus X^0 \tag{12.28c}$$

With these definitions, the difference equation (12.26) is a multiple-phase dynamic process governed by

$$y_{t+1} = \theta(y_t) = \begin{cases} \theta_0(y_t), & y_t \in X^0 \\ \theta_1(y_t), & y_t \in X^1 \\ \theta_2(y_t), & y_t \in X^2. \end{cases} \tag{12.29}$$

12.3.1.1   Relationship with Walras's Producer's Tatonnement   Notice that

$$y_{t+1} - y_t = \min\{\beta y_t, \tfrac{1}{c}\pi_t\},$$

which is a form analogous to equation (2.1) for Walras's idea of producer's tatonnement.

12.3.2 Graphical Analysis

A very good idea of how this process works can be obtained from the graphs of total revenue and cost. Consider the total revenue and total cost curves shown in figure 12.3. Also shown just above the total cost curve is a curve representing the maximum allowable investment in current production in a given period given the production level in the previous period. This is obtained by calculating the cost of the maximum production level that will be considered given previous production, which is

$$C[(1 + \beta)y] = h + c(1 + \beta)y. \tag{12.30}$$

We therefore have the constraint

$$C(y_{t+1}) \leq C[(1 + \beta)y_t]. \tag{12.31}$$

Using (12.30), you can see that (12.26) can be given an equivalent form in revenue/output space

$$h + cy_{t+1} = \min\{h + c(1 + \beta)y_t, yD^{-1}(ny_t)\}\Delta(y_t, \backslash X^0), \tag{12.32}$$

where $\Delta(y_t, X_0) = 0$ if $y_t \in X_0$ and $= 1$ if $R_t \in \backslash X_0$, that is, $\Delta(x, S) = 1 - \chi_S(x)$. This enables us to trace out how market feedback leads to a sequence of adjustments in expenditure and output levels as shown in the sequence of steps on the diagrams in figure 12.3.

12.3.2.1 The Effect of Unit Cost Reductions on Performance   The phase zones are $X^0 = X^{0\prime} \cup X^{0\prime\prime}$, X^1, and $X^2 = X^{2\prime} \cup X^{2\prime\prime}$. In figure 12.3a adaptive process leads to an asymptotically stable competitive equilibrium. In figure 12.3b bounded fluctuations emerge after a period of growth; in figure 12.3c a market collapse occurs because price has fallen below unit cost, and in figure 12.3d bankruptcy occurs after a period of growth.

It is easy to see from the diagrams that, up to a point, the higher marginal cost is (*ceteris paribus*), the more likely are convergence and the smaller equilibrium output, and vice versa. Conversely, declining cost increases equilibrium output but eventually leads to increasing instability and collapse.

The elasticity of demand plays a special role here. If demand is elastic, total revenues increase as output expands so firms' financial resources increase. Retained earnings grow until the level where the elasticity of demand is one.

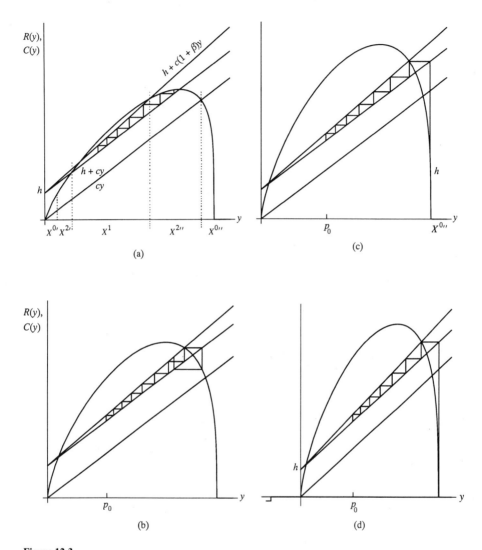

Figure 12.3
Cost, revenue, and production adjustments. (a) Expansion and convergence. (b) Expansion and
fluctuation. (c) Expansion until the market becomes unprofitable. (d) Expansion and collapse.

After that, they decline and this leads to fluctuations. Transitory dividends increase and then decline. If a stationary state exists at an output level with an elastic demand, production will converge to it. If, on the other hand, the stationary state exists in the region where the elasticity of demand is less than unity, then sales revenue will eventually decline. This forces a cutback in production and subsequent fluctuations that may or may not converge, or that may end in a market collapse.

12.3.3   The Effect of Caution on Performance

Figure 12.4 shows three diagrams in which the flexibility coefficient β has been varied when all other parameters have been fixed. In figure 12.4a, β is relatively small and increases successively in figures 12.4b and 12.4c as the decision maker becomes more flexible. In the most cautious case, growth in zone $\mathcal{R}_1$ is relatively slow. When fluctuations emerge, they are confined to a trapping set within which the slope of $\theta(\cdot)$ is greater than unity in absolute value so the fluctuations are strongly ergodic. Greater caution still would obviously prolong growth and reduce the amplitude of the fluctuations that ultimately emerge.

In figure 12.4b growth is accelerated in the regime $\mathcal{R}_1$, price falls below unit cost, and the null regime is entered. For other initial conditions, fluctuations would emerge. The reader can show that there exists an escape set. Because the slope of $\theta(\cdot)$ is greater than one, the null regime must be entered almost surely. (Recall Theorem 8.10.)

In figure 12.4c growth is even more rapid and fluctuations can emerge still sooner. Such a great fall in price occurs that the firm goes bankrupt and again exits the industry. What is true for one firm is, given our simplifying assumptions, true for all. We get an industrial collapse. This result also occurs almost surely.

It is clear then that in this model, relatively cautious behavior slows growth, prolongs the growth phase, and therefore prolongs the time during which transitory dividends are paid; it also dampens the fluctuations that may eventually emerge. Conversely, relative daring accelerates growth but shortens the period of transitory dividends, hastens the emergence of fluctuations, increases their amplitude, and, when extreme, leads to a collapse in price and bankruptcy. In short, cautious enough but not too cautious behavior permits growth, prolongs profitability, stabilizes fluctuations, and prevents disaster.

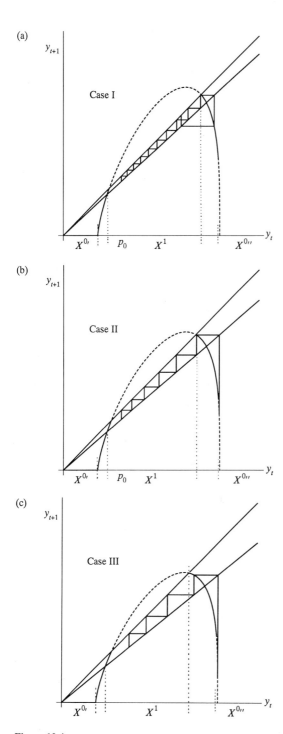

Figure 12.4
The effect of caution on the change in output. (a) Cautious growth and strongly ergodic fluctuations. (b) Faster growth and demise due to negative profits. (c) Very rapid growth, overshoot, and bankruptcy.

These effects have occurred in the particular setting of demand and cost given in the numerical simulations, but it is easy to see that within the framework of the model they are quite general in character, though the particular results will vary with other parameters of demand. In particular, if the equilibrium occurs where demand is elastic so that the adjustment process is asymptotically stable, relative caution has no affect on fluctuations because they do not occur. Even in this case, however, it does prolong growth and the period of positive transitory dividend payments.

12.3.4 Stability Analysis

12.3.4.1 Existence of Stationary States   If demand is regular normal, it is easy to show that $R(\cdot)$ is single-peaked and that $\theta(\cdot)$ is also. This can be seen by considering the derivative

$$R'(y) = ny\frac{dD^{-1}(ny)}{dy} + D^{-1}(ny). \tag{12.33}$$

It also follows that $\lim_{y \to \infty} \theta_2(y) = h/c$ and $\theta_2(0) = -h/c$. Therefore, if there exists a point y such that $\theta(y) > y$ and if $h > 0$, then there must be two positive stationary states. For this to happen we must have $\theta_2(y) = \frac{1}{c}(R(y) - h) > y$ or

$$R(y) - cy - h > 0. \tag{12.34}$$

The term on the left is maximized at the point, say y'', where $R'(y'') = c$. Consequently, if

$$R(y'') \geq cy'' + h$$

then there are two positive stationary states, say y^ℓ and y^u with $y^\ell < y^u$.

12.3.4.2 Stability   The first of these must occur where demand is elastic, that is where total revenue increases as output increases. Therefore,

$$\theta_2'(\tilde{y}^\ell) > 1,$$

so $\tilde{y}^\ell$ is unstable. If $y_0 < \tilde{y}^\ell$, then $\theta(y_0) < y_0$ and $\theta^n(y_0) = 0$ for finite n. This is the situation when output does not exceed the break-even point, which would occur if the initial capitalization is too small.[15]

Now consider $\tilde{y}^u$. If demand is elastic so that $\tilde{y}^u < y''$, then $\theta'(\tilde{y}^u) > 0$.

But $\theta(y) \geq y$ for $\tilde{y}^\ell \leq y \leq \tilde{y}^u$, so $\theta'(\tilde{y}) < 1$. Consequently, if $\tilde{y}^u$ occurs where demand is elastic, then it is asymptotically stable.

If $\tilde{y}^n$ occurs where demand is inelastic, then $\theta'(\tilde{y}^u) < 0$, so fluctuations occur in its neighborhood. If

$$\theta'(\tilde{y}^u) = \tfrac{1}{c} \left[\tilde{y}^u P'(\tilde{y}^n) + P(\tilde{y}^u) \right] > -1,$$

then these fluctuations will dampen out near $\tilde{y}^u$ and trajectories close to this competitive equilibrium will converge to it. If the inequality is reversed, they will diverge and fluctuations will be perpetuated, or the system will self-destruct.

12.3.4.3   Chaos and Strong Ergodicity   Consider normal demand and assume that $R(\cdot)$ is concave on the range $[0, y^0]$ where $y^0 = D(0)$. Of course, $R(0) = R(y) = 0$, $y \geq y^0$. Suppose

$$\theta_2'(\tilde{y}^u) < -1. \tag{12.35}$$

Then there is a largest constant ϵ (depending on $\tilde{y}$), such that $\theta_2'(y) < -1$ for all $y \in (\tilde{y}^u - \epsilon, y^0)$. (This follows from the concavity of $R(\cdot)$.) Let β^ϵ be the unique value of β, such that

$$\theta_1(\tilde{y} - \epsilon) := (1 + \beta^\epsilon)(\tilde{y} - \epsilon) = \theta_2(\tilde{y} - \epsilon).$$

Then, remembering that $\beta > 0$ so $\theta_1'(y) = 1 + \beta > 1$, it follows that

$$|\theta'(y)| > 1 \quad \text{for all} \quad y \in (0, y^0). \tag{12.36}$$

Before jumping to any conclusions, at this point we have also to consider the viability of the process. To this end let $y(\beta)$ be the function satisfying $(1 + \beta)y = \theta_2(y)$ and define

$$y^M(\beta) = (1 + \beta)y(\beta).$$

Then for any such β, given that all the remaining parameters are fixed, the maximum possible output is

$$y^M(\beta) = \max_{y \geq 0} \theta(y). \tag{12.37}$$

The maximum possible overshoot is $\theta[y^M(\beta)]$. If

$$\theta[y^M(\beta)] > \tilde{y}^\ell, \tag{12.38}$$

then $T = [\tilde{y}^\ell, y^M(\beta)]$ is a trapping set. By construction $\theta(\cdot)$ is expansive on $(0, y^0)$, so the dynamic process is strongly ergodic on T. It is very easy to show that the Li-Yorke conditions are also satisfied so, following the argument of Theorem 8.8, trajectories in T are chaotic almost surely.

Suppose that (12.38) is violated. If $\theta[y^M(\beta)] < \tilde{y}^\ell$, then some trajectories must eventually enter the null regime, because $\theta(y) < y$ for all $y < \tilde{y}^\ell$. If $\theta[y^M(\beta)] > y^c$, then some output levels can become unprofitable, i.e., price will fall below unit cost and the null regime will be entered. Finally, if $\theta_2[y^M(\beta)] < 0$, then the firm goes bankrupt and $\theta[y^M(\beta)] = 0$ (which is a stationary state in the null regime). Note that $y^c > \tilde{y}^u > \tilde{y}^\ell > 0$ and choose β so that

$$\theta[y^M(\beta)] = y^c.$$

Denote this value by β^c. Then by construction

$$T = \left[\theta[y^M(\beta^c), y^M(\beta^c)]\right]$$

is a trapping set, $\theta(\cdot)$ is expansive on this set, and the process is strongly ergodic. This result will hold for all $\beta < \beta^*$, so it can be said that our result is robust with respect to the degree of caution.

Now consider changes in unit cost and in the strength of demand μ. That is, let $D_\mu(p) = \mu D(p)$ for any given $D(p)$. Then

$$R(\mu D(p)) = \mu D(p) D^{-1}(y)$$
$$= \mu y D^{-1}(y).$$

Let y'' be the maximizer of θ_2. Then $\mu y'' P'(y'') + \mu P''(y'') = 0$, so y'' is unchanged by changes in μ or c. Moreover, y^0 is unchanged by changes in μ. Consequently,

$$\frac{dy^M}{dc} = \frac{d\theta(y'')}{dc} < 0 \quad \text{and} \quad \frac{dy^M}{d\mu} = \frac{d\theta(y'')}{d\mu} > 0.$$

This means that (up to a point) increases in c and decreases in μ stabilize the system and vice versa, and that given either μ or c, an interval of values for the other parameters (c or μ) exists so that $\tilde{y}^u$ is unstable for all parameters in that interval. But for any such (μ, c) pair, we know that there is a range of β's yielding strong ergodicity.

12.3.4.4   Simple and Complex Dynamics Robustly   To summarize:

PROPOSITION 12.1

(i) Both simple and complex dynamics for individual firms and for aggregate industry dynamics occurs robustly.

(ii) Given all other parameters held fixed, simple dynamics occur robustly for

(a) sufficiently large unit cost c;

(b) sufficiently weak demand, i.e., sufficiently small μ.

(iii) Complex dynamics occurs robustly for

(a) sufficiently small (but not too small) unit cost c;

(b) sufficiently large (but not too large) μ;

(c) given small enough c or large enough μ, for all sufficiently small flexibility coefficients β.

12.4   Profitability in Disequilibrium

In equilibrium

$$\tilde{y} = \theta(\tilde{y}) = \frac{1}{c}(\tilde{p}\tilde{y} - h),$$

which implies that

$$\pi(\tilde{y}) = \tilde{p}\tilde{y} - c\tilde{y} - h = 0,$$

so net profits are zero.

In disequilibrium when $\tilde{y}^u$ is unstable and fluctuations are perpetuated, then profits fluctuate. Gross profits are always positive. Otherwise, the firm and industry go out of business. Net profits, however, fluctuate, sometimes being negative, sometimes positive. This raises the question of their average value in the long-run.

Assume that the process is ergodic in a trapping set $T \subset X^2$. This includes the case for which stable cycles occur and the case when the process is strongly ergodic. Then

$$E(\pi) = \lim_{T \to \infty} \frac{1}{T} \sum_{t=0}^{T-1} \pi(y_t).$$

This limit exists and is finite (by the Birkhoff Theorem 8.2).

Notice that profits as defined in equation (11.9) can be reexpressed as

$$\pi(y_t) = c\,(\theta(y_t) - y_t)$$
$$= c(y_{t+1} - y_t).$$

We find that because $y_t < y^M$ for all t,

$$\lim_{T\to\infty} \frac{1}{T} \sum_{t=1}^{T} \pi(y_t) = \lim_{T\to\infty} \frac{1}{T} c\,[y_T - y_1]$$
$$= 0$$

Thus, when the long-run dynamics is ergodic in the financial regime X^2, the statistical expectation of profit is zero.

Now consider the case for which $\tilde{y}^u$ is unstable and for which the trapping set intersects both X^1 and X^2. This will occur for some interval $[0, \beta^c]$ constructed above. Then for all $y_0 \in T = \left[\theta[y^M(\beta)], y^M(\beta)\right]$, the behavior is viable and

$$y_{t+1} = \min\left\{(1+\beta)y_t, \frac{1}{c}[y_t D^{-1}(y_t) - h]\right\}, \quad y_t \in T,$$

or

$$y_{t+1} = \begin{cases} (1+\beta)y_t, & y_t \in X^1 \cap T \\ \frac{1}{c}\left[y_t D^{-1}(y_t) - h\right], & y_t \in X^2 \cap T. \end{cases}$$

As $y_{t+1} = (1+\beta)y_t < \frac{1}{c}\left[y_t D^{-1}(y_t) - h\right]$ for $y_t \in X^1$ and since $C(y)$ is monotonically increasing, it follows that

$$C(y_{t+1}) = c(1+\beta)y_t + h < y_t D^{-1}(y_t).$$

Proceed now as follows:

$$E(\pi) = \lim_{T \to \infty} \frac{1}{T} \sum_{t=0}^{T-1} \pi(y_t)$$

$$= \lim_{T \to \infty} \frac{1}{T} \sum_{t=0}^{T} \left[y_t D^{-1}(y_t) - C(y_t) \right]$$

$$= \lim_{T \to \infty} \frac{1}{T} \left\{ \sum_{s|y_s \in X^1} \left[y_s D^{-1}(y_s) - C(y_s) \right] \right.$$

$$\left. + \sum_{s|y_s \in X^2} \left[y_s D^{-1}(y_s) - (y_s) \right] \right\}$$

$$> \lim_{T \to \infty} \frac{1}{T} \left\{ \sum_{s|y_s \in X^1} \left[y_s D^{-1}(y_s) - y_{s-1} D^{-1}(y_{s-1}) \right] \right.$$

$$\left. + \sum_{s|y_s \in X^2} \left[y_s D^{-1}(y_s) - y_{s-1} D^{-1}(y_{s-1}) \right] \right\}$$

$$= \lim_{T \to \infty} \frac{1}{T} \sum_{t=1}^{T} \left[y_t D^{-1}(y_t) - y_{t-1} D^{-1}(y_t) \right]$$

$$= \lim_{T \to \infty} \frac{1}{T} \sum_{t=1}^{T} \left[y_t D^{-1}(y_t) - y_{t-1} D^{-1}(y_t) \right]$$

$$= \lim_{T \to \infty} \frac{1}{T} \left[y_T D^{-1}(y_T) - t_1 D^{-1}(y_1) \right]$$

$$= 0.$$

Hence,

$$E(\pi) > 0.$$

To summarize:

PROPOSITION 12.2   *If the competitive disequilibrium process is ergodic and*

$$T \cap X^1 \neq \emptyset$$

(so that the caution constraint is binding part of the time), then profits are positive in the long-run, i.e.,

$E(\pi) > 0.$

Comparing this with the equilibrium result and with the unstable case for which $T \subset X^2$, we have the following corollary.

PROPOSITION 12.3   *Suppose the competitive equilibrium $\tilde{y}^u$ occurs where demand is inelastic and is unstable (i.e., $\frac{1}{c}$ and μ are sufficiently large) but globally stable on the trapping set*

$$T'' = \left[\theta^2(y''), \theta(y'') \right] \subset X^2,$$

where y'' is the maximizer of $\theta_2(\cdot)$. Let β'' be defined by

$$(1 + \beta'')y'' = \theta^2(y'').$$

Then for all $y_0 \in T''$,

$E(\pi) = 0,$ *all $\beta > \beta''$*

$E(\pi) > 0,$ *all $\beta < \beta''$.*

Notice that as $\beta \to 0$, $\pi(y_t) \to \pi(\tilde{y}) = 0$, and that for β large enough so that $T \subset X^2$, $\pi(\tilde{y}) = 0$. This suggests that there is some precautionary level β^{**} that will maximize $E(\pi)$ over all positive π.

However, for $\beta = 0$, $y_t = y_0$ for all t. If every firm *knew* perfectly the structure of the system, and if each chose y_0 optimally with respect to π so that

$$\pi(y_0) = \max_{y \geq 0} \pi(y)$$

and then set $\beta = 0$, and if each firm could count on all the others to behave likewise, then ny_0 would be the maximum industry profit, which each firm would share equally.[16]

12.5   Revenue Maximization

12.5.1   The Modified Model

In the model presented so far, firms were assumed to choose the output level that maximized estimated gross profit. When the elasticity of demand is relatively small so that an overshoot of equilibrium occurs, the market price may fall below marginal cost, so that a loss is estimated to occur in the subsequent period and the firm exits. Because all firms are similar, they all exit even though none are bankrupt, and the industry collapses even though a competitive equilibrium exists. In a situation with no overhead costs, you can see that such a collapse always occurs because the competitive equilibrium occurs for that output $\tilde{y}$ where $\tilde{p} = D^{-1}(\tilde{y}) = c$.

Other behavioral strategies could avoid this extreme instability. As a simple example, suppose that firms maximize sales revenues instead of gross profits. Then it is easy to see that the phase structures governing production are still those given in equation (12.27) but the phase zone X^0 is modified to be

$$X^0 = \left\{ y \mid \left[y D^{-1}(ny) - h \right] < 0 \right\}. \tag{12.39}$$

Phase zones X^1 and X^2 are modified accordingly. Note that revenue maximization is equivalent to an estimated profit-maximizing strategy when profits are estimated to be positive. Otherwise, it is an output-maximizing strategy.

Given this modification, (12.29) still describes the multiple-phase dynamics. An industrial collapse can now occur only in the case of bankruptcy. Because firms are forced to cut back production whenever output enters the inelastic region, and so long as revenue does not fall below overhead costs, the decline in production causes a rise in price, a recovery in working capital, and a resumption of growth. Compared to the estimated profit-maximizing rule, the financial zone is widened and viability enhanced.

12.5.2   A Comparison with Profit Maximizing

An example shows this effect. Consider the Case II situation shown in figure 12.4b. It is reproduced as figure 12.5a. For profit maximizing, losses must inevitably occur, leading firms to abandon the industry even though a competitive equilibrium exists. Revenue maximizing for exactly the same demand and cost situation has the effect of widening zone X^2. The null zone is moved to the right. Instead of abandoning the industry, firms scale back production. Fluctuations persist with positive long-run average profits.

12.5.3   Zero Fixed Costs

Now look at the case mentioned above where a collapse always occurs for the profit-maximizing model, that is, when $h = 0$. In this case, it is easy to see that $\tilde{p} = c$, so, if $\tilde{y}$ lies in the region of inelastic demand, price must fall below c; growth culminates in an abrupt exit almost surely. In this case, (12.32) becomes

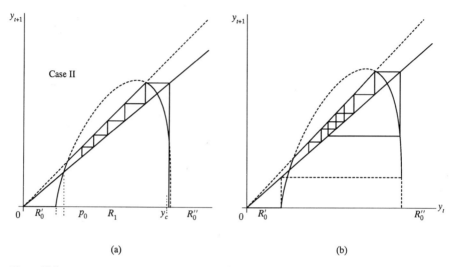

Figure 12.5
Profit versus sales maximizing behavior. (a) Profit-maximizing demise due to losses. (b) Revenue-maximizing viability and strong ergodicity.

$$y_{t+1} = \theta(y_t) = \min\{(1 + \beta)y_t, \frac{1}{c}y_t D^{-1}(ny_t)\}. \tag{12.40}$$

The change is minor but the stabilizing effect of revenue maximization is dramatic.

12.6 Summary

The theory of this chapter shows that financial feedback can exert a powerful influence on the dynamic performance of business firms in a competitive market environment. Caution (or flexibility) also plays a crucial role, as does the objective maximized. Sufficiently cautious behavior yields positive long-run profits when excess daring would not. A revenue- or sales-maximizing strategy provides a wider zone of viability than does profit-maximizing and, coupled with caution, yields positive long-run profits. Excess daring (or excess flexibility) yields faster growth but can lead to zero profits and a greater chance of bankruptcy.

In general, the market mechanisms and firm behavior studied in these three chapters explain salient features of real-world experience in terms of intrinsic economic interactions at the microeconomic level. Competitive equilibria are stationary states that can be approximated asymptotically under just the right conditions. Our analysis shows, however, that nonconverging fluctuations can yield more favorable long-run results for both marketing firms and producers if outages and bankruptcy can be avoided. These conditions can be prevented by sufficient inventories, cash reserves, and caution. The initial levels of these crucial variables required to insure viability do exist theoretically. They could not, however, be known by decision makers in the real world, who may fail because of insufficient initial capitalization or because they pursue growth too aggressively.

To keep markets working, an external source of funding may be needed from time to time to reinitialize a given sector. Cost-reducing technical change could exacerbate the problems of instability by speeding growth and spoiling the market through excessive production.

Our models, therefore, appear not just to provide amusing examples of mathematical artifacts. They would seem also to enhance as well our understanding of qualitative aspects of real business phenomena.

Notes

Preface

1. Lorenz (1963a, 1963b, 1964), Smale (1967), May (1976), May and Oster (1976), and Feigenbaum (1978).

2. Li and Yorke (1975).

3. Georgescu-Roegen (1950) and Benhabib and Day (1980).

4. Samuelson (1958), Gale (1973), and Benhabib and Day (1980).

1 Introduction

1. See, for example, various issues of the *Survey of Business Conditions* published by the U.S. Department of Commerce.

2. See Day (1979), p. 150.

3. An early representative of this approach is Frisch (1933). Others who have followed this path include, for example, Lucas (1979) and Sargent (1979) among many others.

2 Dynamics

1. Barraclough (1984).

2. See, for example, the U.S. Department of Commerce's monthly *Survey of Business Conditions*, the Council of Economic Advisors' Annual *Economic Report to the President*, and the World Bank's series of annual *World Reports*.

3. State variables describe one essential aspect of a system in the sense that the dynamics of a system can be determined in terms of its state variables alone. The set of state variables may not be unique and the dynamics may be describable in terms of alternative sets of state variables. In such cases one set of state variables can be transferred into another set of the same dimension.

   Another class of variables is that of the *auxiliary variable*. A variable belonging to this class is useful for describing a system and its structural relationships but can be eliminated by substitution so it is not essential. These are a fine points so far as we are concerned in this book.

4. See Walras (1926, pp. 242, 476). Tatonnement is usually associated with Walras's *market* tatonnement. We discuss that concept in chapter 9.

5. In the interest of simplicity we have ignored possible negativities in output. Later we shall be quite fastidious about such things.

6. The parameters were as follows in the examples shown in figure 2.2: for figure 2.2a, $a = 4.0$, $b = 2.0$, $c = 0.5$, $d = 0.7$, $h = 0.1$; for figure 2.2b the parameters were the same except $a = 4.2$; for figure 2.2c the parameters were the same except $a = 4.5$. Note that the scales on the three diagrams are also different.

7. Strictly speaking, for this to be true the interval containing $\bar{x}$ must not be too large because, as we have seen, for initial conditions far enough from $\bar{x}$, the system may self-destruct. In general, many different behaviors might occur for initial conditions far enough from the periodic or stationary state in question.

8. That is, subject to the proviso of note 7 above.

9. An example is the irrational rotation on the circle.

10. For an excellent discussion see Lasota and Mackey (1985, §4.3).

11. Given the mixing conditions mentioned above.

12. "As Wilken has pointed out in a masterly analysis, this moment of decision by Alexander is one of history's great proofs that individuals, not mere economic forces, can change the destinies of mankind" (Renault, 1975, p. 116).

13. For example, Hawking (1988, p. 174) asks, "Is the theory so compelling that it brings about its own existence?" My own philosophical position comes closest to Immanuel Kant who remarked that "the mathematician, the natural philosopher [scientist] . . . are merely artists, engaged in the arrangement and formation of concepts" (p. 471). This view was shared—among physicists—by Einstein, Plank, and Schroedinger.

3 Methodological Issues

1. A more general type of relationship, the set valued function or *correspondence* associates with a given "cause" a *set* of possible effects. See Debreu (1959, p. 6). I have considered dynamical systems based on this more general concept in Day (1978) and in Day and Kennedy (1970). For a very advanced treatment see Aubin and Frankowska (1990).

2. As Feynman observed, it is physical attraction that keeps things together; it is physical repulsion that keeps us from falling through the floor. See Feynman (1963, 1:12–16).

3. One is induced to wonder if Balzac was aware of Poincaré?

4. This method was originated by Cournot, Marshall, and Hicks and subsequently by Benassy (1975) and Grandmont (1976).

5. See, for example, Hirsch and Smale (1974).

6. "Just as no velocity can exceed that of light c, no mechanical motion can be smaller than elementary length λ and no time interval can be shorter than elementary duration λ/c." Gamov (1966, p. 161) probably meant *measured* velocity and *measured* length and that no time interval shorter than λ/c could be perceived and measured.

7. Hirsch and Smale (1974).

8. Marsden and McCraken (1976).

9. For a watershed survey of this broad evolutionary view in various fields, see *American Scientist*, 65, 1977.

10. See, for example, Hawking (1988, p. 146).

4 Dynamical and Semidynamical Systems

1. For a classic, general background in dynamics, see Samuelson's *Foundations*, part II. Other texts are also useful, not only for illustrating the basic ideas of simple dynamics, but also for showing how far the subject has come. See Goldberg (1961), Levy and Lessman (1961), and Baumol (1970).

2. Note here that the symbol for infinity is not treated as belonging to $\mathbb{R}$.

3. Lorenz (1963a) used (4.2d′) in his original work on irregular fluctuations.

4. A purely formal way of resolving this problem is to consider that the dynamical system operates on the power set $\mathcal{P}(D)$. By taking account of the fact that the empty set $\emptyset \in \mathcal{P}(D)$, then flows exist in $\mathcal{P}(D)$. But that is a mere formalism. To arrive at a more useful construct, let (θ, D) be a semidynamical system and define $D^* = \{y \in D | \theta^{-n}(y) \neq \emptyset \text{ all } n\}$. Obviously, $D^* \subset D$.

But D^* can be "small" relative to D, or even empty. For example, the affine map with $b > 0$ and domain $D := \mathbb{R}$ has an inverse everywhere. In this case $D^* \equiv D$, so $\{\theta, D\}$ can be thought of as a dynamical system with nonempty images. But when $D := \mathbb{R}^+$, then $D^* = [b, \infty]$ and there are no preimages in D for $[0, b]$.

5 Simple Dynamics

1. Samuelson (1943, p. 61) gives a nice discussion inspired by Schumpeter's (1934) description of the circular flow.

2. See for example, Courant (1934, p. 66).

3. By this notation is meant that as x approaches b_1 from above, $\theta(x)$ increases without bound.

4. Using the notation of the general piecewise linear map set

$$b_0 = 0, b_1 = b \quad \text{and} \quad b_2 = 0$$

$$a_0 = 0, a_1 = a \quad \text{and} \quad a_2 = c.$$

Let $\beta_1 = \pi$ and $\beta_2 = \rho$. Then we can write the tent map as shown in (5.7).

5. This theorem holds for n-dimensional dynamical systems but is based on the one-dimensional argument of Li and Yorke (1975). See Diamond (1976).

6. To prove Theorem 5.4, show that the Li-Yorke conditions imply (5.10)–(5.11). Let a be a Li-Yorke point with $b = \theta(a)$, $c = \theta(b)$ and $d = \theta(c)$. Let $I = [b, c]$. By continuity, θ must assume all values between $\theta(b)$ and $\theta(c)$. Therefore, $\theta(I) \supset [d, c]$. Let $J = [d, c]$, then using Lemma 5.2, there exists a compact set $Q \subset [b, c]$ such that $\theta(Q) = [d, c]$. Let $Y = Q$. Now use the lemma again. $I = [a, b]$ and $J = Y \subset \theta[a, b]$. So there exists an X such that $\theta(X) = Y$, but $\theta(Y) = [d, c] \supset [a, b] \cup [b, c] \supset X \cup Y$.

By construction X and Y have at most one point in common, which is b. This can happen only if $b = \max_{x \in [a, c]} \theta(x)$. In this case we can choose for the initial application of Lemma 5.2 the *open* interval (a, b) for I and repeat the argument. Likewise, in the subsequent step. This shows that both conditions of the chaos theorem hold.

7. The origin of this theorem is Švarkovskii (1964).

8. For a detailed analysis of this equation in an economic context, see Day (1967).

9. There are actually many concepts of stability in use and terminology varies among authors. I have tried to be consistent with my usage within this book.

6 Multiple-Phase Dynamics I

1. The term "multiple-phase dynamics" seems to have been introduced into economics by Georgescu-Roegen (1950) who, building on Leontief's (1953) subsequently published work, gave a lucid introduction. The basic idea was perhaps first used explicitly by Malthus. I gave a general treatment with an emphasis on technological change and on the switch among behavioral rules in Day (1963, 1978) and in Day, Morley, and Smith (1974). Malinvaud (1980), for example, gives a discussion in terms of macrodynamics.

2. Recall that $\chi_x(S) = \begin{cases} 1 & \text{if } x \in S \\ 0 & \text{if } x \notin S \end{cases}.$

3. Standard references are Halmos (1950) and Kelley (1955).

7 Chaos

1. The term "chaos" was introduced to describe a precise class of mathematical trajectories by Li and Yorke (1975). The discussion in this chapter is based on that paper. Their work was inspired in part by Lorenz (1963a) whose own work evolved from the theory of hydrodynamics and of turbulent flow. The term chaos was also used by the founders of thermodynamics in the mid-nineteenth century to denote random behavior generated by deterministic laws. See Gibbs (1901,

p. vi). It is important to note that it is the generated behavior that has the disorderly character—not the underlying process generating it. For a good pedagogical introduction to chaos, see Saari (1991). For a more technical and more comprehensive introduction, see Collet and Eckmann (1980).

2. Since our maps are exclusively in the real domain, "compact" is equivalent to closed and bounded.

3. Define

$$Q_{n+1} = \theta_0^{-1} \cdot \theta_1^{-1} \cdots \theta_n^{-1}(X_{n+1}).$$

Then

$$Q_{n+1} \subset \theta_0^{-1} \cdot \theta_1^{-1} \cdots \theta_n^{-1} (\theta(X_n)) = \theta_0^{-1} \cdots \theta_{n-1}^{-1}(X_n) = Q_n.$$

4. On the relation of continuity, compactness, and the finite intersective property, see Dunford and Schwartz (1988), vol. 1, p. 17, and Berge (1963, pp. 69, 83).

5. In general, since $x \in Q \subset Q_n$ we get

$$\theta^n(x) \in \theta^n(Q) \subset \theta^n(Q_n) = \theta^n \left(\theta_0^{-1} \cdots \theta_{n-1}^{-1}(X_n) \right)$$

$$= \theta^{n-1}(\theta \cdot \theta_0^{-1})\theta_1^{-1} \cdots \theta_{n-1}^{-1}(X_n)$$

$$= \theta^{n-1} \cdot \theta_1^{-1} \cdot \cdots \cdot \theta_{n-1}^{-1}(X_n)$$

$$\vdots$$

$$= \theta \cdot \theta_{n-1}^{-1}(X_n)$$

$$= X_n.$$

6. This theorem is the essence of the widely cited theorem of Li and Yorke (1975), which I have broken into pieces for pedagogical convenience.

7. Also part of the Li-Yorke Theorem.

8 Statistical Dynamics

1. Discussion with Wayne Shafer and Giulio Pianigiani were especially helpful in developing this chapter, and I have drawn on our joint work, namely, Day and Shafer (1987) and Day and Pianigiani (1991). In addition to the references cited in the text, the reader who wants to explore the background and details of the topics covered should consider Lasota and Mackey (1985) and, for a more advanced treatment, Dunford and Schwartz (1988), part I, chap. 8. A good text on measure theory is also useful such as Halmos (1950).

2. On the origin of statistical mechanics, see Gibbs (1901). On the mathematical theory, see Dunford and Schwartz (1958, pp. 726–730).

3. See Lasota and Mackey (1985, pp. ix–x).

4. See Dunford and Schwartz (1958, pp. 661–684). This combines Theorem 9, p. 667, with Corollary 10, p. 668. See also Lasota and Mackey (1985, pp. 57–59).

5. The results summarized here were derived in Kowalski (1975) and Li and Yorke (1978). See Day and Shafer (1987, p. 353).

6. This result was first derived by Ulam and von Neumann (1947). See Pianigiani (1979) or Lasota and Mackey (1985, p. 47).

7. As a useful background on laws of large numbers and central limit theorems, see Rao (1973, chap. 2).

8. Three formulae are used here:

$$\sum_{i=1}^{n} i = \frac{n(n+1)}{2} \quad \text{and} \quad \sum_{i=1}^{n} i^2 = n(n+1)\frac{(2n+1)}{6}$$

$$\sum_{i=1}^{n} i^3 = \frac{n^2(n+1)^2}{4}.$$

The first one is found by adding the series $1 + 2 + \cdots + n$ to the series $n + (n-1) + \cdots + 1$ which by factoring equals $n(n+1)$. Dividing by 2 gives the formulae. In the other cases the method is essentially the same. Obtaining the common factors, however, requires some effort.

9. This result was obtained in Hofbauer and Keller (1982) and Ziemien (1985). For a discussion see Day and Shafer (1987).

10. See Pianigiani (1979).

9 Multiple-Phase Dynamics II: Further Analysis

1. See Day and Walter (1989) for further details.

10 Tatonnement

1. Actually, Walras formulated two kinds of price adjustment process: one called producer's tatonnement, which was discussed in §2.1.2, and another referred to as consumer's tatonnement, which is the form to be studied in this chapter. See Walras (1926, p. 477).

2. Samuelson (1947, p. 263) actually formulated the model in continuous time. For a textbook discussion see Varian (1984, p. 245). Advanced analyses of tatonnement in discrete time will be found in Saari and Simon (1978), Saari (1985), Saari and Williams (1986), and Bala and Majumdar (1992). The idea that Walrasian tatonnement could produce chaotic price sequences was presented in my lecture at the Institut Henri Poincaré in Paris, June 1981. This chapter is an outgrowth of the notes prepared for that conference.

3. Walras (1926, p. 477).

4. See Samuelson and Nordhaus (1989, p. 560). Their curve, drawn on Marshallian axes, is essentially like Walras's. For an application in the context of the fishing industry, see Copes (1970) and Crutchfield and Farmer (1982).

5. Parameters used for computing the curves shown in figure 10.5 are

$A = 7.0,$ and 15.5

$a = 1.1,$

$B = 10,$

$\gamma = 1.5$

$b = 1.75,$

$p' = .3,$

$\delta = 1.0$

6. Parameters used in computing figure 10.10 are

$$\lambda = \tfrac{1}{2}, \quad \alpha = \tfrac{1}{2}, \quad \beta = \tfrac{1}{2}, \quad \bar{y} = \tfrac{3}{5}, \quad \mu = \tfrac{1}{2}.$$

These did not vary. For $\bar{x}$ the parameters were (a) 1.0, (b) 1.65, (c) 1.96, (d) 2.04, (e) 2.05, and (f) 2.06.

7. For a discussion of the problems of disequilibrium involved in tatonnement, see Fisher (1983). Arrow emphasizes that equilibrium is only "the end result of a process . . . [and] that inequalities between demand and supply are . . . an integral part of the process by which the market reaches its equilibrium position," quoted by Saari (1985, p. 1117). Arrow's statement, like Walras's exposition cited above in note 1, presumes that *markets do reach equilibrium*. For an illuminating discussion, see Weintraub (1979), especially chapters 6 and 7. Another approach is simply to deny the problem and to assume that markets in effect always work in equilibrium, a view that has been followed by a substantial school of macroeconomists. See, for example, Lucas (1987).

11 Market Mediation

1. Slightly paraphrased from Clower and Friedman (1984, p. 115).

2. For general discussions of market mediation, see Clower and Friedman (1984) and Day (1984).

3. My interest in the market for equities was very much stimulated by conversations with John Burr Williams over many years, whose classic work was published more than half a century ago. See Williams (1938). John Burr Williams, Jr., has also made available to me his father's extensive notes and unpublished manuscripts dealing with various aspects of the stock market and other competitive economic sectors. Barbara Gordon introduced me to the role played by the specialist and to Richard Ney's provocative (if inflammatory) analysis of that role. As I thought about the topic more, it seemed to me that here, even more than elsewhere in economics, the equilibrium method that underlies the "efficient market hypothesis" is misleading. With growing conviction I have come to the view that a more useful approach for understanding what goes on in the market for equities could be based on Keynes' lucid if informal description of the speculative component in investor behavior. I was glad to learn from later discussions with Professor Corinne Bronfman that I was not completely alone in this view. I finally sketched the present theory at the Istituto di Matematica of the University of Siena in Spring 1988 and incorporated it subsequently in joint work with Weihong Huang. See Day and Huang (1990).

4. This is a standard stock market term. A shortcut formula suggested by Fischer Black (1986, p. 533) would be the current earnings multiplied by a suitable price-earnings ratio. The current earnings capitalized at a rate that consisted of the current interest rate plus a risk factor would be similar.

5. Also a standard term. See Williams (1938) for the classic work on the determination of investment value and for advice on how α-investors should behave.

6. For a related conception of the β-investor, see Schwartz (1988). Our usage in effect combines his "sheep" and "exaggerators" but in a way that makes possible some precise and quite interesting inferences. Sheep have also been called "simple extrapolators."

7. The market maker is a stylized version of the so-called specialist, as described for example by Stoll (1985) who gives a concise survey of the system used by the New York Stock Exchange. This system is not used on all stock markets and it may not be continued much longer. Nonetheless, the current model will serve well as an example of how market dynamics are derived from economic strategies.

8. In the real world stock market mediators charge a transaction fee to both buyers and sellers, but it is a very small fraction of the price, so we shall assume here that its effect on supply and demand is negligible. Demand and supply, hence excess demand, can then be expressed as shown

in (11.19). However, the transaction fee does play a crucial role in determining the profitability and viability of mediation which is investigated below.

9. The parameters are as follows:

$u = v = .5$

$p^B = 0,$

$a = .2,$

$\lambda = 1,$

$p^T = 1,$

$A = 1,$

$b = .88,$

$\epsilon = .01,$

$d = .5.$

12 Financial Feedback

1. The cobweb idea goes back at least to Henry Moore in the early part of this century. Theoretical and empirical analyses were contributed by many authors in the 1930s. In 1934 Leontief in effect used iterated, nonlinear maps, probably the first application in economics. See Leontief (1966) for the English version of this classic note.

2. This is tantamount to assuming a rapidly convergent tatonnement process. On this "temporary equilibrium" approach, see Samuelson (1943, p. 265).

3. For empirical work using adaptive expectations, see, for example, Nerlove (1958).

4. See Arlington Williams (1987) and the references therein and Sterman (1989).

5. Or, lagging (12.5) and substituting into (12.4), we get the sequence of temporary equilibrium market quantities generated by

$$Y_{t+1} = \psi(Y_t) := S\left[D^{-1}(Y_{t+1}) \right].$$

These equations give alternative but equivalent versions of the cobweb model of competitive price adjustments with a production lag.

6. This example is interesting. Using our formal definition of §5.3.6, equilibrium price is *unstable* even though prices converge to it in finite time. This is a special kind of stability. For a discussion of this kind of behavior and other exotic types of stability, see Cherene (1978).

7. For a discussion see Day and Hanson (1991).

8. The model is an outgrowth of early work discussed in Day (1967). The earliest numerical experiments with my approach were computed around 1970 by Richard Benson, who produced irregular fluctuations. At that time we were unaware of the work on irregular fluctuations by Lorenz. With the mathematical tools now available, it is possible to give a much more complete analysis than was possible then.

9. The term h includes deductions for depreciation, interest on long term debt, property taxes, executive compensations, and "locked-in dividends." Note that $C(0) = h$. The term $c(y)$ includes labor, materials, and interest on working capital.

10. Except for Carlsson (1939) and Williams, Jr. (1967) and my own early work alluded to in note 8 above, a curious asymmetry has been maintained until recently in much of the microeconomic

analysis of demand and supply. The households endowment of money is assumed to matter in determining its demand as in the pure exchange economy analyzed in §10.2.1, but the budget of the firm has been ignored in determining the supply of commodities. More recent developments, for example by Greenwald, Kohn, and Stiglitz (1993) and Woodford (1988), are rectifying this situation. On the sales maximizing strategy, see Baumol (1967, chap. 6), and Day (1967).

11. Thus, the production decision is a simple primal linear programming problem

$$\max_{y \geq 0}(p^e - c)y$$

subject to

$$y \leq y^u$$

$$cy \leq m - h.$$

Its dual is

$$\min_{c^u, p \geq 0} c^u y^u + \rho(m - h)$$

subject to

$$c^u + c\rho \geq p^e - c.$$

The production level y is the primal variable; the uncertainty premium c^u and the internal rate of return are the dual variables.

12. This expression does not imply that managers of individual firms know market demand $D(\cdot)$, aggregate supply, or the number of firms; but only that they observe and receive the price p_t that emerges on the market.

13. This adaptive, behavioral approach to representing uncertain choice was developed in the study of the dynamics of agricultural production. See Day (1963).

14. See note 12.

15. Note that the elasticity of demand $\left|\frac{dp}{dy}\frac{y}{p}\right|$ is not a parameter but a variable in all demand functions except the constant elasticity function, $p = Ay^{-\alpha}$.

16. The results described in this section were obtained in collaborative work with Weihong Huang.

Bibliography

Arms, Richard W. Jr. 1983. *Volume Cycles in the Stock Market*. Homewood, IL: Dow Jones–Richard D. Irvin, Inc.

Aubin, Jean-Pierre, and Helené Frankowska. 1990. *Set Valued Analysis*. Boston: Birkhäuser.

Bala, Vinkatesh, and M. Majumdar. 1992. "Chaotic Tatonnement." *Economic Theory*, 2(4), 437–446.

Balzac, Honoré. 1989. *The Rise and Fall of César Birotteau*. Trans. Ellen Marriage. New York: Carroll and Graf Publishers, Inc.

Barraclough, G., et al. (eds.). 1984. *The Times Atlas of World History*. Rev. ed., Maplewood, NJ: Hammond, Inc.

Baumol, William J. 1959. *Business Behavior, Profits and Growth*. New York: The Macmillan Company.

Baumol, William J. 1967. *Business Behavior, Value and Growth*. Rev. ed. New York: Harcourt, Brace and World, Inc.

Baumol, William J. 1970. *Economic Dynamics*. 3d ed. New York: The Macmillan Company.

Benassy, Jean-Pascal. 1975. "Neo-Keynesian Disequilibrium Theory in a Monetary Economy." *The Review of Economic Studies*. 42, 503–523.

Benhabib, Jess, and Richard H. Day. 1980. "Erratic Accumulation." *Economics Letters*, 6(2), 113–117.

Berge, Claude. 1963. *Topological Spaces*. New York: The Macmillan Company.

Black, Fisher. 1986. "Noise." *Journal of Finance*, 41, 519–543.

Blatt, J. M. 1978. "On the Econometric Approach to Business-Cycle Analysis." *Oxford Economic Papers*, 30, 292–300.

Buccola, Steven T., and Vernon Smith. 1987. "Uncertainty and Partial Adjustment in Double Auction Markets." *Journal of Economic Behavior and Organization*, 8, 587–602.

Carlsson, Sune. 1939. *A Study on the Pure Theory of Production*. Reprint. New York: Augustus Kelly, Bookseller, 1965.

Cherene, Louis, J., Jr. 1978. *Set Valued Dynamical Systems and Economic Flow*. Berlin: Springer-Verlag.

Clower, Robert, and Daniel Friedman. 1984. "Trade Specialists and Money in an Ongoing Exchange Economy." Chap. 5 in R. Day and G. Eliasson (eds.), *The Dynamics of Market Economies*. Amsterdam: North-Holland Publishing Company.

Collet, P., and J. Eckmann. 1980. *Iterated Maps on the Interval as Dynamical Systems*. Basel: Birkhäuser.

Copes, Parzival. 1970. "The Backward-Bending Supply Curve of the Fishing Industry." *The Scottish Journal of Political Economy*, 17, 69–77.

Courant, Richard. 1934. *Differential and Integral Calculus*. New York: John Wiley and Sons, Inc.

Cournot, Augustin. 1838. *Researches into the Mathematical Principles of the Theory of Wealth*. Trans. Nathaniel T. Bacon (English ed. 1897). New York: The Macmillan Company. Reprint. Homewood, Illinois: Richard D. Irwin, Inc., 1963.

Crutchfield, J. P., and J. D. Farmer. 1982. "Fluctuations and Simple Chaotic Dynamics." *Physics Report*, 92, 45–82.

Cugno, F., and L. Montrucchio. 1984. "Teorema della Ragnatela Aspettative Odattine & Dinamiche Caotiche." *Rivista Internazionale di Scienze Economiche & Commerciali*, 31(8), 713–724.

Day, Richard H. 1963. *Recursive Programming and Production Response*. Amsterdam: Elsevier North-Holland, Inc.

Day, Richard H. 1967. "A Microeconometric Model of Business Growth, Decay, and Cycles." *Unternehmensforschung*, 11(1), 1–20.

Day, Richard H. 1978. "The Structure of Recursive Programming Models." Chap. 2 in R. H. Day and A. Cigno, *Modelling Economic Change*. Amsterdam: Elsevier North-Holland, Inc.

Day, Richard H. 1979. "Technology and the Agro-Industrial Complex: A Global View." in R. H. Day and N. Kamrany (eds.), *Economic Issues of the Eighties*. Baltimore, MD: Johns Hopkins University Press.

Day, Richard H. 1984. "Disequilibrium Economic Dynamics: A Post Schumpeterian Contribution." *Journal of Economic Behavior and Organization*, 5, 57–76.

Day, Richard H. 1985. "Dynamical Systems Theory and Complicated Economic Behavior." *Environment and Planning B: Planning and Design*, 12, 55–64.

Day, Richard H. 1987. "The General Theory of Disequilibrium Economics and of Economic Evolution." Chap. 3 in D. Batten, J. Casti, and B. Johansson (eds.), *Economic Evolution and Structural Change*. Berlin: Springer Verlag.

Day, Richard H., and Kenneth A. Hanson. 1991. "Cobweb Chaos." In T. J. Kaul and J. K. Sengupta (eds.), *Economic Models, Estimation and Socioeconomic Systems: Essays in Honor of Karl A. Fox*. 175–192. Amsterdam: North-Holland, Elsevier Science Publishers, B.V.

Day, Richard H., and Weihong Huang. 1990. "Bulls, Bears and Market Sheep." *Journal of Economic Behavior and Organization*, 14, 299–329.

Day, Richard H., and Peter Kennedy. 1970. "Recursive Decision Systems: An Existence Analysis." *Econometrica*, 38, 666–681.

Day, Richard H., Samuel Morley, and Kenneth R. Smith. 1974. "Myopic Optimizing and Rules of Thumb in a Micro Model of Industrial Growth," *American Economic Review*, 64, 11–23.

Day, Richard H., and Giulio Pianigiani. 1991. "Statistical Dynamics and Economics." *Journal of Economic Behavior and Organization*, 16, 37–84.

Day, Richard H., and Wayne Shafer. 1987. "Ergodic Economic Fluctuations." In A. Medio (ed.), *Advances in Dynamic Economics,* special issue of the *Journal of Economic Behavior and Organization*, 8, 339–362.

Day, Richard H., and Jean-Luc Walter. 1989. "Economic Growth in the Very Long Run: On the Multiple-Phase Interaction of Population, Technology, and Social Infrastructure." Chap. 11 in W. Barnett, J. Geweke, and K. Shell (eds.), *Economic Complexity: Chaos, Sunspots, Bubbles and Nonlinearity*. Cambridge: Cambridge University Press.

Debreu, Gerard. 1959. *Theory of Value*. New York: John Wiley and Sons, Inc.

Diamond, Phil. 1976. "Chaotic Behavior of Systems of Difference Equations." *International Journal of Systems Science*, 7, 666–681.

Dunford, Nelson, and Jacob T. Schwartz. 1988. *Linear Operators Part I: General Theory*. New York: John Wiley and Sons, Inc.

Dury, K. 1981. "National Bureau of Economic Research on the Theory of General Economic Equilibrium." *Rapporteur's Report*, University of Berkeley, February 13–15.

Feigenbaum, M. J. 1978. "Quantitative Universality for a Class of Nonlinear Transformation." *Journal of Statistical Physics*, 19, 25–52.

Feynman, Richard. 1963. *The Feynman Lectures on Physics*. 3 vols. Reading, MA: Addison-Wesley.

Fisher, Franklin. 1983. *Disequilibrium Foundations of Equilibrium Economics*. Cambridge: Cambridge University Press.

Forrester, Jay W. 1961. *Industrial Dynamics*. Cambridge, MA: MIT Press.

Friedman, M. 1962. *Price Theory*. Chicago: Aldine Publishing Company.

Frisch, Ragnar. 1933. "Propagation Problems and Impulse Problems in Dynamic Economics." In *Essays in Honor of Gustav Cassel*, 171–205. London: George Allen and Unwin.

Gale, David. 1973. "Pure Exchange Equilibrium of Dynamic Economic Models." *Journal of Economic Theory*, 6, 12–36.

Gamov, George. 1966. *Thirty Years That Shook Physics: The Story of Quantum Theory*. Reprint. New York: Dover Publications, 1985.

Georgescu-Roegen, Nicholas. 1950. "The Theory of Choice and the Constancy of Economic Laws." *Quarterly Journal of Economics*, 64, 125–138.

Gibbs, Willard. 1901. *Elementary Principles in Statistical Mechanics*. Reprint. Woodbridge, CT: Ox Bow Press.

Goldberg, Samuel. 1961. *Introduction to Difference Equations*. New York: Science Editions, Inc.

Grandmont, Jean-Michel. 1976. "On Keynesian Temporary Equilibrium." *Review of Economic Studies*, 43, 53–67.

Grandmont, Jean-Michel. 1985. "On Endogenous Competitive Business Cycles." *Econometrica*, 53, 995–1045.

Greenwald, Bruce C., Meir Kohn, and Joseph E. Stiglitz. 1993. "Financial Market Imperfections and Productivity Growth." Chap. 9 in R. H. Day, G. Eliasson, and C. Wihlborg (eds.), *Markets for Innovation, Ownership and Control*. Amsterdam: North-Holland, Elsevier Science Publishers, B.V.

Guckenheimer, J., and P. Holmes. 1983. *Nonlinear Oscillations, Dynamical Systems and Bifurcations of Vector Fields*. New York: Springer-Verlag.

Haavelmo, Trygve. 1956. *A Study in the Theory of Economic Evolution*. Amsterdam: North-Holland Publishing Company.

Halmos, Paul R. 1950. *Measure Theory*. New York: Springer-Verlag.

Hardy, Thomas. 1983. *Tess of the D'Urbervilles*. Reprint. London: Cathay Books.

Hawking, Stephen W. 1988. *A Brief History of Time*. Toronto: Bantam Books.

Heisenberg, Werner. 1983. *Tradition in Science*. Seabury Press. Republished as *Encounters with Einstein*. Princeton, NJ: Princeton University Press, 1989.

Hicks, John R. 1946. *Value and Capital*. 2d ed. London: Oxford University Press.

Hirsch, N. W., and Steve Smale. 1974. *Differential Equations, Dynamical Systems and Linear Algebra*. New York: Academic Press.

Hofbauer, F., and G. Keller. 1982a. "Equilibrium States for Piecewise Monotonic Transformations." *Ergodic Theory and Dynamical Systems*, 2, 23–43.

Hofbauer, F., and G. Keller. 1982b. "Ergodic Properties of Invariant Measure for Piecewise Monotonic Transformations." *Mathematische Zeitschrift*, 20, 119–140.

Jeans, Sir James. 1943. *Physics and Philosophy*. Cambridge: Cambridge University Press. Reprint. New York: Dover Publications, 1981.

Jensen, R. V., and R. Urban. N.d. "Chaotic Price Behavior in a Nonlinear Cobweb Model." Yale University, Department of Applied Physics.

Kelly, John L. 1955. *General Topology*. Princeton, NJ: D. Van Nostrand Company, Inc.

Kirman, Alan P. N.d. "On Ants and Markets." Manuscript, European University Institute, San Domenico di Fiesole, Italy.

Kowalski, Z. 1975. "Invariant Measure for Piecewise Monotonic Transformations." In Z. Ciescelski, U. Uvbanik, and W. A. Woyczinski (eds.), *Probability Winter School*. Berlin: Springer-Verlag.

Lasota, Andrzej. 1977. "Invariant Measures on Topological Spaces." *Bollettino U.M.I.*, 14-B, 592–603.

Lasota, Andrzej, and Michael C. Mackey. 1985. *Probabilistic Properties of Deterministic Systems.* Cambridge: Cambridge University Press.

Lasota, Andrzej, and James Yorke. 1973. "On the Existence of Invariant Measures for Piecewise Monotonic Transformations." *Trans. of the American Mathematical Society*, 186, 481–488.

Leontief, Wassily W. 1953. *Studies in the Structure of the American Economy.* Chaps. 1–3. New York: Oxford University Press.

Leontief, Wassily W. 1958. "Theoretical Note on Time, Preference, Productivity of Capital, Stagnation and Economic Growth." *American Economic Review*, 48, 105–111.

Leontief, Wassily W. 1966. "Delayed Adjustment of Supply and Partial Equilibrium." In W. W. Leontief, *Essays in Economics: Theories and Theorizing.* (Original in German, 1934.) New York: Oxford University Press.

Levy, H., and F. Lessman. 1961. *Finite Difference Equations.* New York: The Macmillan Company.

Lin, Tzong-Yau. 1988. *Studies of Economic Instability and Irregular Fluctuations in a One-Sector Real Growth Model.* Ph.D. Dissertation, University of Southern California, Los Angeles.

Li, Tzong-Yau, M. Misiurewicz, G. Pianigiani, and J. Yorke. 1982. "Odd Chaos." *Physics Letters*, 87A, 271–273.

Li, Tzong-Yau, and James A. Yorke. 1975. "Period 3 Implies Chaos." *American Mathematical Monthly*, 82, 985–992.

Li, Tzong-Yau, and J. Yorke. 1978. "Ergodic Transformations from an Interval into Itself." *Trans. of the American Mathematical Society*, 135, 183–192.

Lorenz, E. 1963a. "Deterministic Nonperiodic Flow." *Journal of the Atmospheric Sciences*, 20 (March), 130–141.

Lorenz, E. 1963b. "The Predictability of Hydrodynamic Flow." *Transactions of the New York Academy of Sciences*, Series II, 25, 409–432.

Lorenz, E. 1964. "The Problem of Deducing the Climate from the Governing Equations." *Tellas*, 16, 1–11.

Lucas, Robert E., Jr. 1979. "An Equilibrium Model of the Business Cycle." *Journal of Political Economy*, 83, 113–144.

Lucas, Robert E., Jr. 1987. *Models of Business Cycles.* Oxford: Basil Blackwell, Ltd.

Malinvaud, Edmund. 1980. *Profitability and Unemployment.* Cambridge: Cambridge University Press.

Marsden, J. E., and M. McCracken. 1976. *The Hopf Bifurcation.* New York: Springer Verlag.

Marshall, Alfred. 1920. *Principles of Economics.* 8th ed. New York: The Macmillan Company.

May, R. M. 1976. "Simple Mathematical Models with Very Complicated Dynamics." *Nature*, 261, 459–467.

May, R. M., and G. F. Oster. 1976. "Bifurcations and Dynamic Complexity in Simple Ecological Models." *American Naturalist*, 220, 573–599.

Misiurewicz, M. 1980. "Absolutely Continuous Measures for Certain Maps of an Interval." *Publications Mathematiques*, 53, 17–51.

Müller, G., and Richard H. Day. 1978. "Cautious Rolling Plans with Forecasting and Market Feedback." In R. Day and A. Cigno (eds.), *Modelling Economic Change: The Recursive Programming Approach.* Amsterdam: Elsevier North-Holland Inc.

Nerlove, Marc. 1958. *The Dynamics of Supply.* Baltimore: Johns Hopkins University Press.

Ney, Richard. 1975. *Making It in the Market.* New York: McGraw-Hill.

Pais, Abraham. 1982. *"Subtle Is the Lord—": The Science and the Life of Albert Einstein.* Oxford: Oxford University Press.

Pianigiani, Giulio. 1979. "On the Existence of Invariant Measures." In V. Lankshmikartan (ed.), *Applied Nonlinear Analysis*, 374–378. New York: Academic Press.

Pianigiani, Giulio, and James Yorke. 1979. "Expanding Maps on Sets Which Are Almost Invariant: Decay and Chaos." *Transactions of the American Mathematical Society*, 252, 351–360.

Poincaré, Henri. 1952. *Science and Method.* Reprint. New York: Dover Publications.

Prigogine, Ilya. 1980. *From Being to Becoming.* San Francisco: W. H. Freeman.

Rao, C. Radhakrishna. 1973. *Linear Statistical Inference and Its Applications.* New York: John Wiley and Sons, Inc.

Renault, Mary. *The Nature of Alexander.* New York: Pantheon Books.

Ruelle, D., and F. Takens. 1971. "On the Nature of Turbulence." *Communs Math. Phys.*, 20, 167–192.

Saari, Donald G. 1985. "Iterative Price Mechanisms." *Econometrica*, 53, 1117–1131.

Saari, Donald G. 1991. "Erratic Behavior in Economic Models." *Journal of Economic Behavior and Organization*, 16, 3–35.

Saari, Donald G., and Carl Simon. 1978. "Effective Price Mechanisms." *Econometrica*, 46, 1097–1125.

Saari, Donald G., and Steve Williams. 1986. "On the Local Convergence of Economic Mechanisms." *Journal of Economic Theory*, 40, 152–167.

Samuelson, Paul A. 1943. "Dynamics, Statics and the Stationary States." *The Review of Economics and Statistics*, 25, 58–68.

Samuelson, Paul A. 1947. *Foundations of Economic Analysis.* Rev. ed. 1983. Cambridge, MA: Harvard University Press.

Samuelson, Paul A. 1958. "An Exact Consumption-Loan Model of Interest with or without the Social Contrivance of Money." *The Journal of Political Economy*, 66, 467–482.

Samuelson, Paul A., and William Nordhaus. 1989. *Economics.* 13th ed. New York: McGraw-Hill, Inc.

Sargent, Thomas J. 1979. *Macroeconomic Theory.* New York: Academic Press.

Schumpeter, Joseph. 1934. *Theory of Economic Development.* Cambridge, MA: Harvard University Press.

Schwartz, R. 1988. *Equity Markets.* New York: Harper and Row, Publishers.

Smale, Steve. 1967. "Differential Dynamical Systems." *Bulletin of the American Mathematical Society*, 73, 747–817.

Soar, Robert. 1972. "Teacher Behavior Related to Pupil Growth." *International Review of Education*, 18, 508–528.

Sterman, John. 1989. "Deterministic Chaos on Experimental Economic Systems." *Journal of Economic Behavior and Organization*, 12, 1–28.

Stoll, Hans R. 1985. *The Stock Exchange Specialist System: An Economic Analysis.* Monograph Series in Finance and Economics, 1985:2. New York: New York University, Graduate School of Business Administration.

Stutzer, M. 1980. "Chaotic Dynamics and Bifurcations in a Macro Model." *Journal of Economic Dynamics and Control*, 2, 353–376.

Švarkovskii, A. N. 1964. "Coexistence of Cycles of a Continuous Map of a Line into Itself." *Ukrainian Mathematics Journal*, 16, 61–71.

Ulam, S. M., and John von Neumann. 1947. "On Combination of Stochastic and Deterministic Processes." *Bulletin of the American Mathematical Society*, 53, 1120.

Varian, Hal R. 1984. *Microeconomic Analysis*. New York: W. W. Norton and Company.

Walras, Léon. 1926. *Elements of Pure Economics or the Theory of Social Wealth*. Definitive ed. Trans. William Jaffé. Homewood, Illinois: Richard D. Irwin, Inc.

Weintraub, E. Roy. 1979. *Microfoundations: The Compatability of Microeconomics and Macroeconomics*. Cambridge: Cambridge University Press.

Williams, Arlington. 1987. "The Formulation of Price Forecasts in Experimental Markets." *Journal of Money, Credits and Banking*, 19, 1–18.

Williams, John Burr. 1938. *The Theory of Investment Value*. Amsterdam: North-Holland Publishing Company.

Williams, John Burr. 1967. "The Path to Equilibrium." *Quarterly Journal of Economics*, 81, 241–255.

Williams, John Burr. N.d. *The Current Assets Mechanism: A Financial Theory of the Firm*.

Woodford, Michael. 1988. "Expectations, Finance, and Aggregate Instability." In M. Kohn and S. C. Tsiang (eds.), *Financial Constraints, Expectations, and Macroeconomics*. Oxford: Clarendon Press.

Ziemien, K. 1985. "Almost Sure Invariant Principle for Some Maps of an Interval." *Ergodic Theory and Dynamical Systems*, 5, 625–640.

Index